BEETHOVEN

BEETHOVEN

THE PHILOSOPHY OF MUSIC

Theodor W. Adorno

Fragments and Texts
edited by Rolf Tiedemann

Translated by Edmund Jephcott

Stanford University Press
Stanford, California
1998

Stanford University Press
Stanford, California
©1993 Suhrkamp Verlag
This translation ©1998 Polity Press
First published in Germany as *Beethoven:*
   Philosophie der Musik by Suhrkamp Verlag
Originating publisher of English edition
   Polity Press in association with Blackwell Publishers Ltd
First published in the U.S.A. by Stanford
   University Press, 1998
Printed in Great Britain
ISBN 0-8047-3515-8
LC 98-60570
This book is printed on acid-free paper.

CONTENTS

Contents

EDITOR'S PREFACE

'To great writers, finished works weigh lighter than those fragments on which they work throughout their lives.' Benjamin's aphorism from *One-Way Street* sounds as if it had been coined for the book Adorno wanted to write decades later on Beethoven. Adorno pursued – one might even say: courted – few of his literary projects as long or intensively as this. And none came to a stop, for almost a lifetime, at a similarly early stage of its composition. His first texts on Beethoven were produced, as yet without any idea of writing a book on the composer, in 1934, the second year of the Nazi regime, and shortly before the beginning of his exile. According to Adorno, he planned to write a 'philosophical work on Beethoven' from 1937; the earliest surviving notes for it date from spring or summer 1938, immediately after his move to New York. He seems to have formed the plan after completing the '*Versuch über Wagner*', or even in parallel to it. Two years later, in June 1940, a letter to his parents, mainly about the defeat of France, contains the statement: 'The next major piece of work I intend to take on will be the Beethoven.' The work on Beethoven had actually been started long before, though only in the form of notes on individual compositions and, usually, on isolated aspects of Beethoven's music. But the real work, which for Adorno began only with the formulation of the connected text, had not even been started, doubtless because of the daily pressures to which the *émigré* writer was exposed. At the end of 1943 – by now Adorno was living in California – he was still far from having started to write the book, as emerges from a letter to Rudolf Kolisch. Referring to 'my long-planned book on Beethoven', Adorno writes: 'I think it ought to be the first thing I do after the war.' But even when the war was over and Adorno was back in Frankfurt-on-Main, he continued to write notes of the kind he had been accumulating more or less continuously since 1938. In 1956, however, these broke off rather abruptly; after that, only a few additions were made. In a letter of July 1957 to the pianist and Beethoven scholar Jürgen Uhde, Adorno remarked wistfully: 'If only I could get on with writing my book on Beethoven, on which I have copious notes. But heaven alone knows when and whether I shall be able to complete it.' In October 1957 Adorno finally wrote the essay 'Verfremdetes Hauptwerk' ['The Alienated *Magnum Opus*'] on the *Missa Solemnis*. After dictating the first draft he wrote in his diary, with quite uncharacteristic emotion: 'Thank heaven I have done it at last.' By this time he had clearly given up hope of completing his Beethoven project. When he included the essay on the *Missa Solemnis* in the miscellany *Moments musicaux* in 1964, he referred in the Preface to his 'projected philosophical work on Beethoven' as follows: 'It has yet to be written, primarily because the author's exertions have foundered continually on the *Missa Solemnis*. He has therefore attempted, at least, to explain these difficulties, to state the question more clearly, without presuming to have answered it.' The hope of solving the problems which not only the *Missa* but Beethoven's music as a whole posed to philosophical interpretation seemed to Adorno increasingly forlorn; but there were times when he entertained it all the same. In an impromptu radio talk on Beethoven's late style in 1966, his last work concerned with Beethoven, Adorno no longer mentioned his plan for a book at all. But not long before his death, in January 1969, he included *Beethoven. The Philosophy of Music* as the last in a series of eight books he still intended to complete. It is hard here to distinguish the gentle irony with which the sixty-five-year-old author committed himself to writing eight more books, from his unshakable belief in his own productivity, which for others was, indeed, hardly imaginable. Up to the end, the work on Beethoven was not 'written down', nor was its final drafting even begun. The present edition brings together the very numerous preparatory notes for that work, as well as a few completed texts: fragments on which the author worked throughout his life, or at least throughout its most productive phase.

The book now at the reader's disposal contains, on the one hand, every word Adorno wrote for his *Beethoven* study and, on the other, nothing written by anyone else, at least in the text section. All the same, it is not a book by Adorno. It lacks the closed, integrated structure of a completed work; it has remained a fragment. Adorno's *Beethoven* is fragmentary in a far more literal sense than his *Aesthetic Theory*, for example. If the latter has been aptly called a 'great fragment' – it breaks off before the final stage of formulation – the fragments in *Beethoven* are of a lesser kind. They are first drafts which were put aside before Adorno had attempted to combine them into a whole, or had even sketched a plan for the entire work. None of the notes on Beethoven was written for a reader; they were all intended for the author himself, as *aides-mémoire* for the time when he would apply himself to the final composition, a task he never began. Many of the notes are merely programmatic in nature, hardly more than what Adorno called a formal indication of what he intended to write. And even when, in some cases, individual ideas and motifs go far beyond this stage, they usually trace the path ahead rather than covering the ground itself. Much of the material, which does not go beyond the mere impression or idea, Adorno would never have approved for printing. While he knew what he intended to say, the reader can only surmise it. The reader of the fragments must always bear in mind that Adorno is not speaking directly to the reader. What is only hinted at, sometimes in a private idiom, the reader must translate into a language in which it can be understood by all. The receptive exertion that any text by Adorno demands of its readers is required in potentiated form by the fragments presented here.

To the Editor, Adorno described his fragments on Beethoven as a diary of his experiences of Beethoven's music. They occur in the same arbitrary sequence in which one is accustomed to hear, play or read music. Their chronological sequence follows the contingency of the abstract passage of time we experience empirically from day to day. The Editor has not retained this sequence in the printed version, but has replaced it by an order of his own. In doing so he has not attempted to organize the material as Adorno himself might have done, had he written the projected book. Instead, the existing notes on Beethoven, however fragmentary or provisional they might appear in relation to a book that does not exist, have been evaluated in terms of their internal structure or logic. The order in which they are presented to the reader is an attempt to make this structure visible. Benjamin spoke of the capacity of neglected historical phenomena to 'attain legibility' as a process in time. In a similar way, fragmentary texts may become legible as a kind of spatial configuration: a signature that can only be deciphered if the surviving fragments and drafts are arranged in a constellation determined by their *inherent meaning*, whereas it would remain unknowable had the notes been left in the sequence in which they were produced. The present arrangement of Adorno's fragments on Beethoven in no way claims to make good what the author failed to achieve and which has thus been lost for ever. Rather, it attempts to bring the kaleidoscope of material to a standstill, so that the logic behind its chronology can emerge. This procedure is not inappropriate to a philosophy like Adorno's, which from the outset saw its task as that of 'arranging its elements in changing constellations until they form a figure which can be read as an answer while the question simultaneously vanishes'. Just as each of the following fragments on Beethoven contains a question to answer which nothing less than the unwritten book on the composer would be needed, the constellation which the fragments form objectively together cannot, of course, replace that book or answer the question; but it may cause that question, in the way described by Adorno, to 'vanish', by composing itself as a figure which 'can be read as an answer'.

The figure or answer that Adorno's fragments on Beethoven present through their arrangement includes the few texts on the composer that were completed, and these are reproduced with the fragments in what follows. In a conversation in 1964 the author called these texts 'advance payments' on his Beethoven book. At that time the essay 'Spätstil Beethovens' ['Beethoven's Late Style'] had been published; its author wrote of it that it might 'expect to receive some attention in view of Ch. VIII of *Doctor Faustus*'. Such attention is merited hardly less by the other parts of Adorno's *Beethoven*. Moreover, the essay later published with the title 'Verfremdetes Hauptwerk' had already been written. Adorno expressly included the passages from the *Introduction to the Sociology of Music* devoted to Beethoven among those which, he said, constituted a partial anticipation of his projected book. The editor has therefore incorporated extracts from the *Introduction to the Sociology of Music* on the mediation between Beethoven's music and society and on Beethoven's symphonic style in the text of the present volume. A text on the late Bagatelles for piano (op. 126) has also been included; written about the same time as the essay on the late style, it had not been printed at that time and had slipped Adorno's memory, as had an extract from *Der getreue Korrepititor* and two pieces written shortly before his death and inserted into his *Aesthetic Theory*. Whereas all these texts took their places within the structure of the Beethoven project, three other studies which were further removed from the book's plan but could not be omitted have been added in an appendix.

The extensive notes section also contributes to the aim of illuminating Adorno's theory on Beethoven as fully as possible, no matter how undeveloped its formulation may have been. In it the literary and historical sources mentioned by Adorno in his fragments are set out. Documentation and references were an integral part of his project, making extensive quotations necessary. The reader should be aware of material to which the author is referring or alluding, and should also be advised of passages which do not succeed in conveying what Adorno intended. The notes on particular fragments or parts of fragments also refer to variants and parallel passages which are to be found in Adorno's completed works. He referred back later to many of the ideas first expressed in his notes for the Beethoven book, often in quite different contexts. The unsatisfactory character which many of the fragments will necessarily have for the reader is not infrequently compensated for, or at least alleviated by, the reworking of the same idea. However extensively the metamorphoses undergone by countless of Adorno's ideas on Beethoven are documented, the listing of parallel passages was never intended to be exhaustive. Priority has always been given to variants in which the argument of the Beethoven fragments is taken further or modified.*

'We do not understand music – it understands us. This is as true for the musician as for the layman. When we think ourselves closest to it, it speaks to us and waits sad-eyed for us to answer.' Although Beethoven's name is not mentioned in it, this note by Adorno in the earliest of the notebooks containing his fragments on Beethoven is placed directly before the first note explicitly dealing with him. Now and then, with splendid immodesty, Adorno had given his book on Beethoven the subtitle *The Philosophy of Music*. When he later published the *Philosophy of Modern Music*, he wrote, in a prominent place: 'A philosophy of music is only possible today as a philosophy of modern music.' All the same, it is conceivable that he was also hinting in coded form at the reason why he had not yet written his philosophy of Beethoven's music. If, as he wrote elsewhere in the *Philosophy of Modern Music*, 'no music today can speak in the tone of *Dir werde Lohn* [Yours be the reward]', then no philosophy can today 'answer' a music which, like Beethoven's, could still speak truly in that tone. It is the tone of humanity, whose relation to the mythical Adorno's book on Beethoven would have made its theme. Myth, as Adorno does not tire of emphasizing, means, in the terms used by Benjamin, the entanglement of the living in guilt, fate encumbered by nature. Humanity, however, does not stand opposed

---

* Additions by the editor are enclosed in square brackets. Details on the preparation of the text and on the chronology of the fragments can be found in the Editorial Afterword and in the Comparative Table following it.

to myth in an abstract contradiction, but converges with myth's re-conciliation. Adorno, who used the term humanity reluctantly and rarely on account of its false consecration, was nevertheless once prepared, prompted by Goethe's *Iphigenia*, to offer the definition that to be human was 'to have escaped the spell, to have pacified nature rather than subjecting it to the inflexible domination which only perpetuates fate'; but such an escape took place only 'in great music, in Beethoven's "Leonore" aria and in moments of some *adagio* movements like that of the first "Razumovsky" Quartet, eloquent beyond all words'. To this, Adorno's book on Beethoven sought to respond. The fragments, which bear witness only to the attempt, are hardly more than the first stammered beginnings of an answer. The answer itself could no longer be found in an age when the 'better worlds' of which Florestan sang were no more than a blood-stained mockery of this present world, beside which Pizarro's dungeon appears idyllic. This, ultimately, may be the reason why Adorno's book on Beethoven remained unwritten, and why its fragments could only mournfully reflect the mourning with which Beethoven's music mystically 'speaks' to humanity, in vain awaiting its answer.

ACKNOWLEDGEMENTS

The publishers gratefully acknowledge permission to reproduce copyright material as follows:

Newspaper cutting from 1945, 'Beethoven's Birthplace in Bonn Now in Ruins', reprinted by kind permission of Associated Press.

Extracts from *Introduction to the Sociology of Music* by Theodor Adorno, English translation © 1976 by The Continuum Publishing Company. Reprinted with permission.

Material from pp. 14–15, 19 of *Dialectic of Enlightenment* by Theodor Adorno, trans. John Cumming, Verso, London, 1979. Reprinted with permission.

Every effort has been made to trace all copyright holders, but if any have been inadvertently overlooked the publishers will be pleased to make the necessary arrangement at the first opportunity.

Fragments
and
Texts

ONE

PRELUDE

Reconstruct how I heard Beethoven as a child.   [1]

From my childhood I can clearly remember the magic emanating
from a score which named the instruments, showing exactly what
was played by each. Flute, clarinet, oboe – they promised no less
than colourful railway tickets or names of places.[1] If I am entirely
honest, it was this magic far more that the wish to know music as
such that induced me to learn how to transpose and read scores
while still a child, and which really made a musician of me. So
strong was this magic that I can still feel it today when I read the
Pastoral, in which, probably, it first manifested itself to me. Not,
however, when it is *played* – and that is no doubt an argument
against musical performance as such.[2]   [2]

Of my childhood experience of Beethoven I know that I first (when
certainly no more than 13) came across the 'Waldstein' Sonata and
mistook its theme for an accompaniment which was to be joined
only later by the melody. – My favourite piece for a long time was
the *Adagio* from op. 2, no. 1. I heard about the chamber music,
especially the quartets, so early, from Rosé,[3] that I never actually
experienced its newness. I probably did not really understand the
quartets until Vienna,[4] although I had long half-known them by
heart. – The violin sonatas, which move me indescribably, go back
to my *early* childhood ('Kreutzer', the small Sonata in A minor [op.
23] and two slow movements: the D major section from the Sonata
in A major [op. 30,1] and the E major minuet movement from the

Sonata in G major [op. 30,3].) – My first real experience of the late
Beethoven was through op. 109 and op. 119; I heard both of them,
with a short interval between them, played by d'Albert and
Ansorge.[5] I discovered and cherished the first movement of [op.] 101
on my own. – I played trios (the first [op. 1,1] and the 'Geister' Trio)
while still a schoolboy.   [3]

On my childhood image of Beethoven:[6] I thought the 'Hammerklavier' Sonata must be an especially *easy* piece, associating it with
toy pianos with little hammers. I imagined it had been written for
one of those. My disappointment when I could not play it. –
Another part of the same stratum: as a child I thought the
'Waldstein' Sonata portrayed the *name* Waldstein; in the opening
bars I imagined a knight entering a dark wood. Was I not, perhaps,
closer to the truth in this than I ever was later when I could play the
piece by heart?   [4]

The difficulty of any musical analysis lies in the fact that the more
the piece is dissected into its smallest units, the closer one comes to
mere sound, and all music consists of mere sounds. The most specific thus becomes the most general, abstract in the wrong sense. But
if this detailed analysis is omitted, the connections elude us. Dialectical analysis is an attempt to sublate [*aufheben*] each danger in the
other.   [5]

NB: In the study of Beethoven the appearance of giving primacy to
the whole must be avoided at all costs, the subject matter being
shown as genuinely dialectical.   [6]

It will not be possible to avoid completely certain scientific procedures relating to the logic of proportions. The approach used by
Rudi [Rudolf Kolisch] in his typology of tempi,[7] only subtler. For
example: comparisons between main themes, transitions, second
subject groups, closing themes, codas, and so on, of different (naturally comparable) works. What such shapes have in common may be
abstract and empty, but it can sometimes throw light on the *essence*
of these shapes, as when pedal points, shifts to the subdominant,
and so on, occur in closing sections. Follow up.   [7]

The fundamental error in Bekker's book [Paul Bekker, *Beethoven*,
2nd edition, Berlin 1912] is that he regards the content [*Gehalt*] of
Beethoven's music and its objective musical form as largely independent of each other – and the latter as subordinate to the former,

whereas any statement about content remains mere verbiage unless it is wrung from technical findings. That is the methodological rule in my work. Evidence of the contrary in Bekker [ibid., p. 140], where he refers to the Funeral March in op. 26 as: 'a piece of music of thrilling power, with an imposing grandeur of feeling. And yet – a piece of music. Its special charm, the reason for its popularity, lies in its objective musical values. As a confession it hardly concerns us'. (Note the condescending tone.) Paul Bekker is a barbarian of progress; his concept of historical development constantly obscures his view of the specific quality and encourages him to pontificate. On the Rondo from op. 31,1 (p. 150): 'the work concludes with a charming Rondo, an inconspicuous late bloom of an obsolete genre.' Once again, the attitude of *nil admirari*, on the basis that, if you know where it all leads, you always know better.   [8]

'Developing variation.' But the aim is not, as is often the case in the analyses of René [Leibowitz],[8] to show what is contained in what, but what *follows* what, and why. Not mathematical but 'historical' analyses are needed – René usually thinks he has 'proved' a piece of music by demonstrating thematic relationships. But the task begins only after that. Cf. Valéry's book on Degas.[9]   [9]

How undiscriminating our means of analysing musical meaning still are can be seen from a straightforward question such as: Why does so simple and in some ways masterful a piece as the introduction of Act III of the *Meistersinger*, when compared to a piece expressing 'resignation' by Beethoven – for example, the first movement of op. 101 – have an embarrassed, turgid, Pharisaical quality? And yet this is *objectively* the case, regardless of the mere taste of the listener, or the psychology of Wagner – in which the categories of genuine and ungenuine remain ambivalent, changeable – and even regardless of its theatrical function. I shall attempt to indicate a number of objective moments in the composition.

The[10] formal idea of the piece is the contrast of three elements: subjective-expressive theme, folksong (in the Shoemaker's song) and chorale. The Chorale is meant to have affirmative power, especially through its cadences. But the relationship of these elements is an outward one. Folksong and chorale give the effect (in extreme contrast to Bach, for example) of a *quotation*, because we *know*: this is a folksong and this a chorale; and this knowledge, this reflexion on naivety, dissolves the latter, making it something manipulated. 'Look, I'm a plain, true-hearted master' – 'I have a German soul': simplicity as artifice. (Nietzsche doubtless felt all this but always argued it *ad hominem*, never really in relation to the 'artist'.) The incongruity manifests itself, however, in purely musical terms. In the true chorale the cadence is taken for granted and never especially emphasized. From the standpoint of *Tristan*, where it no longer really commands belief, and where straightforward diatonic harmony seems banal, the cadence has to be exaggerated in order to be felt at all. It's like a parson intoning: Verily I say unto you, my dear brethren, amen, amen, amen. And this gesture is at the same time in contradiction to the chorale's melody, which it overstates to the point of expressing, not faith, but: Look, I believe. – Similarly with the folksong. As a melody it does not convey the deeply fractured expression (intended as a stroke of genius) of hopeless tenderness, of renunciation's sweetness, that Wagner ascribes to it. He therefore has to introduce this effect from outside, by harmonization, by modulation to E major, by the chord of the ninth, by overstretching – all of which procedures are foreign to the musical phenomenon itself. But it is not thereby assimilated but rather, for the sake of effect, *stands still* as something heterogeneous. The whole has something of the Child Jesus in Flanders, 'where the star stops' – Monsieur Timmermans is teleologically immanent in Wagner (his assimilation of precisely this element is dubious even in Mahler). *The technical reflection on expression in Wagner is a negation of its own content.* But it should be added that this is not the whole truth, and that precisely this fractured quality, the truthful image of untruth, has about it something wholly splendid, and even infinitely touching. That is to say that untruth, depending on the point it occupies on the sundial of history, is at the same time *truth* – a fact that Nietzsche misjudged, registering it merely by categories such as charm and refinement. And finally: *all* musical characters are really quotations. Alexandrinism is the principle of art that has attained self-awareness . . .   [10]

A prominent and fundamental motif of the work must be that Beethoven – his language, his substance and tonality in general, that is, the whole system of bourgeois music – is irrecoverably lost to us, and is perceived only as something vanishing from sight. As Eurydice was seen.[11] *Everything* must be understood from that viewpoint.   [11]

The ideological essence of music, its affirmative element, does not lie, as with other arts, in its specific content, or even in whether or not its form operates in terms of harmony. It lies merely in the fact that it is *a voice lifted up*, that it is music at all. Its language is magical in itself, and the transition to its isolated sphere has *a priori* a quality of transfiguration. The suspension of empirical reality and the forming of a second reality *sui generis* seem to say in advance: all is well. Its tone is by origin consoling, and to that origin it is bound. But that does not apply unambiguously to music's status as *truth*. It can be said that it stands, as a *totality*, more directly and completely under the sway of appearance. But this *a priori* condition encompasses it as if from outside, like a kind of general clause, whereas inwardly, in its immanent movement, through its lack of objective substance and unequivocal relationships, music is more *free* than other arts. Its remoteness from reality does, it is true, cast on the latter a reflected, conciliatory glow, but keeps music itself *purer* of subservience to reality, which affects it primarily, not in its essence, but as a context of interrelated effects. Once it has consented to be music at all, it can, to an extent (that is, as far as it is not aimed at consumption), do as it thinks fit. – From this standpoint, Beethoven's work would be seen as an attempt to *revoke* the *a priori* untruth of music's voice, of its being music at all, through the immanent movement of the concept as an *unfolding* truth. Hence, perhaps, the insignificance of the starting point:[12] this is nothing but the untruth, the appearance inherent in music as such. – The late style would signify that music becomes aware of the *limit* of this movement – of the impossibility of cancelling its own premises by virtue of its own logic. The late style is the μετάβασις εἰς τέvος. [12]*

Perhaps the pure, strict concept of art can be derived only from music, while great literature and great painting – and especially great literature and painting – necessarily contain something material, projecting outside the charmed aesthetic circle, not dissolved in the autonomy of form. – It is precisely the logical, profound aesthetic which is fundamentally *inappropriate* to *significant* literature, as it is to novels. Hegel, unlike Kant, had some awareness of this. [13]

Benjamin's concept of aura,[13] which may touch on the music-like quality of *all* art, could be scarcely better explicated than by some turning points in *An die ferne Geliebte* (and similarly in the last violin sonata [op. 96]), such as the shift between the first and second songs, which opens a limitless horizon, and the passage with semi-quaver-triplets in 'Nimm sie hin denn, diese Lieder' [bars 21–5].[14] [14]

The dispute whether music can portray anything definite, or is only a play of sound-patterns in motion,[15] no doubt misses the point. A far

* [Above the text:] (Beethoven, perhaps for Introduction.)

closer parallel is with dream, to the form of which, as Romanticism
well knew, music is in many ways so close. In the first movement of
Schubert's Symphony in C major, at the beginning of the development, we feel for a few moments as if we were at a rustic wedding;
an action seems to begin unfolding, but then is gone at once, swept
away in the rushing music which, once imbued with that image,
moves onwards to a quite different measure. Images of the objective
world appear in music only in scattered, eccentric flashes, vanishing
at once; but they are, in their transience, *of music's essence*. The programme is, so to speak, the musical residue left over from the day's
dealings. While the music lasts we are *in* it much as we are in dream.
We are at the rustic wedding, then are carried away in the musical
flood, heaven knows where (it may be similar with death – perhaps
the affinity between music and death has its locus here). – I believe
the images flitting past to be *objective*, not mere subjective associ-
ations. The anecdote told by Decsey about the poem 'Lieblich war die
Maiennacht' and the post-horn passage in Mahler's Third Symphony,
is relevant here (though doubtless too rationalistic).[16] Within the
framework of such a theory, a *rescue* of programme music might be
attempted. Perhaps with reference to the *Pastoral*.   [15]

Beethoven may represent an attempt to *circumvent* the ban on
images. His music is not an image of anything, and yet is an image
of the whole: an imageless image.   [16]

The task of the book will be to resolve the riddle of humanity as a
dialectical image.[17]   [17]

Copied from a notebook:[18] The element of *praxis* in Beethoven.
Humanity in his work means: you should behave as this music
behaves. It shows how to lead a life which is active, outwardly productive without being narrow – a life of solidarity. And the injunction to 'strike sparks from a man's soul'[19] – no 'emotional effusions'.
Against Tolstoy's 'Kreutzer Sonata'. However: this does not *exhaust*
the meaning of Beethoven. – The metaphysics of 'gallantry' and
amusement: a way to defeat boredom. This was a feudal need. The
bourgeoisie took it over and adapted it. By work, time is killed *in
earnest*. Similarly, Beethoven forces aimlessly passing time to stand
still. By work it is conquered twice over. Precisely what is a lie in
reality is truth in ideology. Extremely important: to be taken further.
– Beethoven's *rhythm* and tonality. Syncopation is relative to the
down-beat as dissonance is to consonance. The problem of tonality
cannot be grasped deeply enough. It is *both* the surface as opposed

to the subcutaneous, *and* the general principle which itself constitutes the subcutaneous.[20] – Emancipated rhythm today is in the same
position as harmony: it is nullified by the absence of a distinguishing
principle. NB: Schoenberg *latently* sustained musical metre. –
Jemnitz's remark on rhythmical monotony, arising from the occurrence of complementary events on each beat.[21]   [18]

To come closer to understanding the *Missa*, it is doubtless necessary
to study the Mass in C major. – There is Schenker's analysis of the
Fifth.[22] – Bekker quotes a movement composed by Beethoven for a
projected mythological opera: in it all the dissonances were to
remain unresolved.[23]   [19]

On considering the original manuscript of Beethoven's 'Geister'
Trio: the extraordinarily extensive abbreviations cannot be
explained by haste. Beethoven composed relatively little. Nor –
unlike Schubert – does he make countless changes in the MS. What
is striking, however, is the *haziness* of the script. It looks like a mere
support for the real substance – that is, the sound it represents. The
written form clearly betrays an aversion to a process which does not
itself form part of the musical imagination (so that in Beethoven the
visual appearance of the notation has little influence on the composition, unlike the case with many, especially modern, composers). In
this context, one should think first of the primacy of the whole over
the individual part in Beethoven. In the written image the 'idea' or
'inspiration', the clearly defined individual melody, recedes into the
flow of the whole. But something deeper is also involved: the image
of the *objectivity* of music, which Beethoven conceived as something
existing in itself, not originally made by him, as φύσει, not θέσει. He
is the stenographer of the objectified composition, which is something detached from the arbitrariness of individuation. In
Benjamin's phrase: 'the clerk recording his own inner life.'[24] What
the handwriting reveals is, really, the *shame* of the accidental subject before a truth which has been granted him as the whole. The
secret of his impatience, and of his harsh, aggressive trait.
Beethoven's script seems to mock the beholder for not having
known *beforehand* the music which is here noted down for the first
time. In this connection, Beethoven's irritation with the man who
misspelled Haydn's name: 'Haydn – Haydn – everyone knows
that.'[25] – Likewise: 'Everyone knows the "Geister" Trio.'   [20][26]

Title of the book: either *Beethoven's Music*, or *The Music of
Beethoven*.[27]   [21]

TWO

MUSIC AND CONCEPT

Apossible epigraph for a chapter of the book on Beethoven: Clemens Brentano. The echo of Beethoven's music (I, 105f[28]), especially:

> Selig, wer ohne Sinne
> Schwebt, wie ein Geist auf dem Wasser
> [Happy is he who floats like a spirit over the water]

and

> Selbst sich nur wissend und dichtend,
> Schafft er die Welt, die er selbst ist.
>   [Knowing and singing himself alone,
>   he creates the world that he himself is.]

Might well be an epigraph for Chapter 1.   [22]

Music can express only what is proper to itself: this means that words and concepts cannot express music's content *directly*, but only in mediated form, that is, as philosophy.   [23][29]

In a similar sense to that in which there is only Hegelian philosophy, in the history of western music there is only Beethoven.   [24][30]

The will, the energy that sets form in motion in Beethoven, is always the *whole*, the Hegelian *World Spirit*.   [25]

The Beethoven study must also yield a philosophy of music, that is, it must decisively establish the relation of music to conceptual logic. Only then will the comparison with Hegel's *Logic*, and therefore the interpretation of Beethoven, be not just an analogy but the thing itself. Perhaps one comes closest to this by following up the ancient comparison between music and dream. Except that the analogy is concerned less with the play of representations – which appear only intermittently in music, like flower garlands in pure ornamentation – than with logical elements. The 'play' of music is a play with logical forms as such: those of statement, identity, similarity, contradiction, the whole and the part; and the concreteness of music is essentially the force with which[31] these forms imprint themselves on the material, the musical sounds. They, the logical elements, are largely unambiguous – that is, as unambiguous as they are in logic, but not so unambiguous that they have a dialectic of their own. The theory of musical forms is the theory of such unambiguity, and of its sublation. The boundary between music and logic is not, therefore, located within the logical elements, but in their specifically logical synthesis, in *judgement*. Music does not include judgement, but a synthesis of a different kind, constituted[32] solely by the constellation of its elements, not their predication, subordination, subsumption. This synthesis, too, is related to truth, but to one which is quite unlike apophantic truth, and this non-apophantic truth will probably be definable as the aspect through which music coincides with dialectics. This discussion should terminate in a definition such as: *Music is the logic of the judgement-less synthesis.* Beethoven should be tested against this, in the twofold sense that, on the one hand, such logic is demonstrated through his work; and, on the other, that the work is determined 'critically' as music's mimesis of judgement, and therefore of language. The meaning of the work with regard to the philosophy of history is understood in terms both of the ineluctability of this mimesis and of music's attempt to escape it – to revoke the logic which pronounces judgement.[33]   [26][34]

If the relationships between Beethoven and major philosophy are to be revealed, some of the most fundamental categories will have to be clarified.

1 Beethoven's music is an image of that process which great philosophy understands the world to be. An image, therefore, not of the world but of an interpretation of the world.

2 The sensuous component of music, which is devoid of qualification yet is mediated within itself and sets the whole in motion, is the motivic-thematic dimension.

Question: Interpret the difference between motif and theme.

3 The 'spirit', the mediation, is the whole as form. The category which, in this context, is identical between philosophy and music, is *work*. What is called conceptual exertion or work in Hegel[35] is thematic work in music.

The recapitulation: the return to oneself, the reconciliation. Just as this remains problematic in Hegel (in that the conceptual is posited as the real), in Beethoven, where the dynamic element is set free, the recapitulation is also problematic.

One needs to counter the objection that all this is mere analogy, since music lacks the conceptual medium which forms the very essence of philosophy. Here I shall just note a few points to be used against this objection. (NB: It is *no* part of Beethoven's intention or idea to refute humanity, and so on, which is itself constituted only by music's complexion.)

1 Beethoven's music is immanent in the same way as is philosophy, bringing forth itself. Hegel, who has no concepts outside philosophy, is, in that sense, likewise concept-less in face of the 'heterogeneous continuum'.[36] That is to say, his ideas, like those of music, are explained only by each other. This idea must be followed up exactly, since it leads to the innermost depths.[37]

2 The form of music as *language* in Beethoven's work must be analysed.

3 The pre-philosophical concept in philosophy corresponds to the conventional musical *formula*, on which the work is done.

A concise answer must be given to the question: what *are* immanently musical concepts? (NB: Make quite clear that these are not concepts *about* music.) The answer can only be attained *against* traditional aesthetics, the doctrine of the visual-symbolic-monistic nature of art, which provides the dialectical force setting the Beethoven theory in motion.

The whole study might possibly be introduced by a discussion of music and concept.

NB: The difference between music and philosophy must be defined in the same way as their identity.*   [27]

In one place [cf. fr. 225], I described each piece by Beethoven as a *tour de force*, a paradox, a *creatio ex nihilo*.[38] That may be the deepest connection with Hegel and absolute Idealism. What I described as the 'floating' element in my study of Hegel is at bottom precisely this.[39] And that might be decisive for the construction of the book on Beethoven. Might the late style, finally, be a critique of

---

* [Added later:] Against the 'philosophy of art' and an interpretation of art through something foreign to it.

Just *that* – of the possibility of keeping music alive out of pure spirit, as an absolute becoming? Dissociation and 'maxims' point to this. Hegel had eliminated precisely the 'dictum' which lacks a contradiction . . .[40]   [28][41]

Towards a Theory of Beethoven

1 In the totality of its form, Beethoven's music represents the social process. In doing so it shows how each individual moment – in other words, each individual process of production within society – is made comprehensible only in terms of its function within the reproduction of society as a whole. (Decisively connected to the aspect of reproduction is the nullity of the individual element, the fortuitousness of the initial material, which yet, at the same time, is more than just fortuitous. The theory of the Beethovenian theme should be added here.) Beethoven's music is, in a sense, a means for putting to the test the idea that the whole is the truth.[42]

2 The special relationship between the systems of Beethoven and Hegel lies in the fact that the unity of the whole is to be understood merely as something mediated. Not only is the individual element insignificant, but the individual moments are estranged from each other. This can be exemplified by the antithetical relationship of Beethoven's music to folksong, which also represents a unity, but an unmediated one – that is, one in which there is no boundary between the thematic kernel, or motif, the other motifs and the whole. By contrast, the Beethovenian unity is one which moves by means of antitheses; that is to say, its moments, taken individually, seem to contradict each other. But therein lies the meaning of Beethovenian form as process, so that, through the incessant 'mediation' between individual moments, and finally through the consummation of the form as a whole, the seemingly antithetical motifs are grasped in their identity. The analysis of the first movement of the String Quartet in E minor [op. 59,2] as the history of the opening fifth, and more generally as a demonstration of the mediated identity of the first and second themes, belongs here. The Beethovenian form is an integral whole, in which each individual moment is determined by its function within that whole only to the extent that these individual moments contradict and cancel each other, yet are preserved on a higher level within the whole. Only the whole proves their identity; as individual elements they are as antithetical to each other as is the individual to the society confronting him. That is the real meaning of the 'dramatic' element in Beethoven. Recall Schoenberg's formula about music being the history of a theme.[43] This, however,

should be shown historically to be a social relationship, by demonstrating that the antithesis between *tutti* and solo is at the origin of thematic dualism both in Beethoven's music and in the sonata form in general. The concept, especially, of the mediating phrase and the 'entry phrase' should also be developed in this context. The theoretical interpretation of the closing section has still to be worked out.

3 Beethoven's music is Hegelian philosophy: but at the same time it is truer than that philosophy. That is to say, it is informed by the conviction that the self-reproduction of society as a self-identical entity is not enough, indeed that it is false. Logical identity as immanent to form – as an entity at the same time fabricated and aesthetic – is both constituted and criticized by Beethoven. Its seal of truth in Beethoven's music lies in its suspension: through transcending it, form takes on its true meaning. This formal transcendence in Beethoven's music is a representation – not an expression – of hope. At this point a precise analysis of the D major passage from the slow movement of the great String Quartet in F major [op. 59,1; third movement, bars 70ff] must be given. In the formal sense this passage appears superfluous, since it comes after a quasi-retransition, after which the recapitulation is expected to follow immediately. But when the recapitulation fails to appear it is made clear that formal identity is insufficient, manifesting itself as true only at the moment when it, as the real, is opposed by the possible which lies outside identity. The D^b major theme is new: it is not reducible to the economy of motivic unity.[44] This throws light on phenomena incomprehensible to traditional interpretations of Beethoven, such as the introduction of the E minor theme in the great development section of the *Eroica* [first movement, bars 284ff], and on major expressive moments in Beethoven, such as the second subject group in the slow movement of the Piano Sonata, op. 31, no. 2 [second movement, bars 31ff], and certain passages in *Fidelio* and in the third *Leonore* Overture.

4 The key to the very late Beethoven probably lies in the fact that in this music the idea of totality as something already achieved had become unbearable to his critical genius. The material path taken by this realization within Beethoven's music is one of contraction. The developmental tendency in those works of Beethoven which precede the late style itself is opposed to the principle of transition. The transition is felt to be banal, 'inessential'; that is, the relation of disparate moments to a whole which holds them together is seen as no more than a prescribed convention, no longer tenable. In a sense, the dissociation found in the last works is a consequence of the moments of transcendence in the 'classical' works of the middle period. The element of humour in Beethoven's last works can probably be

equated with his discovery of the inadequacy of mediation, and is their truly critical aspect. [29]

Beethoven's critical procedure, the 'self-criticism' so often invoked, arises from the critical sense of the music itself, whose principle is the immanent negation of all its postulates. That has nothing to do with Beethoven's psychology. [30]

The expression of the main theme of the Ninth is not, as Bekker [*Beethoven*, p. 271] fatuously maintains, 'like a gigantic shadow of the demon that has been conjured up ... dissonances crying out in pain' (where??).[45] It is a pure representation of *necessity*. But perhaps it is precisely here that the contrast to Hegel becomes palpable. This contrast marks the demarcation between art and philosophy. To be sure, in Beethoven, too, necessity is produced by consciousness – it is, in a sense, a necessity of thought. But when contemplated by aesthetic subjectivity, it does not become reconciled to it, is not that contemplation. The gaze of the work of art, which is manifested in this theme, and wants, through its meaning, to be gazed upon in turn, has something withstanding, resistant about it which is really unknown to idealistic philosophy – for which everything is its own work. In this way the work of art, in the dualism constituted between itself and the beholder (a dualism posited by the art-work itself), is more real, more critical, less 'harmonistic' than philosophy. Of course, this theme is the World Spirit, but as an appearance it remains in one aspect external, distanced from the person perceiving it. The Ninth Symphony puts less faith in identity than does Hegel's philosophy. Art is more real than philosophy in that it acknowledges identity to be appearance.*[46]

In this connection cf. note on Rembrandt in this notebook.[47] [31]

The following definition of the nature of philosophy from the Preface to the *Phenomenology of Mind* looks like a *direct* description of the Beethovenian sonata:

> For the real subject matter is not exhausted in its *purpose* but in working the matter out; nor is the mere *result* attained the concrete whole itself, but the result along with its Becoming. The purpose by itself is a lifeless universal, just as the general drift is a mere activity in a certain direction, which is still without its concrete realisation; and the naked result is the corpse of the system which has left its guiding

---

* [In margin:] cf. Bekker's good formulation [*Beethoven*, p. 273]. Cf. Hegel, *Ästhetik*, I [ed. Hotho, 2nd edition, Berlin 1842], p. 63.

tendency behind it. (G.W.F. Hegel, *The Phenomenology of Mind*, transl. by J.B. Baillie, London 1971, p. 69)

In relation to my study, this passage is quite inexhaustible – almost too good to be used as an epigraph:

1 Regarding 'purpose', consider Schoenberg's definition of the fate of a theme.[48] What matters is precisely the *exposition* of this fate. The theme is not an end in itself, but neither is it simply incidental – that is to say, without the theme there is no development. The theme is (in true dialectical fashion) *both*: it is not independent, in that it is a function of the whole, *and* it is independent – that is, memorable, vivid, and so on. Consider, in addition, the difference between themes, on the one hand, and fields of tension and disintegration, on the other. In the equidistance of all elements from the centre which I have claimed to be a characteristic of modern music,[49] the dialectic comes to a standstill.

2 Directly connected to this is the critique of 'tendency' – of development in itself – as 'mere activity'; that is, development exists only as development of a theme, in which it 'exhausts' itself through work (the concept of thematic work, and of work in Hegel); as development of something existent (touched on in the *Philosophy of Modern Music*[50]). But what makes development in Beethoven more than mere activity is the affirmed re-emergence of the theme.

3 Against results: final chords, or codas, are in a sense results, without which the activity would be empty bustle, but on their own they are – through their thing-like nature – literally the 'corpse which has left its guiding tendency behind it'.[51]

(Regarding all this, consider Max [Horkheimer]'s objection: philosophy is not supposed to be a symphony.)

On the problem of the recapitulation: Beethoven made it a kind of guarantee of the *idealism* informing his music. Through it the result of the work, of the universal mediation, proves itself *identical* to the immediacy which is dissolved by the reflection which is its immanent development. That Beethoven derived this element from tradition in no way negates what has been said, since, firstly, the influence of tradition is deeply linked to the blinding effect of ideology* (work alienated from itself being transfigured as creation; this idea needs to be explored in detail); secondly, Beethoven, like Hegel, made the imprisonment of the bourgeois spirit within itself into a *driving force*, and thus 'incited' the recapitulation. In the work of both, we find the bourgeois spirit exalted to the utmost. But it is profoundly

* [Added at foot of page:] (Problem of fetishism.)

revealing that, *nevertheless*, the recapitulation in Beethoven remains aesthetically dubious in the same fundamental way as does the thesis of identity in Hegel; by a deep-seated paradox these elements are, in both, abstract and mechanical.   [32][52]

Out of the recapitulation Beethoven produced the identity of the non-identical. Implicit in this, however, is the fact that while the recapitulation is in itself the positive, the tangibly conventional, it is *also* the moment of untruth, of ideology.   [33]

In his last works Beethoven did not abolish the recapitulation; he actually *emphasized* the moment of it which has just been mentioned. – It must be stated that, *in itself*, the recapitulation is not *only* bad but has, tectonically, an extremely positive function in 'pre-critical' music. Really, it only became bad through being made into the good, that is, through being metaphysically *justified* by Beethoven. This is a pivotal aspect of dialectical construction. [34][53]

The idealistic 'system' within Beethoven's work is tonality, through the specific function it takes on as fully worked out moments. Aspects to be considered are:

1 Subsumption: everything comes *under* tonality; it is the abstract concept governing this music – everything is its 'business'. It is the abstract identity of Beethoven's work; that is, all its moments can be defined as basic characters of tonality. Beethoven 'is' tonality.
2 Against this: it does not remain abstract but is *mediated*: it is *becoming*, and is thus constituted only through the coherence between its moments.
3 These interrelationships are the *negation* of the moments through reflection on themselves.
4 Like abstract concepts and assumptions, tonality, being concretely mediated, is the *result* of Beethoven's work. This is, really, the moment which I call the 'full working-out' of tonality. Herein lies the moment of Beethoven's work which relates to the philosophy of identity – its trust, its harmony; but also, for better or worse, its compulsive character.
5 The *ideological* moment appears to me to lie in the fact that tonality, although merely given and pre-existent, appears to emerge 'freely', as if from the musical meaning of the composition itself. But, again, this is also a *non*-ideological moment since tonality is not, of course, contingent, but is *really* 'reproduced' by Beethoven as *a priori* synthetic judgements are reproduced by Kant.[54]

6 The category of the *tragic* in Beethoven is the – harmonistic – resolution of negation in identity.
7 Like Beethoven's music, tonality is the *whole*.
8 Affirmation within tonality is identity as expression. The result: It is so.

NB: The relation of tonality to the subject–object problem.   [35]

In *Kant*, the system versus the 'rhapsodistic'. In this context, consider especially the introductory sections of the *Architecture of Pure Reason*.[55]   [36]

On the concept of homoeostasis. The biological resolution of tensions – cf. Fenichel, [*The Psychoanalytic Theory of Neurosis*, New York 1945, p. 12] (consult sources).[56] In Schoenberg's *Style and Idea*, precisely this is defined as the meaning of music (entirely Hegelian, by the way: the Idea as the whole).[57] This has the following consequences:

1 In this respect even imageless music is 'image'; perhaps this is the true *stilo rappresentativo*.
2 Homoeostasis contains an (inseparable) moment of musical *conformism* – not excepting Schoenberg. Is an 'allostatic' music at all possible?
3 Herein lies the real coincidence with Hegel: from this standpoint, their relationship can be defined as one of logical unfolding, *not* of analogy. This is, no doubt, the missing link between them. [37]

The preponderance of totality is seen in the fact that in the classical models of Beethoven's solemn style – the C minor Sonata op. 30 [no. 2; for violin and piano], the Fifth Symphony, the 'Appassionata', the Ninth Symphony – the main theme *descends* on the music with the anticipated force of the whole; against this the individual subject, as the second theme, *defends* itself. Almost too distinctly in that Sonata in C minor for violin and piano.   [38]

The developmental law of Beethoven's music: through its preeminence, the idea is anticipated, takes on a *decorative* aspect, as if produced by the composer's cast of mind rather than through-composed. The through-composition then catches up, but only gradually. Again, compare the Violin Sonata [that is, op. 30,2].   [39]

Beethoven. In relation to him, the concept of *negation* as that which drives a process forward can be very precisely grasped. It involves a *breaking off* of melodic lines before they have evolved into something complete and rounded, in order to impel them into the next figure. The opening of the *Eroica* is one example, but the tendency is seen most clearly in the Eighth Symphony, first movement, where the opening theme, marked *tutti*, is broken off [bar 33] to make room for the octaves and then the second theme. – Within the same complex we find interrupting, interpolating themes, such as the figure

Example 1

from the first movement of the *Eroica* [bar 65]. Throughout this passage, just as in Hegel, it is the whole, a power ruling behind the scenes, which really intervenes.

Still to be worked out: where does this coincidence originate and what does it mean? The experience which nourished the concept of the World Spirit; on this point, see a note in Q [cf. fr. 79].   [40]

Music and dialectical logic. One form – the form? – of negation in music is *obstruction*, where progression gets stuck.* The C♯ early in the *Eroica* [bar 7]. In it the force making the music *proceed* is pent up. But this note also has a *motoric* function, through the processive effect of the minor second, E♭–D. This is obstructive in that it does not form part of the scale, and thus conflicts with tonality as the objective spirit, which the individuated, thematic element here *opposes*. Central.   [41]

The relationship between Beethoven and Hegel can be explained very precisely with reference to the conclusion of the development of the 'Hammerklavier' Sonata, when, after the B major episode, the main theme is exploded by the low F♯ as the new quality [first movement, bar 212]. The retransition which follows has something gigantic about it, a kind of inordinate stretching. Compare this with the passage from the Preface to the *Phenomenology of Mind*, concerning the new quality which gathers beneath the germ layer, then bursts violently forth[58] (the same inordinateness is found at the end of the Fugue). The whole recapitulation of the first movement is especially important, since the force of the preceding music subjects

---

* [Added at foot of note:] Another form of negation is *interruption*. Discontinuity = dialectic.

it to the widest modifications. Discuss this passage, for example, the chord of the diminished seventh below the F in the phrase [bar 234]:

Example 2

To be interpreted in the slow movement: the critical B in the chord of the Neapolitan sixth [bar 14]. The indescribable effect of the dissected triad as the closing group, and the mystical passage preceding it, where the right hand crosses over.   [42]

Beethoven's work contains an exact equivalent of the Hegelian category of *Entäusserung* [objectification]: one might speak of a home-coming: 'I am the earth's once more';[59] utmost remoteness must 'come back into the world'. In the first movement of the Piano Concerto in E♭ major, to the passage of unworldly rapture in which the piano, in its highest register, is more flute-like than any flute [bars 158–66], the march which follows is juxtaposed with harsh abruptness [bars 166ff]. – In the same movement, of incomparable grandeur, we find a character of *fulfilment*, of a pledge redeemed – precisely that which is refused by Stravinsky; as in:[60]

Example 3

etc.

A true theory of musical form would need to elaborate such categories fully. – The rhapsodic exuberance at the end of the Rondo: now there is fear no longer (quite unlike the case with Mozart's music, which knows no fear). – The transition from the second to the third movement is deeply related to the junction (which is *not* mediated) between the Finale and the *Largo* in the 'Geister' Trio: the dawning, the sacredness of *day*. – The Rondo is very closely related to *Le Retour* [Piano Sonata in E♭ major, op. 81a, third movement], even in the details of its passage-work.   [43]

The truly Hegelian quality of Beethoven is, perhaps, that in his work, too, mediation is never merely something *between* the moments, but is immanent in the moment itself.   [44]

'[. . .] and holds the opposites, so to speak, close together' – on op. 2 no. 1 [Wolfgang A.] Thomas-San-Galli, *Ludwig van Beethoven*, Munich 1913, p. 84.   [45]

The configuration of Beethoven's *oeuvre* in pairs of works assists interpretation as an external sign of its dialectical nature. Through it the Beethoven of the middle period (Fifth and Sixth; Seventh and Eighth) transcends the closed totality of the *oeuvre*, as the very late Beethoven transcends it *within* the individual work. The truth of Plato's dictum that the best writer of tragedies must also be the best writer of comedies[61] lies in the insignificance of each work *qua* work. The solemnity of the Fifth and the dialect of the Sixth do not 'complement' each other, but represent the self-movement of the concept. [46]

A discussion of the dialectic in Beethoven requires an account of stillness through motion, as in the first movement of the 'Pastoral' Sonata op. 29 [now op. 28], and in the first movement of the Violin Concerto.   [47]

On music and dialectical logic. It can be shown how Beethoven only gradually attained a fully dialectical mode of composing. In the C minor Violin Sonata from op. 30 – one of the first fully Beethovenian conceptions, and a work of the highest genius – the antagonism is still *unmediated*, that is, the thematic complexes are set out in splendid contrast, like armies or pieces on a chessboard, then collide in a dense developmental sequence. In the Appassionata the antithetical themes are at the same time identical in themselves: identity in non-identity.
'The Absolute' in Beethoven is tonality. And it is no more absolute than Hegel's absolute. It is also: spirit. Consider Beethoven's remark that one need not give any more thought to *basso continuo* than to dogma.[62]   [48]

In music everything individual is ambivalent, oracular, mythical – while the whole is unambiguous. This is music's transcendence. But it is from the single meaning of the whole that the multiple individual meanings can be identified.   [49]

After a performance of the second *Leonore* Overture under

Scherchen,[63] the following, probably decisive link in the structure of my argument became clear to me: the negation of the individual detail in Beethoven, the insignificance of the particular, has its *objective* reason in the nature of the material: it is insignificant *in itself*, and not as a result of the immanent movement of the music's form. That is to say that the more one delves into any particular element in tonal music, the more this is seen as merely an examplar of its concept. An expressive minor triad states: I am something, I mean something; and yet it is only a group of sounds which has been placed here, as if heteronomously (cf. Beethoven's remark on an effect due to the skilful placing of a chord of the diminished seventh, and wrongly ascribed to the composer's natural genius[64]). Beethoven's autonomy cannot endure such mis-attribution: it is the very point at which the category of autonomy becomes musically concrete. He draws the logical conclusion from both – from the particular's claim to be something, and from its actual triviality. Its meaning is rescued through its nothingness: the whole in which it is absorbed realizes the precise meaning which the particular wrongly claims. This is the core of the dialectic between part and whole in Beethoven. The whole redeems the false promise of the individual detail.   [50][65]

The priority of the whole in Beethoven is widely understood; my task is to trace and interpret its origin in relation to particular moments. The current state of knowledge is summed up in Riemann's trite formulation: 'The classical mode of composition' (here he does *not* distinguish Beethoven from Mozart and Haydn) 'always has the *overall development*, the broad outline, in view. Critics concur in their general admiration for the mighty effects the classical masters are able to draw from initially unpretentious thematic material, through developing it further.' Hugo Riemann, *Handbuch der Musikgeschichte*, vol. II, part III, Leipzig 1922, p. 235.   [51]

On the affirmative, harmonistic element in the negation of the details by the whole, cf. Bekker, *Beethoven*, p. 278.[66] – Also, the 'more agreeable' element in the bass recitative [that is, Ninth Symphony, fourth movement].[67] More agreeable for the audience, that is, through concealment. Important.   [52]

The nullity of the particular; the fact that the whole means everything and – as at the close of op. 111 – that it retrospectively conjures up as accomplished facts details which were never actually there: this remains a central concern of any theory of Beethoven's music. It is based, really, on the fact that no values exist 'in nature', and that they are solely the result of *work*. This view combines quint-essentially bourgeois (ascetic) elements with critical components: the sublation of the individual moment in the totality. – In Beethoven, the particular is intended always to represent the unprocessed, pre-existing natural stuff: hence the triads. Precisely its lack of specific qualities (unlike the highly 'qualified' material of Romanticism) makes possible its complete submergence in the totality. – The negativity of this principle later manifests itself in the diatonic natural themes, the false primal phenomena, of Wagner. In Beethoven this principle is still sustainable

1 through the homogeneity of the material. Even its smallest features are differentiated through the economy of the whole. Banality is definable only in relation to a pre-existing principle opposed to the material which has become banal;
2 in Wagner, the trivial individual element is supposed to mean something in itself; never in Beethoven.

The supreme example of what is at issue here is the opening of the recapitulation of the 'Appassionata' [first movement, bar 151]. In isolation it is in no way striking. In conjunction with the development it is one of the great moments in music.   [53]

In the Violin Concerto* the melody, resembling a closing group, over the dotted D of the horns [second movement, bars 65ff and bars 79ff], is the most overwhelming expression of spaciousness, of gazing into the distance (how feeble, by contrast, is Siegfried on Brunhilde's rock!); at the same time, it shows an extreme 'lack of inspiration': the almost meaningless, melodically unformed quality of the dissected chords and formulaic seconds of the principal voice. This paradox contains the whole of Beethoven; to resolve it would be to raise an understanding of him to the level of theory.   [54]

When Eduard [Steuermann][68] had played the Four Impromptus [op. 90] by Schubert (with the matchlessly great one in C minor), I raised the question why this music was so incomparably *sadder* than even the most sombre pieces by Beethoven. Eduard thought it was due to Beethoven's *activity*, and I defined this, with his agreement, as totality, as the indissoluble union of whole and part. This would mean that Schubert's sadness results not just from the expression (which is itself a *function* of musical temper), but from the liberation of the

* [Above the line:] slow movement.

particular. The liberated detail is abandoned, exposed, just as the liberated individual is also alone, sorrowful – the negative. From this follows something about the twofold nature of Beethoven, which must be emphasized: that is, the totality gives a quality of the particular *holding its own* (which is lacking in Schubert and in the whole of Romanticism, especially Wagner); at the same time, it imparts to the particular an ideological, transfiguring quality which reflects Hegel's doctrine of the positivity of the whole as the summation of all individual negativities – that is, it imparts a moment of *untruth*.

[55]

On the *difference* to Hegel: the dialectical movement of music from nothing to something is possible only if and as long as the nothing is *unaware* of its nothingness: that is, as long as the quality-less themes are content to be themes, without being given a bad conscience by the melody of the *Lied*. Once this bad conscience has arisen – as in Schubert, in Weber and even, to an extent, in Mozart's *Singspiel* element – the trivial theme is open to criticism instead of unfolding within the totality to become its own critique: it is experienced as trite, meaningless. Schubert's great instrumental works are the first manifestation of this awareness, which is *irrevocable*: after that, triadic themes became *really* impossible, in terms of their internal structure. They had strength only as long as that different awareness did not exist, and the subtlest analysis would be needed to define concretely why this was so. But once[69] the theme has taken on substance, the totality becomes a *problem* (not simply impossible). The whole of Brahms's music later crystallized around this problem.

[56][70]

Beethoven's achievement lies in the fact that in his work – and in his alone – the whole is never external to the particular but emerges solely from its movement, or, rather, is this movement. In Beethoven there is no mediation *between* themes, but, as in Hegel, the whole, as pure becoming, is itself the concrete mediation. (NB: In Beethoven there are really no transitional elements, and the inventive richness of, especially, the young Beethoven has the essential purpose of dissolving the topological existence of individual themes. There are so many that none can make itself autonomous. This may be shown, for example, with reference to the first movement of the early Piano Sonata in E♭ major [op. 7].)

This achievement becomes impossible if the development of the *material as a whole* (NB: not just of the particular inspirational idea), if its increasing richness, enforces an emancipation of melodies. To the emancipated melody the whole is no longer

immanent. But it remains as a task confronting this bad individuality. In this way the whole does violence to the particular. This is true
not only of Schumann's formalism or of the deformation of themes
by the 'New Germans' (Siegfried's horn theme in the *Götterdämmerung*). It applies, too, to the most intimate figures; for example, when, in Schubert's B minor Symphony, the second theme is
reinterpreted to give it a symphonic *forte* character, violence has
already been done to it. This theme is so thetic in character that it
rebels against the change – especially since this change of character
does not evolve but is merely placed before us. It is very instructive
to compare this to changes in the character of a *single* theme in
Beethoven. An example is the close of the String Quartet in F major,
op. 59,1, when the Russian theme emerges slowly and in a quite
unharmonized form. Here, the change of character, the way in
which the folksong theme is made interchangeable, acts both as a
means of creating tension and as a disguise which brings about the
resolution. The theme *is* not so, but *presents* itself so, and the sweetness of the harmonization is that of dissimulation – as if the theme,
looking back, had disclosed this one, last, alluring possibility, but
had not succumbed to it. It is precisely this renunciation which also
marks the boundary dividing Beethoven from Romanticism. The
close of the 'Kreutzer' Sonata is also relevant. In this context it is
worth noting the paradox whereby the tendency towards fungibility
(or interchangeability) – as the organizing principle of a musical
whole – increases together with the impossibility of fungibility, that
is, with the uniqueness of the particular detail.[71] This paradox circumscribes the whole recent history of music up to Schoenberg. The
twelve-tone technique is probably its totalitarian resolution – hence
my misgivings about this technique.

Wagner knew of this paradox in his own production. His music is
an attempt to resolve it by reducing the particular to fungible basic
forms – fanfares and chromatic elements. But the historical state of
the material gave him the lie. The fanfares merely impersonate arid-
ity. Not even poverty can be reinstated – what in Beethoven was
bare but significant in the sense used by Goethe can look merely
threadbare even in Schubert; in Wagner it has become theatre and in
Strauss kitsch.   [57][72]

The works of great composers are mere caricatures of what they
would have done had they been allowed. One should not assume
any pre-established harmony between the artist and his time, inseparable as the two may be. Bach – the destroyer of organ music rather
than its consummator – is infinitely more *lyrical* than is allowed by

the repressive 'style' of the trudging *basso continuo*: how recalcit-
rantly the Fugue in F♯ major, the 'Well-Tempered Clavier', I [BWV
859], the 'French' Suite in G major and the 'Partita' in B♭ major sub-
mit to its dictates. At the same time, the joy in dissonance, especially
in less-known works like the motets. This is still more true of
Mozart. His music is a sustained attempt to outwit convention. In
piano pieces such as the B minor *Adagio*, the Minuet in D major; in
the 'Dissonance Quartet'; in passages of *Don Giovanni* and heaven
knows where else, traces of the dissonance he intended can be discerned. His harmony is not so much an expression of his nature as
an effort of 'tact'. Only Beethoven dared to compose as he wanted:
that, too, is a part of his uniqueness. And it was, perhaps, the mis-
fortune of the Romanticism which followed that it no longer faced
the tension between the permitted and the intended: this is a position of *weakness*. Now, they could dream only what was *allowed*.
Wagner.   [58]

The significance of the element of *Haydn* in Beethoven, not only in
the first pieces but in more mature works such as the Sonata in D
major, op. 28 (formation of chromatic inner voices and their implications). Cf. the *Presto* of the C major Sonata (Peters, no. 21) by
Haydn. Also its first movement.   [59]

In Beethoven everything can become anything, because it 'is' nothing; in Romanticism everything can represent anything, because it is
individuated.   [60]

Beethoven's music does not merely contain 'Romantic elements', as
music historians maintain, but has the whole of Romanticism and its
critique within itself. This must be shown in detail. The relationship
to Hegel. Chopin; 'Moonlight' Sonata, first movement. Mendelssohn, middle movement in G minor of the G major Sonata [op. 79].
'Les Adieux'. – *Ferne Geliebte*, the passage of semiquaver-sextuplets
['Nimm sie hin denn, diese Lieder', bars 21–5].[73]   [61]

With reference to the first movement of op. 27, no. 2, it must be
shown how Beethoven, in Hegelian fashion, bears within himself the
whole of Romanticism – not merely its 'mood' but its cosmos of
forms – in order both to cancel it and to preserve it at a higher level.
For example, the Romantic element of crepuscular shading (the shift
from D♯ to D); the preservation of 'atmosphere'; the hybrid form
between instrumental music and *Lied*; the absence of contrasts (in
the sustained triplets) as a reduction to subjectivity. Only Schoenberg was again able, with such genius, to disregard possibilities he

had once taken up. – At the close the principal motif is reflected
from the depths, a model for the conclusion of Chopin's Fantaisie
Impromptu. [62]

Schumann's *humour* as 'gallows humour' – 'Was kost die Welt?'
[What price the world?], and so on, expresses the incompatibility
between the subject and what it says, feels, does. It is directed
against the composing subject, and is deeply connected to a certain
negligence. Relation to Beethoven? Difference? [63]

The affirmative gesture of thanksgiving at the end of the 'Spring'
Sonata has, through its character, become a formula of
Romanticism, as in the coda of the first movement of Schumann's
Fantasia in C major. It could be shown how this gesture has been
debased to one of 'transfiguration', as at the end of Liszt's
Liebesträume or in the Overture of the *Flying Dutchman*. [64]

On the relationship between Beethoven and Romanticism: Euripides
is accused (by Mommsen) of 'slovenliness' in his manner of tying the
dramatic knot in the prologue and untying it by divine intervention.[74] What happened after Beethoven is analogous, while
Schoenberg leads the attempted reconstruction. [65]

It may be fruitful to ask which of Beethoven's achievements passed
over into *Berlioz* – who, compared to him, represents something like
the early history of modernity. As far as I can see, it was the unexpected rhythmical obstructions and *sforzati*, and the 'inserted'
expression marks; both amount to the same thing – a revolt against
the idiomatic element from *within* the idiomatic, without replacing
the threadbare idiom by another. (This, by the way, exactly describes the principle of the *late* Beethoven.) All this emerged as the
shock of modernity in Berlioz, whereas in Beethoven it had been
concealed beneath the germ layer of tradition. In Berlioz such tendencies are set free, but by the same token become detached, undia-
lectical, absurd – the moment of *madness* in his work. He is related
to Beethoven much as Poe is to German Romanticism. To him
Valéry's observation about all that has been *lost* to art through
modernity[75] applies emphatically. (Also the remark in a letter of
Jacobsen's, to the effect that *Niels Lyhne* was composed badly by
intention.)[76] [66]

On the 32 Variations [WoO 80]: have not the *grace notes* in
Beethoven already an element of shock, which also drives the music
forward? A physiognomy of all Beethoven's embellishments will

need to be given. The long trills of the late style: the superfluous element, reduced to the most cursory formula. – Analysis of the changing functions of these mannerisms would probably allow Beethoven's treatment of traditional musical elements to be studied as if under a microscope.   [67]

The concept of 'musical' music, which Busoni derides in his essay on aesthetics,[77] has a very precise meaning. It refers to the purity of the musical medium and to its logic, in contrast to language. It locates the strength of the musical configuration in its extreme remoteness to language. Music speaks because it is pure of language – it communicates, not through its expression or content, but through the *gesture* of speech. In this sense Bach's is the most musical music. That is equivalent to saying that his composition does the least violence to music, becomes meaningful through its immersion in the meaning-less. The opposite type is Beethoven. He forces music to speak, not merely through expression (which is no less present in Bach) but by bringing music closer to speech through its own disposition. Therein lies his power – that music is able to speak, without word, image or content – and also his negativity, in that his power does music violence, as indicated on p. 113 of this notebook [cf. fr. 196]. Conversely, the musical musician is in danger of becoming a specialist, an expert, a fetishist – from Bach to Schoenberg. Underlying this is a genuine paradox: the limit set to both tendencies is that of all music, indeed of art itself. – Music is able to speak through both its remoteness and its closeness to language. – In this respect, Mozart represents a kind of indifference point.   [68]

THREE

SOCIETY

To convince oneself of the inconceivable greatness and stature of Beethoven's work, it should be compared to the achievement of literary classicism in Germany around 1800. If Goethe was able to write isolated poems such as 'Über allen Gipfeln', stanzas like the first of 'Füllest wieder Busch und Tal', in Beethoven *everything* produced after about op. 18 is of this standard, leaving aside 'palette waste' (of which there is *very* little in Beethoven). And the mighty sweep, the momentum of its highest flights, as in 'Pandora', is actually also the *formal law* of Beethoven's work. A classicism without plaster of Paris; mysteriously immune to the outmoded, even where it is beginning to become uninterpretable. Of course, this cannot be ascribed simply to superior talent (neither Goethe nor Jean Paul was a dunce); it is due both to the pristine state of his medium, by which it was predestined to depict the human as nature, and to the historical moment, when music and not poetry converged with philosophy, at least in Germany.   [69]

The affinity between Beethoven's humanity and a certain type of family-album poetry deserves precise analysis; for example:

> Wer ein treues Weib errungen,
> Stimm in unseren Jubel ein,[78]
> [Who a loyal wife has won, let him join in our rejoicing,]

or:

Und ein liebes Herz erreichet,
Was ein liebes Herz geweiht.[79]
[And a loving heart attains what a loving heart has hallowed.]

In such lines the grandeur and the ideology of the bourgeoisie are so intertwined that neither is conceivable without the other. Thoughts of marriage and children are found even in the songs addressed to the *Ferne Geliebte*.   [70]

Schiller has something of the man risen from a lowly station who, embarrassed in good society, starts shouting to make himself heard. 'Power and impudence' – the bragging of the petty-bourgeois, which may be a general characteristic of the brutal bourgeois craving for ostentation, as observed by Max Horkheimer. Included in this gesture is the self-incited, pealing, violent laughter and a certain tendency to 'explode'. This lies at the source of the solemn tone, and underlies the whole of idealism – a certain nobility in the sense of grandeur, sovereignty over nature,[80] compensates for the vulgar, inferior element. Behind the maxims lie the letters about woollen stockings exchanged with their mothers by pastors' sons working as private tutors. This element must be defined as an objective aspect of bourgeois bombast. It is usually linked to the fiction of *strength*. In Schiller it is held in check by a strong intellect, but what remains of it is finally pure weakness. Beethoven is not immune to this – though his work is saved by the enormous density of its purely musical substance.   [71]

What we know about Beethoven as a private person suggests that the grim, unfriendly aspect of his character had to do with shame and rejected love. An extreme contrast to Wagner in the formation of the bourgeois character. A man who becomes a monad and clings to the monadological form to preserve his humanity. Wagner, by contrast, becomes inordinately loving because he cannot withstand the monadic situation. – Associated with the boorishness is an open-handed generosity, but also mistrust. – The aloofness derives from the fact that for the proper human being, as represented by Beethoven, all human relationships have a moment unworthy of humanity. – This is allied to strong traits of aggression, sadism, of noisy, blustering laughter, of insult. Coupled to an element of will: he commands himself to laugh. The demonic is always self-imposed, never quite 'genuine', or 'natural'. Musicians' humour, in which laughter is emancipated from spirit, almost always has this trait. –

The confinement of humanity to music alone is linked to shame. How brusque someone needs to be in order to write 'Dir werde Lohn' [Yours be the reward].[81] – This complexion of Beethoven's humour leads again and again to polyphony. Canons such as 'Bester [Herr] Graf, Sie sind ein Schaf[!]' [WoO 183]. Polyphony in Beethoven has an entirely new meaning: a solution enforced by yoking together disparate, disintegrated elements. It has to work. Hence the canons.   [72]

'Even the early Beethoven was the foremost living composer.' Thomas-San-Galli, *Ludwig van Beethoven*, p. 88.   [73]

On the formation of the bourgeois character in music, see Chopin, *Briefe* [ed. by Alexander Guttry, Munich 1928], pp. 382f: 'The bourgeois class wants to be amazed, dazzled by mechanical virtuosity, which I am unable to do. Genteel folk who travel a lot are arrogant; but they are also educated and judicious when they are prepared to look closely at themselves. Yet they are always so caught up and isolated within their conventional boredom that they care little whether music is good or bad, as they have to listen to it from morning till night in any case', and so on. In this connection, Beethoven's mode of notation, aiming at a mechanical effect, as in the ms of the 'Geister' Trio.[82]   [74]

It is conceivable that Beethoven actually *wanted* to go deaf – because he had already had a taste of the sensuous side of music as it is blared from loudspeakers today. 'The world is a prison in which solitary confinement is preferable.' Karl Kraus.[83]   [75]

On the theory of Beethoven's *deafness*, cf. Julius Bahle, *Eingebung und Tat im musikalischen Schaffen* [*Ein Betrag zur Psychologie der Entwicklungs- und Schaffensgesetze schöpferischer Menschen*], Leipzig 1939, p. 164:

> We should not, therefore, dismiss out of hand the link drawn by Romain Rolland between Beethoven's deafness and his immense inner concentration, his incessant auditory seeking and grasping. This was confirmed to Rolland by Dr Marage, in his diagnosis of the post-mortem findings. He wrote to Rolland: 'The cause of Beethoven's deafness seems to me to lie in a congestion of blood in the inner ear and the auditory centres, caused by overstrain of the organ through excessive concentration, and in the pitiless inevitability of thought, as you put it so beautifully. A comparison with Indian yoga seems to me entirely apt.' (R. Rolland, *Beethovens Meisterjahre*, Leipzig 1930, p. 226.) According to this diagnosis, therefore, Beethoven had

sacrificed himself on the altar of deafness in order 'to draw nearer than others to God, and from that vantage point to spread the divine radiance among mankind'.   [76]

'O you physicians, scholars and sages,' he cried in ecstasy, 'do you not see how the Spirit creates form, how the inner god made Hephaestus lame in order to make him repulsive to Aphrodite and so to preserve him for the art of fire and crafts; how Beethoven went deaf so that he could hear nothing but the singing daemon within him . . .' Georg Groddeck, *Der Seelensucher*, Leipzig/Vienna 1921, p. 194.[84]   [77]

That Beethoven never goes out of date is connected, perhaps, to the fact that reality has not yet caught up with his music: 'real human-ism'.[85]   [78]

To say that Beethoven's music expressed the World Spirit, that it was the content of that Spirit or suchlike, would undoubtedly be pure nonsense. What is true, however, is that his music expressed the same experiences which inspired Hegel's concept of the World Spirit.   [79]

The reluctance of the Age of Enlightenment to deal with bourgeois life in the drama, its inclination to reserve it to comedy and finally to smuggle it ironically into drama as *comédie larmoyante*,[86] or to excuse the *bürgerliches Trauerspiel* as an anomaly – all this may not perhaps reflect simply the consequence of court convention under Absolutism, but also an awareness of the *non-representability* of the bourgeois world, of the contradiction between the decay of images within objects and their presentation as image. The novel and com-edy were possible to the extent that they made this contradiction their theme. And it is conceivable that the unparalleled upsurge of music in the same period is connected to the fact that it lent voice to the empirical subject without *initially* being affected by that paradox or aporia. In Beethoven, a middle-class person can speak, without shame, like a king. Underlying this, to be sure, is the profound indi-gence of all musical classicity, Beethoven's '*Empire* bombast' – per-haps one of the most fundamental points on which he is open to critique.   [80]

It is peculiar to the bourgeois Utopia that it is not yet able to con-ceive an image of perfect joy without that of the person excluded from it:* it can take pleasure in that image only in proportion to the unhappiness in the world. In Schiller's 'Ode to Joy', the text of the Ninth Symphony, any person is included in the circle provided he is able to call 'even a single soul his own in this wide world'; that is, the person who is happy in love. 'But he who has none, let him steal weeping from our company'. Inherent in the bad collective is the image of the solitary, and joy desires to see him weep. Moreover, the rhyme word in German, *stehle* [steal], points rightly to the property relationship. We can understand why the 'problem of the Ninth Symphony' was insoluble. In the fairytale Utopia, too, the step-mother who must dance in burning shoes or is stuffed into a barrel spiked with nails is an inseparable part of the glorious wedding. The loneliness punished by Schiller, however, is no other than that produced by his revellers' community itself. In such a company, what is to become of old maids, not to speak of the souls of the dead?[87] [81]

My study on Beethoven will have to offer a critique of Pfitzner's theory of the creative 'idea' in support of my view of the dialectical nature of great music. Cf. Bahle [*Eingebung und Tat*] p. 308; quotation from Pfitzner: 'In music ... a passage always *is* and *affects us* just as it is in itself, and is not altered by any change in its position or its context' (refute this with reference to opp. 57 and 111); 'ultimately, music should be judged by *it*, the small unit (the melody); not by the effect of this or that piece of music as a whole; just as gold(!!) is assayed in terms of its carat number, and not by the objects made from it' (cf. Pfitzner, *Gesammelte Schriften* [Augsburg 1926], vol. II, pp. 23 and 25). Here, the relationship between the Romantic postulation of the individual lyrical subject as absolute, and the notion of the theme as possession or value (gold!), is quite obvious. Cf. 'Musical Thieves, Unmusical Judges'.[88] Bahle, p. 309, uses the term '*atomistic*'. [82]

The Mozartian 'divine *frivolity*' refers, in terms of the philosophy of history, to the moment when the libertine freedom and sovereignty of the feudal order passed over into that of the bourgeoisie, which, however, at this stage still resembled the feudal. The double meaning of '*Herr*' (Mr; lord). Humaneness still coincides here with libertinism. Utopia appears in the form of this identity. Mozart died just before the French Revolution lapsed into repression. The affinity of this aspect with traits of the young Goethe. The 'Muses' son'[89] is a kind of Mozartian prodigy, a primal phenomenon. [83]

---

* [Marginal note:] On this point: Thomas More's Utopia includes slaves recruited among convicts, prisoners of war and 'criminals worthy of death' bought from foreign countries. There are also 'foreign wage labourers': cf. Elster, *Wörterbuch der Volkswirtschaft*, Jena 1933, p. 290.

Regarding Beethoven and the French Revolution: *Wagner-Lexikon* 262 (Mozart's half-cadences as *Tafelmusik* – mealtime entertainment).[90] – Symphonic themes are not absolute antitheses, ibid. 439.[91] – NB: Beethoven's relationship to the French Revolution is to be understood in terms of specific *technical* concepts. – I should like to hold one thing fast: just as the French Revolution did not create a new social form but helped a structure already formed to break through, in the same way Beethoven relates to *forms*. His work involves not so much the production of forms, as their reproduction out of freedom (something very similar happens in Kant). This reproduction out of freedom has, however, at least one strongly ideological trait. The moment of untruth lies in the fact that something appears to be in the process of creation which in fact is already there (that is exactly the relationship between precondition and result that I have tried to define). Hence, also, the 'impudent' quality: the pretension to freedom of someone who, in reality, was *obeying*. The expression of necessity in Beethoven is incomparably more substantial than that of freedom, which always has something fabricated about it (as with the mandatory joy). Freedom is real in Beethoven only as hope. That is one of the most important social links. The passage: 'Yours be the reward' should be compared, for example, to the close of *Fidelio*.[92] The 'unattainability of joy'.[93]   [84]

Fichte passage in original: Rochlitz, IV, p. 350. – Beethoven and the French Revolution, Rochlitz III, p. 315. – Beethoven's physiognomy as that of the idealist, Rochlitz IV, p. 353.[94] In the same connection, certain passages from Hegel's *Philosophy of History*, such as that on the Chinese.[95]   [85]

Beethoven reveres Seume; Thomas-San-Galli, *Ludwig van Beethoven*, p. 68.[96]   [86]

The history of great bourgeois music at least since Haydn is the history of the interchangeable, or fungible: that no individual thing exists 'in itself', and everything only in relation to the whole. The truth and untruth of this music can be determined from the solution it offers to the question of fungibility – which has both a progressive *and* a regressive tendency. The question in all music is: How can a whole exist without doing violence to the individual part? The answer to this question depends, however, on the general state of the productive forces of music at a given time; more specifically: the more highly developed these forces are, the greater are the difficulties presented to a composer. In Beethoven (and Haydn) the solution is bound up with a certain *bareness* of the material, a kind of upright, middle-class frugality. In this respect Beethoven represents a particular moment: the melody is not yet emancipated, yet the individual part is already substantial; but, again, its substance derives from the bareness of the whole. Melody achieves emancipation only in moments of transcendence. Only at this stage is 'classicism' in music possible at all, and cannot be reconstructed. (These moments of transcendence do not occur in Haydn, nor do we find in his work the substantiality of the human individual, the eloquence of the detail, however meagre. This gives rise to an element of constriction, even of narrow-mindedness in Haydn, despite all the grandeur. The functional interconnections present throughout Haydn's music give an impression of competence, active life and suchlike categories, which ominously call to mind the rising bourgeoisie.) NB: This universal fungibility expresses itself in late capitalism in the passion for organization, the incessant rearranging. It is as if no brick were to be left on any other, especially when all novelty is precluded by the foundation. You need only watch them at work with their blue pencils, their red ink, their scissors. [87]

The way in which music produces itself in Beethoven represents the totality of social *work*. Go back to Haydn. His works often resemble those mechanical models of early factories in which everyone plays his part in the great whole – as in the Salzburg fountain displays. In Beethoven, however, the totality of work has a critical aspect; that is, work consists primarily of a *paring down* for the sake of totality. It already includes the appropriation of surplus value; that is, something is *subtracted* from each individual theme to make it serve the whole. But that, too, is then negated once more. Musical relationships in *Mozart* never have the character of work: that distinguishes him from Beethoven *and* Haydn. [88]

In the great epic, in the epic as such and in all narrative, there exists, as an intrinsic element of their truth, a certain stupidity, an incomprehension, a not-being-in-the-know – something by no means adequately conveyed by the traditional notion of naivety.* Perhaps, at the deepest level, it is the refusal to accept fungibility, an attachment to the Utopian belief that there is something worth reporting. For fungibility repudiates the mythical world to which narrative from the outset is addressed. Myth, after all, is the unchanging. At the origin of all myths is something anachronistic. But the paradox is that precisely this stupidity is the precondition of epic reason, and even,

---

* [Marginal note, perhaps relating to the text as a whole:] NB: 'Objectivity', blind gazing, epic positivism.

in a sense, of cognition itself, of experience in the sense elaborated here, whereas clevernesss destroys such knowledge and thus, in fact, converges with stupidity, a narrow-minded fixation on the here-and-now. In this context, we should think not only of Gotthelf, whose stupidity is not entirely wise, but of Goethe, Stifter and Keller. In *Martin Salander*, for example, it is very easy to recognize the stupidity of the attitude: 'Look how bad people are today', and to point out that Keller knew nothing of the economics of the period of German unification with their attendant crisis. But it is only this stupidity which allows Keller to write a narrative and not merely a report about the beginnings of high capitalism and, this being so, the two crooked lawyer brothers tell us more about fungibility that any theory except the one which is wholly true.[97] Perhaps it is this very stupidity which is indispensable to the epic temper, and has now been lost. (Today, epic itself has been taken over by fungibility, in its praise of any intellectual, though he resemble a yokel; and Brecht's gestic art amounts to a technical abuse of epic stupidity. Even in Kafka, it is faked to a certain extent.) But this loss leads us to one of the deepest questions of art. It is the question concerning the dubious nature of technical progress, which is always progress in the domination of nature.[98] My musicological study of 1941 does not go nearly far enough in this respect.[99] In a painting by a German primitive or by an early Italian master, it is easy to explain this or that characteristic by an inadequate mastery of perspective. But would this same painting be conceivable at all if the perspective were improved? Is not the identification of errors of perspective a mark of positivist obtuseness? Is not the constellation formed by the technical imperfection of the painting and what it expresses, in fact, indissoluble? Or take the famous contention that Beethoven was bad at instrumentation, which can be backed by such cogent evidence as the insufficiency of natural horns and trumpets, and thus the 'holes' in the writing of orchestral parts. Indeed, could his instrumentation have been *better*, without a profound conflict arising between the greater mastery of nature and the core of Beethoven's experience? One need only call to mind the inane, wholly superficial assertion that Strauss had the technique and Beethoven the content, to realize how nonsensically rationalistic[100] is the very concept of technique, as I have used it up to now. – Poverty is of importance here. – In capitalism, always too little and too much. – NB: Walser. The *provincial*, backward element, which Kafka mobilized.   [89][101]

It is very easy to demonstrate defects of instrumentation in Beethoven; over-thin passages caused by insufficient knowledge of woodwinds; obese *tutti* (for example, in the Seventh) which swamp the thematic events. But in his work, as in all significant art, the faults are inseparable from the substance. This means that they are incorrigible. The unison solo of the bassoons in the coda to the Finale of the Fifth [bars 317–19] is, of course, preposterous – ecstatic bassoons are comic. But one need only imagine them replaced by a trombone: still more preposterous. This is a very large subject; it concerns the true location of that which alone deserves to be called style.   [90]

The symphonic principle of the contraction of time, of 'development' in the deeper sense, of 'work', corresponds to epistasis in the drama. Today, under direct domination, both are in decline. Only a fine distinction will decide whether such decline means the liquidation of resistance or its ubiquity.   [91]

The theory of musical development – a primary concern of criticism – ought to deal with the introduction to Act I of *Siegfried*. Mime's fruitless work. His theme is a classical model of symphonic development, from the Scherzo of Schubert's Quartet in D minor. But in Wagner the elaboration of the model, as expression, takes on the character of a fruitless, compulsive circling.[102] In this, Wagner revealed something of the nature of musical development itself: that the futility which he made explicit is objectively implicit in development as such. This, however, is linked to the *social* nature of work, which is both 'productive', in that it keeps society alive, yet also fruitless, in its blind marking of time (the tendency to regress to mere reproduction). If the change in the principle of development between Beethoven and Wagner reflects a developmental tendency of the bourgeoisie as a whole, the later phase also tells us something about the earlier one: that development was always inherently impossible, and could succeed only by a momentary paradox. – Work is to be understood as a central concept in Beethoven. Indeed, the principle of work's symphonic objectivity reflects its *social* objectivity as well.   [92]

On the subject of the musical development – work – bourgeois bustle – intrigue: Figaro's aria in the *Barber*, especially the growing seriousness towards the end, almost as in a symphony of Beethoven.[93]

The principle of the development as 'doing', accomplishing, something; society's production process finally traceable back to the nature of *bustle*, as it is found in Haydn. There, however, it is also *mythical*: the bustling of spirits, pixies, music's poltergeist commotion, its ultimately spooky activity. This is the musical equivalent of the relationship of idealism to myth.[103]   [94]

For the bourgeois: animation = a bustling eagerness to get something done. Study the relation of 'animation' to the mechanical element (for example, Rondo op. 12, no. 3).   [95]

On Beethoven – and various others. In the discussion of the transition from the development-based style to the late style – or perhaps of development as largely insignificant – investigate once more the idea of the imbroglio, of intrigue, and its decline. This decline cannot be attributed solely to the predominance of the realistic, empirical moment, but has its own intrinsic reasons. Just as, in a certain sense, the musical development was never entirely possible, giving rise to insoluble problems and paradoxes, intrigue takes on a foolish, fatuous quality when the characters are fully developed and concretely presented. In this fatuity competition recognizes its own dreadfulness as in a distorting mirror. This can be readily seen in the early Schiller. How inane are the machinations of Eboli and the courtiers, the forced caskets and purloined letters in *Don Carlos*, set against the confrontation between Philip and Posa. How far-fetched is the motivation for the mistaken murder of Leonore in *Fiesko*. How easily could all the havoc in *Kabale und Liebe* [Intrigue and Love] have been cut short if Ferdinand had shown even the faintest scepticism towards the fake love letter addressed to a figure of fun, and if Luise, even if she wanted to respect an enforced vow of silence, had found a way to apprise him of the feebly concealed truth. This foolishness reached its height in dramatists who took the conflict-form seriously (NB: conflict = unity of action), such as Hebbel (for example, in *Herodes*), and is still detectable in the somewhat inane symbolism of the late Ibsen (the sledge in *Borkman*, under the runners of which the old subordinate and father comes to grief). Admittedly, the whole notion of intrigue is bourgeois in the sense that bourgeois *work* appears as intrigue and the typical bourgeois, its mediator, as a villain. But the viewpoint from which this seems the case is that of the absolutist court. The drama of intrigue is always also about work as a means of social climbing, ignoring and desecrating hierarchies. This is why the drama of intrigue is possible only as an absolutist form, an allegorical ceremony, and not with full bourgeois individuation, since this is precisely what it judges. The greatest French drama of the seventeenth and eighteenth centuries would need to be studied in this context. Goethe balked at the stupidity of intrigue – there is none in his work – which is why his plays are as much less 'dramatic' than Schiller's as they are more lasting. All these problems apply equally to music. Ceremonial intrigue would correspond to the *fugue* – while the sonata would stand for the fully developed intrigue as *successfully achieved* –

though also bearing the seeds of its own demise. Beethoven's *oeuvre* is the theatre of both – accomplishment and dissolution. Two decisive questions remain:

1 In concrete technical terms, what leads to dissolution?
2 Why was the sonata possible, but not the bourgeois tragedy?

The second question seems likely to go very deep.* [96][104]

In many of Schubert's works which are orientated towards Beethoven – not the last, but most of the piano sonatas, the outer movements of both Trios, the Trout Quintet and even certain parts of the Octet – one is struck by a certain threadbare or conventional quality of the material. This is not due to a lack of originality – for who could have had more original ideas? – nor does it result directly from inferior skill in through-composition. It is linked, rather, to a certain pre-given character of the musical language which, though running counter to Romanticism's subjective freedom, dominated the entire movement up to the expressive clichés of Wagner. Even in Schubert, the commodity character of music is indicated by a shopsoiled, shabby, slipshod element, which emerges most clearly where the music seems most Beethovenian. This also has to do with the petty-bourgeois element – as if someone in shirtsleeves were making a political speech in a beer-garden (especially certain openings like that of the E♭ major Trio and of the late Piano Sonata in C minor). These are also the moments in Schubert which seem most dated and nineteenth century. Although they are, without exception, grandly conceived and genuine in their musical language, they employ this language too fluently, are insufficiently distanced, almost too sure of it. Especially in Schubert, as compared to Beethoven, there is an element of reification with regard to the material. Beethoven's greatness lies precisely in his difference from it. There is nothing reified in his work, since he is able to dissolve the ready-made quality of the material – which, nevertheless, is *simpler* in his work than in Schubert's. He does so by reducing it to such elementary forms that it no longer manifests itself as material at all. Beethoven's apparent asceticism towards subjective, spontaneous inspiration is precisely the way to elude reification. Beethoven, the master of positive negation: discard, that you may acquire. The shrinkage of the Beethovenian adagio is to be seen in this context. That in the 'Hammerklavier' Sonata is the last adagio in music. The one in the Ninth is the alternative form. The last Quartets and Sonatas contain

* [Later note:] NB: Cf. my comments on musical stupidity [fr. 140].

only variations on it, or *Lieder*; that is, Beethoven recognizes the incompatibility of the 'theme', as a melody sufficient in itself, with the grand design. The mature Brahms had a very sensitive ear for this critical moment in Beethoven.   [97]

NB: Beethoven's *critical* method of composition stems from the meaning of the music itself, and not from psychology.   [98]

The relationship of logic to tonality and of work to musical dynamics needs to be formulated. Probably logic – always pruning and abstracting – *guarantees* appropriation through work in the reflexive form. This is the innermost question in Beethoven.   [99]

Don Quixote's secret. * – If the disenchantment of the world, which Benjamin described as the destruction of aura by mechanization,[105] – that is, by the spirit of pragmatism (in aesthetic terms, perhaps: by the spirit of the comic) – may be called the original and essential contribution of the bourgeoisie, it is no less true that dream and Utopia are themselves bound to the existence of this spirit as their antithesis. We really know only of bourgeois art, and what we call feudal art – such as Dante – is bourgeois in spirit. In truth, there is only as much art as art is impossible. Hence, the existence of all major art forms is a paradox, and most of all the form of the novel, which is the bourgeois genre χατ᾽ ἐξοχήν. Don Quixote and Sancho are inseparable.   [100]

Perhaps the concept of the 'new', which in 'Likes and Dislikes'[106] I made the yardstick of spontaneous artistic experience, was already itself a distortion in terms of the history of philosophy – that is, it was the way spontaneous experience appeared from the perspective of a world which already precluded it. The moment of the new in Beethoven, which I see as the opposite of the fixed 'pattern', is itself confined to his very late work.   [101]

NB: There is no circumventing the problem of Beethoven's fixed, *formulaic language*. Shorthand forms emerge, and in the very late period are petrified into allegories. This can be demonstrated as early as the first movement of op. 10, no. 2. Something decisively bourgeois in Beethoven is no doubt at work here. Then there is the enormously extensive use of abbreviations in his manuscripts, as I have pointed out with regard to the 'Geister' Trio [cf. fr. 20]. Study

---

* [Above the text:] Probably re. Beethoven.

the literature on this. – The mechanical quality is linked to the solemnity. Cf. the quotation from Chopin on p. 8 of this notebook [cf. fr. 74]. [102]

That the subject of *Fidelio* is fidelity rather than love has often been noted. This should be put into a theoretical context, especially with regard to the anti-sentimental element. The notion of *brio*, of striking fire from the soul,[107] as something directed against the private sphere, and against that of expression. The 'public' quality of Beethoven's work, even in the intimacy of the chamber music. The element of expression as a matter of technique is the real antithesis between him and Romanticism. – In this context, consider Kant's doctrine of marriage and Hegel's concept of respectability as opposed to morality.[108] [103]

Bekker's thesis regarding the 'community-forming power' of the symphony[109] needs to be reformulated. The symphony is the aestheticized (and already *neutralized*) form of the *public meeting*. Categories within it, such as oratory, debate, resolution (the decisive element) and ceremony should be identified. The truth and untruth of the symphony are decided in the *agora*. What the late Beethoven rejects is just this element of the conclave, of bourgeois *ritual*.* [104]

Alienation appears in Beethoven as something quasi administrative, institutional – as 'bustle'. *Beethoven and the State* would not be without sense as a title. Hegelianism. Long stretches of the musical enactment as the self-preservation of the totality – hence the moment of objectification. In addition, the military aspect and the popular assembly. [105]

From a conversation with Max [Horkheimer] and Thomas Mann on 9 April 1949.[110] The subject was Russia, and in face of our very heated attacks, T.M. took up a cautiously apologetic position. In connection with the debate on art he advanced the view that it is questionable whether art could lay claim to complete freedom and autonomy, and that its greatest epochs have probably coincided with its attachment to a higher authority (this motif is touched on in his *Faustus* novel).[111] I did not contest this thesis (although I would say that even Bach, compared to Beethoven, shows a moment of heteronomy, of something not entirely embraced by the subject which,

---

* [Inserted above the text:] Concept of *rhetoric* fundamental here.

despite his superior 'accomplishment', places him, in historico-philo-
sophical terms, *below* Beethoven. However, I did argue that this
ought not to be made into an ideology for Russian repression. The
question whether art has not yet quite shaken off its theological origin and is still, to an extent, naively bound by its forms is one thing;
but for it to be heteronomously *subjected*, from outside, to a
bond from which it is already emancipated by its own meaning is
quite another. In the great religious epochs of art, its theological content represented, for the most progressive minds, the *truth* – that dictated by the Russians is regressive and, in its imposition, is already,
transparently, untruth. T.M. conceded the difference. – Max added
that in the greatest epochs of church art, as in the high Renaissance,
the patrons of artists such as Raphael were of the utmost liberality
(their attitude on the delicate question of Joseph's age). The Party
Secretaries who command art production in Russia have the narrow-
est, most retarded, most benighted of minds – 'blockheads'.   [106]

Music, before the bourgeoisie's emancipation, had an essentially disciplinary function. Afterwards, it became autonomous, centred on
its own formal laws, heedless of effect – a synthetic unity. But these
two destinies mediate each other. For the formal law of freedom,
which determines all moments and thus entirely circumscribes aesthetic immanence – is nothing other than the disciplinary function
turned inwards, reflected, wrenched from its immediate social purpose. It might be said that the autonomy of the art-work has its
source in heteronomy, much as the freedom of the subject arose
from lordly sovereignty. The force enabling the work of art to constitute itself and dispense with a direct outward effect, is the force of
this same effect in altered form; and the law to which it relates is no
other than that which it[112] imposes on others. This can be shown in
detail in the *obbligato* style[113] which Viennese classicism took over
from the practice of fugue. This, however, has a decisive consequence. Autonomous music is not *absolutely* cut off from the
context of effects: it *mediates* this context through its formal law.
This is precisely what Kant called our awe before the sublime,[114]
though he did not yet apply this to art.[115] The moment when the
sublime becomes a totality, something immanent, is that of transcendence. 'The glorious moment' ['Der glorreiche Augenblick']
(Georgiades's idea of the festive),[116] 'striking sparks from the
soul',[117] deriving from totality a sense of *resistance*, authority revert-
ing to negation – all this is, in mediated form, the real function of
the autonomous.   [107]*

---

* [Above the text:] re. Beethoven? – but in general, of the utmost importance. 1956.

The opening of the third *Leonore* Overture sounds as if, from the depths of imprisonment, the ocean had been attained.   [108]

Text 1: The Mediation Between Music and Society

The history of ideas, and thus the history of music, is an autarchic motivational context insofar as the social law, on the one hand, produces the formation of spheres screened off against each other, and on the other hand, as the law of totality, still comes to light in each sphere as the same law. Its concrete deciphering in music is an essential task of musical sociology. Due to such hypostasis of the musical sphere, the problems of its objective content cannot be transformed directly into problems of its social genesis, but society as a problem – as the entirety of its antagonisms – immigrates into the problems, into the logic of the mind.

Let us reflect on Beethoven. If he is the musical prototype of the revolutionary bourgeoisie, he is at the same time the prototype of a music that has escaped from its social tutelage and is esthetically fully autonomous, a servant no longer. His work explodes the schema of a complaisant adequacy of music and society. In it, for all its idealism in tone and posture, the essence of society, for which he speaks as the vicar of the total subject, becomes the essence of music itself. Both are comprehensible in the interior of the works only, not in mere imagery. The central categories of artistic construction can be translated into social ones. The kinship with that bourgeois libertarianism which rings all through Beethoven's music is a kinship of the dynamically unfolding totality. It is in fitting together under their own law, as becoming, negating, confirming themselves and the whole without looking outward, that his movements come to resemble the world whose forces move them; they do not do it by imitating that world.

In this respect Beethoven's attitude on social objectivity is more that of philosophy – the Kantian, in some points, and the Hegelian in the decisive ones – than it is the ominous mirroring posture: in Beethoven's music society is conceptlessly known, not photographed. What he calls thematic work is the mutual abrasion of the antitheses, the individual interests. The totality that governs the chemism of his work is not a cover concept schematically subsuming the various moments; it is the epitome of both that thematic work and its result, the finished composition. The tendency there is, as far as possible, to dequalify the natural material on which the work is confirmed. The motive kernels, the particulars to which each movement is tied, are themselves identical with the universal; they are formulas of tonality, reduced to nothingness as things of their own and preshaped by the totality as much as the individual is in individualistic society. The developing variation, an image of social labor, is definite negation: from what has once been posited it ceaselessly brings forth the new and enhanced by destroying it in its immediacy, its quasi-natural form.

On the whole, however, these negations are supposed – as in liberalist theory, to which, of course, social practice never corresponded – to have affirmative effects. The cutting short and mutual wearing down of individual moments, of suffering and perdition, is equated with an integration said to make each individual meaningful through its voidance. This is why the *prima vista* most striking formalistic residue in Beethoven – the reprise, the recurrence, unshaken despite all structural dynamics, of what has been voided – is not just external and conventional. Its purpose is to confirm the process as its own result, as occurs unconsciously in social practice. Not by chance are some of Beethoven's most pregnant conceptions designed for the instant of the reprise as the recurrence of the same. They justify, as the result of a process, what has been once before. It is exceedingly illuminating that Hegelian philosophy – whose categories can be applied without violence to every detail of a music that cannot possibly have been exposed to any Hegelian 'influence' in terms of the history of ideas – that this philosophy knows the reprise as does Beethoven's music: the last chapter of Hegel's *Phenomenology*, the absolute knowledge, has no other content than to summarize the total work which claims to have already gained the identity of subject and object, in religion.

But that the affirmative gestures of the reprise in some of Beethoven's greatest symphonic movements assume the force of crushing repression, of an authoritarian 'That's how it is,' that the decorative gestures overshoot the musical events – this is the tribute Beethoven was forced to pay to the ideological character whose spell extends even to the most sublime music ever to aim at freedom under continued unfreedom. The self-exaggerating assurance that the return of the first is the meaning, the self-revelation of immanence as transcendence – this is the cryptogram for the senselessness of a merely self-reproducing reality that has been welded together into a system. Its substitute for meaning is continuous functioning.

All these implications of Beethoven result from musical analysis without any daring analogies, but to social knowledge they prove as true as the inferences about society itself. Society recurs in great music: transfigured, criticized, and reconciled, although these aspects cannot be surgically sundered; it looms as much above the activities of self-preserving rationality as it is suitable for befogging those activities. It is as a dynamic totality, not as a series of pictures, that great music comes to be an internal world theater. This indicates the direction in which we would have to look for a total theory of the relation of society and music.

[. . .] A composer is always a *zoon politikon* as well, the more so the more emphatic his purely musical claim. None is *tabula rasa*. In early childhood they adjusted to the goings-on around them; later they are moved by ideas expressing their own, already socialized form of reaction. Even individualistic composers from the flowering of the private sphere, men like Schumann and Chopin, are no exceptions; the din of the bourgeois revolution rumbles in Beethoven, and in Schumann's *Marseillaise* quotations it echoes, weakened, as in dreams.

The fact that Beethoven's music is structured like the society to which – with doubtful justification – we give the name of 'rising bourgeoisie', or at least like its self-consciousness and its conflicts, is premised on another fact: that the primary-musical form of his own views was inherently mediated by the spirit of his social class in the period around 1800. He was not the spokesman or advocate of this class, although not lacking in such rhetorical features; he was its inborn son.

[. . .] In Beethoven's youth it meant something to be a genius. As fiercely as the gestures of his music rose against the social polish of the Rococo, he was backed by a good deal of social approval. In the age of the French Revolution the bourgeoisie had occupied economic and administrative key positions before seizing political power; this is what gave to the pathos of its libertarian movement* the costumed, fictitious character from which Beethoven, the self-appointed 'brain owner' as opposed to the landowner, was not free either.

That this archbourgeois was a protégé of aristocrats fits as neatly into the social character of his oeuvre as the scene we know from Goethe's biography, when he snubbed the court. Reports on Beethoven's personality leave little doubt of his anticonventional nature, a combination of sansculottism with Fichtean braggadocio; it recurs in the plebeian habitus of his humanity. His humanity is suffering and protesting. It feels the fissure of its loneliness. Loneliness is what the emancipated individual is condemned to in a society retaining the mores of the absolutist age, and with them the style by which the self-positing subjectivity takes its own measure.[118]
[. . .] What has been called the obligatory style, rudiments of which are discernible as early as the seventeenth century, contains the tele-

---

* Cf. Max Horkheimer, 'Egoismus und Freiheitsbewegung', in *Zeitschrift für Sozialforschung* 5 (1936), pp. 161ff.

ological call for a wholly, thoroughly formed composition, a call for
– an analogy to philosophy – a systematic composition. Its ideal is
music as a deductive unit; whatever drops out of that unit, unrelated
and indifferent, defines itself as a break and a flaw to begin with.
That is the esthetic aspect of the fundamental thesis of Weber's
musical sociology, the thesis of progressive rationality.

Knowingly or not, Beethoven was an objective follower of this
idea. He produces the total unity of the obligatory style by
dynamization. The several elements no longer follow one another in
a discrete sequence; they pass into rational unity through a continuous process effectuated by themselves. The conception lies all ready,
so to speak, charted in the state of the problem offered to Beethoven
by the sonata form of Haydn and Mozart, the form in which diversity
evens out into unity but keeps diverging from it while the form
remains an abstract sheath over the diversity. The irreducible vision,
in an eye that in the most advanced production of his time, in the
masterly pieces of the other two Viennese classicists, could read the
question in which their perfection transcended itself and called for
something else. This was how he dealt with the crux of the dynamic
form, with the reprise, the conjuring of static sameness amid a total
becoming. In conserving it, he has grasped the reprise as a problem.
He seeks to rescue the objective formal canon that has been rendered impotent, as Kant rescued the categories: by once more deducing it from the liberated subjectivity. The reprise is as much
brought on by the dynamic process as it ex post facto vindicates the
process, so to speak, as its result. In this vindication the process has
passed on what was then going to drive irresistibly beyond it.

But the deadlock between the dynamic and the static element
coincides with the historic instant of a class that voids the static
order and yet cannot yield, unfettered, to its own dynamics without
voiding itself. The great social conceptions of Beethoven's own time,
Hegel's philosophy of law and Comte's positivism, have found
words for this. And that bourgeois society is exploded by its own
immanent dynamics – this is imprinted in Beethoven's music, the
sublime music, as a trait of esthetic untruth: by its power, his successful work of art posits the real success of what was in reality a
failure, and that in turn affects the declamatory moments of the
work of art. In truth content, or in its absence, esthetic and social
criticism coincide. This is how little the relation of music and society
can be superimposed on a vague and trivial zeitgeist in which both
are thought to share. Socially, too, music will be the more true and
substantial the farther it is removed from the official zeitgeist; the
one of Beethoven's epoch was represented by Rossini rather than by
him. The social part is the objectivity of the thing itself, not its affin-

ity to the wishes of the established society of the moment; on that point art and cognition are agreed.

[. . .] The interrelation of music and society becomes evident in technology. Its unfolding is the *tertium comparations* between superstructure and infrastructure. [. . .] As an individual psychology, a mechanism of identification with technology as a social ego ideal evokes resistance and resistance only will create originality. There is nothing immediate in originality. Beethoven expressed that in a truth worthy of him, in the inexhaustible sentence that much of what we attribute to a composer's original genius ought to be credited to his skilled use of a diminished 7th chord.

The adoption of established techniques by the spontaneous subject mostly brings their insufficiencies to light. If a composer tries to correct them, by posing problems in a technologically sharply defined form, the novelty and originality of his solution turns him at the same time into an executor of the social trend. The trend is waiting in those problems, waiting to shatter the shell of the extant. Individual musical productivity realizes an objective potential. August Halm – a man greatly underestimated nowadays – was almost the only one to sense that in his theory of musical forms as forms of the objective spirit, however dubious his static hypostasis of the forms of fugue and sonata may have been otherwise.[119] The dynamic sonata form in itself evoked its subjective fulfillment even while hampering it as a tectonic schema. Beethoven's technical flair united the contradictory postulates, obeying one through the other. As the obstetrician of such formal objectivity he spoke for the social emancipation of the subject, ultimately for the idea of a united society of the autonomously active. In the esthetic picture of a league of free men he went beyond bourgeois society. As art as appearance can be given the lie by the social reality that appears in it, it is permitted, conversely, to exceed the bounds of a reality whose suffering imperfections are what conjures up art.

Extract from *Introduction to the Sociology of Music*, transl. by E.B. Ashton, New York, Continuum, 1976, pp. 209–17

[Newspaper cutting from 1945]

Beethoven's Birthplace In Bonn Now in Ruins

By The Associated Press.

BONN, Germany, March 10— The birthplace of the composer Ludwig van Beethoven, the opening notes of whose Fifth Symphony have been used by the Allies as a symbol for victory, was virtually destroyed in the fight for this old university city.

The university area, too, was hard hit from the searing artillery duels of the final battle and the mighty air blows that had preceded

[109]

FOUR

TONALITY

Beethoven reproduced the meaning of tonality out of subjective freedom.

Philosophy of Modern Music[120]

On the prehistory of tonality we find the following extremely curi-
ous comment by Schumann, *Schriften* I, ed. Simon,[121] p. 36:
'Triad = time periods. The third mediates past and future as present.
– Eusebius.' Below this he wrote: 'Daring comparison! – *Raro*.' [110]

On the theory of tonality in Beethoven, remember above all that
communication with the collective presented itself to him in the pre-
existing form of tonality, that the collective is immanent in his work
through the universality of the tonal. Everything is based on it. [111]

To understand Beethoven means to understand *tonality*. It is fundamental to his music not only as its 'material' but as its principle, its
essence: his music utters the secret of tonality; the limitations set by
tonality are his own – and at the same time the driving force of his
productivity. (NB: The 'insignificance' of the Beethovenian melody
can be expressed as that of tonality.) – *Coherence* in Beethoven is
always achieved through a given formal element's realizing, repres-
enting tonality, while the motive power driving the detail beyond
itself is always tonality's need for what comes next in order to fulfil
itself. The form follows this rule in wider and wider circles. But at
the same time, tonality and its representation circumscribe the social
content of Beethoven's music. It is the music's bourgeois bedrock.
The whole work can only come into being through tonality. [112]

Just as tonality coincides, historically, with the bourgeois era, it is, in terms of its meaning, the musical language of the bourgeoisie. The categories of this meaning will need to be worked out, for example:

1   Substitution of a socially produced system rationalized by force for 'Nature'.
2   Establishment of equilibrium (perhaps the exchange of equivalents underlies the form of the cadence).
3[122]   Show that the particular, the individual, is the universal, that is, the individualistic principle of society. That is, the individual harmonic event is always representative of the whole schema, as *Homo oeconomicus* is the agent of the law of value.
4   The tonal dynamic corresponds to social production and is inauthentic, that is, it establishes equilibrium. Perhaps harmonic progression is itself a kind of exchange process, harmonization a give and take.
5   The abstract time of the harmonic sequence.

All this needs to be pursued in detail.   [113]

What actually *is* tonality?* It must be an attempt to subject music to a kind of discursive logic, a universal concept. This implies that the relations between identical chords must always mean the same thing for them. It is a logic of occasional expressions. The whole history of the new music is an attempt to 'fulfil' this musical logic of mathematical proportions, whereas Beethoven represents the attempt to derive music's content from itself, to develop all musical meaning from tonality. – NB: the nonsensical idea of regarding twelve-tone music as a substitute for tonality, whereas it sublates precisely the universality and the subsuming power of tonal relationships.   [114]

The earliest works – written in Bonn – that Beethoven published with an opus number are the Preludes running through all keys, op. 39, composed in 1789. They represent the purest case of a construction of tonality (the dialectical moment: retardations in modulation to create balance). That Beethoven included them in his *oeuvre* is probably to be explained by the fact that they record a fundamental experience.   [115]

Both things need to be said: that there are themes in Beethoven and that there are no themes. – Banalities, that is, the mere structures of

* [Above the note:] first draft.

tonality, are to be found in his work as much as in Schubert. However, if the triplets arranged around the triad in the transition group of the first movement of the Piano Trio op. 97 are compared to the superficially similar – and especially weak – transition in the first movement of Schubert's A minor Quartet, the difference which emerges is the following: in Beethoven there is a dynamic, which strives towards a goal and reflects the effort to reach it. Hence, the accents point beyond themselves to the whole, whereas those in Schubert merely remain where they are. If, in Beethoven, mere nature – in the form of accents, syncopation, and so on (theory of syncopation needed) – simply stayed put as it does in Schubert, it would degenerate into a commodity, negating itself. Beethoven's process is an incessant repudiation of all that is limited, that merely exists. Everywhere in his music is inscribed the injunction: 'O Freunde, nicht diese Töne' [O friends, no more these sounds].[123]

[116]

The analysis of melody in Beethoven must develop the antagonism between triad and second, and the resulting 'insignificance'.   [117]

The above interpretation [cf. fr. 267] of the 'mystical' as the tangible relationship to a thesis which is, as such, intangible, not 'plastic', forms part of the observation that Beethoven compels the material to avow its essence. For the intangible thematic element I refer to, the pure function of which is to 'speak' – is nothing other than the pure material: triads and certain other harmonic and contrapuntal forms.   [118]

Seconds and triads are the modes by which the principle of tonality realizes itself. Triads are tonality as such, that is, mere nature; seconds are the form in which nature appears when animated, as song. One might say that triads are the objective and seconds the subjective moment of tonality. This seems to me very much in agreement with what Beethoven, according to Schindler, called the resistant (that is, alien) and the suppliant principles (cf. Thomas-San-Galli, *Ludwig van Beethoven*, p. 115 and my notes in that context[124]). Only its *unity* constitutes the system of tonality and brings about the affirmation of the whole (ibid.).[125]

    In this form, however, the thesis is too undialectical. In their relationships within tonality as a whole, moments can revert to their opposites, especially as they become more extreme. Subjectivity can take on the expression of the resistant. This is the technical locus of the demonic. Approaching it, subjectivity veers into wretchedness.

The minor seconds in the 'Appassionata' seem haplessly to *desire* the suffering which extra-human tonality imposes.   [119]

The principle of the demonic in Beethoven is subjectivity in its randomness. – An interpretation of tonality is possible only through a *dialectic*; its moments cannot be defined as such. When the minor seconds expressing the demonic seem to summon fate by their very resistance – hell's laughter as the objectivity of the subject – conversely, it is precisely the large intervals which can express pure subjectivity, long since estranged from itself in the seconds (NB: contrary to Hindemith's theory[126]). But this came a good while after Beethoven.

   In Beethoven, intervals larger than the octave seem to occur essentially only in the last phase, where they always tend to overstretch the subjective principle underlying the music, so that it becomes an objectivity attainable only through self-transcendence. Hence, this always happens in polyphonic structures, such as:

1 the ninth in 'Seid umschlungen Millionen'
2 the tenth in the Fugue of the 'Hammerklavier' Sonata
3 the tenth in the great B♭ major Fugue [op. 133]. Check the *Missa*.

   All of these imply a tacit recognition of the octave as the limit; the octave, so to speak, transcends itself.   [120]

Like every movement, each section in Beethoven helps to constitute tonality, while the negativity driving the music forward always stems from an awareness of the *incompleteness* of what has just been formed. I am thinking especially of the introduction to op. 111. – All Beethoven's closing sections are 'satisfying', even the tragic ones. There are no closes ending on a question (but NB: the curious ending of the E minor Sonata op. 90), none that fade away, very few indeed that end sombrely (first movement of Sonatina for Piano in G minor [op. 49,1]). If darkness falls in Beethoven, it is as night, never as dusk.   [121]

Beethoven's shorthand, his comment on the skilful use of chords of the diminished seventh [cf. fr. 197], and the passages quoted by Rudi [Rudolf Kolisch] concerning the metronome,[127] should be brought together.

   Question: the immensely *incisive* effect of the Arietta variations [of op. 111], *despite* their character as mere paraphrase, faithfully following the *basso continuo*.

The C♯ at the end of the variations [bar 170f] (a 'humane vari-ant', a 'humanized star'). Theodor Däubler, 'Der stummer Freund', from *Der sternhelle Weg* [Leipzig 1919], p. 34.[128]

How decisive the *smallest detail* can be in Beethoven, through its simplicity. For example, in the last recapitulation in the Rondo of the Piano Sonata in D minor [op. 31,2], the stationary A in the soprano voice [bars 350ff], above the theme, or the augmented sec-ond in the first movement of the 'Moonlight' Sonata [bar 19, bar 32, and so on], as a *deviation* from the major and minor second.

Tonality in Beethoven must be presented in a wholly dialectical way, as 'rationalization', in the double sense that, on one hand, it alone makes construction possible – indeed, that it provides the very *principle* of construction – and that, on the other, it opposes con-struction, taking on a certain repressive, compulsive character. In this context the moment of 'superfluity' in all tonal music should be mentioned; that is, the compulsion, for harmonic and tonal reasons, to say *repeatedly* things which, as such, need to be stated only once. Critique of the *recapitulation*. In it tonality is indeed the *inhibiting* principle in Beethoven's work, the barrier. [122]

One of the concerns of this study will be to explain a number of peculiarities of Beethoven's *musical language*. These include the *sforzati*. In all cases they mark a *resistance* of the musical meaning to the general gradient of tonality, while standing in a dialectical relationship to it. That is to say, they often emerge from musical events: in the theme of the variations of op. 30, no. 1, for example, the *sforzato* arises from the delay by one crotchet of the appearance of the tonic in bar four. In a corresponding way, after more pro-tracted tensions the *sforzati* are usually 'resolved'; that is, the strong parts of the bar are, as if to compensate, *over-accentuated*. (Ibid., bars 6 and 7.) Furthermore, there is a habit of closing a crescendo on I, the climax, with a *piano* (as has often been remarked). Probably a means of *linking* – always very difficult within the very ungraduated and limited field of dynamics. Instead of one thing clos-ing and then (fragmentarily) something new beginning, the close is denied by the *p* – one could speak of a dynamic syllogism – while the cadence's gradient is at the same time resisted. – Perhaps the late style was formed by the emergence of such peculiarities – in classicist terms it would be called mannerism. – The violin sonatas are espe-cially rich in such features. [123]

A theory of Beethoven's *sforzati* will need to be developed. They are dialectical nodes. In them the metrical gradient of tonality conflicts

with what is being composed. They are the determined negation of
the fixed pattern. Determined, because they yield their meaning only
when measured against the pattern. And therein lies the problem of
the new music.   [124]

Are not the *sforzati*, which are deployed *systematically* from no later
than op. 30, already *shocks*, expressing a power of mere existence
alien to the self (or of a subjectivity estranged from forms and therefore *from itself*)? Do they not, at any rate, manifest a radical alienation, a loss of experience? If Berlioz sought to outdo Beethoven in
this practice, then, probably, he was teleologically *immanent* in the
earlier composer.[129] However, the whole problem is to explain how
Beethoven made the shocks *immanent*, turned them into moments of
both form and expression. This corresponds exactly to Hegel's theory in part III of the *Logic*, where he states that argumentation
should absorb the strength of its opponent into itself.[130] There is,
altogether, a great deal of this in Beethoven.   [125][131]

The theory that the substance of tonal music consists of a *deviation*
from the schema can perhaps be best corroborated through some
instrumental works by *Bach*, in which the objectivity of the pattern
is especially conclusive. In the fast movements of the Violin Sonata
in C minor (the one with the Siciliano), (especially the second), there
is hardly a note which is not composed 'against the grain', which is
not *unlike* the expectation aroused, surprising, and the power of the
piece lies precisely in this. Particularly with regard to the use of
intervals.   [126]

In Romanticism, and already in Beethoven, there is a definite *proportion* between the melodic and the harmonic elements. Not only
does the harmony support the *melos*, but the latter is very largely a
function of the former, never autonomous, never really 'song'. The
reason for the central importance of the *pianoforte* in the nineteenth
century before Wagner may be that it corresponded most exactly to
this equilibrium of melody and harmony. In the same connection,
the 'inner voices' – like melodies under fly-leaves – in Schubert and
Schumann, and sometimes in Beethoven also (in the *Adagio* of op.
59,1, but also in slow movements for piano). The veiled, absent element of Romanticism is connected to this. The melody never entirely
there (like a violin melody with accompaniment), but projected *into
the distance* by the harmonic dimension of depth. Technical equivalents of the philosophical category of *infinity*. The style of piano-
playing *à la* Schnabel,[132] with its over-vivid rendition of 'sung'
melodies, destroys precisely this element, making it too positivistic.

But exactly the same thing happened in the late phase of Romantic composition; Tchaikovsky as opposed to the melodies of Schumann, which *never* overstate the assertion: 'That's how we are' (for example, the continuation of the march theme in the second movement of the Fantasia in C major). [127]

An example of the false, Romantic fungibility of the theme in Beethoven is the opening of the development in the 'Pathétique' [first movement, bars 133ff]. Here we find both elements: the doing of violence, and illusion. [128]

One of the main problems in interpreting Beethoven: playing very fast phrases (semiquavers) as *melodies* without slackening the tempo. 'Passage-work' hardly exists in Beethoven; *everything* is melodic and has to be played as such – that is, with an immanent moment of *resistance*. Especially striking in the first movement of op. 111. [129]

Tonality is the principle on the basis of which key is possible at all. [130]

The working-out of tonality in composition – a system which is at once prescribed and freely elaborated – can be demonstrated, perhaps, by the opening of the 'Waldstein' Sonata. The *pre-existing*, 'abstract' aspect of tonality is contained in the first bar, C I. But at the same time, in reflecting on itself – through movement (*all* musical elements, including rhythm and harmony, are functionally interrelated) – this harmony reveals itself to be, *not* C I, but G IV, through the theme's tendency to move both forwards and upwards. It thus leads to G I, but because of the ambivalence of the first bar this G, too, is not definitive: hence the sixth. The following B♭ [bar 5] is thus not merely a 'descending chromatic bass'. It is the negation of the negation. In that it belongs to the subdominant region, it implies that the dominant is not a final result (it is actually just another reflection of itself, a possible aspect of the chord of G, not something 'new'. But as, unlike the opening, it does not manifest itself as self-reflection, but as something *posited*, as a quality bringing about a fundamental change, it is emphasized by the structure, both metrically <first note of the half-period> and by its harmonic isolation). The dominant of the dominant is thereby negated; but so, too, retrospectively, is the opening: it is not only G IV but also F V, and only through this double negation does it become concretely that which, through its concept, it was from the first, namely C

major. At the same time, the seemingly new quality, the chromatic-
ally constructed bass, is retained as an achieved principle until the
G, the true dominant of C, is reached. Moreover, the fact that the B♭
with the chromatic step, that is, the new, is only a self-reflection of
the old can be precisely demonstrated. For, again, the chromatic
interval B–B♭ is, *melodically*, only an imitation of the diatonic semitone interval C–B immediately preceding it. The fermata G [bar 13],
too, in not yet being a result of C major, points beyond itself
through the interjection of C minor. The latter, however, is only a
reflection of the chromatic A♭ preceding it in the bass. This, fundamentally, is Beethoven's principle. – What is striking, and in need of
interpretation, is the lack of secondary degrees [*Nebenstufen*].

The second subject is in E, because the most closely related keys
needed for the modulatory construction of C major (which, in the
entire course of the exposition, has never arrived at a full cadence)
have already been used up. It is a free inversion of the main theme:
seconds within the span of a fifth.   [131]

The change from major to minor is rare, as an expression of
Romantic ferment, but highly effective when it occurs, as in the
theme of the rondo in the 'Waldstein' Sonata, and in the closing section of the first movement of the Piano Sonata in G major, op. 31,1.
Also, the closing section of the last Violin Sonata [op. 96].   [132]

It is Bekker's fateful error to have obscured the structural significance of tonality by his risible aesthetic of musical key ('The last
work in F minor that Beethoven was to entrust to the piano'[133]).
Seeming close to an insight, he spoils it by his Romantic faith in
tonal expression. See my critique of the aesthetic of key in 'Zweite
Nachtmusik'.[134]   [133]

The C♯ minor in the Piano Sonata op. 27,2 is already, as in Chopin,
far from the C major norm. Include a theory of keys. – That of the
C♯ minor Quartet [op. 131] is quite different. It is related to B♯ and
to the augmented third. Its model is likely to have been the Fugue in
C♯ minor from the first volume of the 'Well-Tempered Clavier'. An
archaic C♯ minor, as if it were an organ key. Why it has this effect is
difficult to fathom (NB: applies only to the outer movements). [134]

Absurd as it is to ascribe to key in Beethoven the decisive importance which Bekker accords it, there is something to be said for his
view all the same: particular keys, with a certain rigidity, give rise to
identical note-formations, almost as if induced by the arrangement

of the piano keys. For example, in D minor, at very different periods:

Example 4

[Cf. op. 31,2, first movement, bars 139–41 and Ninth Symphony, first movement, bars 25–7, first violin.] If a musical historian set about registering *all* Beethoven's profiles, he could probably trace them back to a limited number of orignal types (some steps towards this in Rudi's [Rudolf Kolisch's] work on tempi).[135] But never reveal to anyone that this might be possible, and under no circumstances should I do it myself. All the same: if someone else were to perpetrate such a bestiality, how much it might help me in my, I hope, more humane undertaking. 'Such is life.'   [135]

By what subtle means is form generated in Beethoven. The main theme of the Eighth Symphony consists of an antecedent and a consequent phrase (both of four bars). The consequent phrase is repeated to lead into the 'entry', which is immediately treated as a transition. The problem with this section, with its extreme dearth of harmonic progressions (practically only I and V; distinct IV only after the 'entry'), is the treatment of the consequent phrase, which gives the entry a formal meaning, that is, one that leads further. This is done melodically [cf. bar 7f, first clarinet]:

Example 5

Although this closes on the tonic, the upward-leading interval G–A seems so weak that the repetition of the consequent phrase is felt to be necessary, since otherwise there would be no conclusion. The complete closure which is then attained in the repetition seems at the same time (one bar too early) like the start of the entry, and this metrical ambiguity continues to operate throughout the entire movement, lending it a further dynamic. And all this because in one place there was an A instead of an F (incidentally, according to a rule of harmony the tonic third is always regarded as weaker than the eighth). But how precisely formed, how thoroughly organized as language in all its values must a system of relationships be for a whole form to be decided by so subtle a feature.   [136]

To understand fully the impulse that drove Beethoven in his last phase to oppose antiphony, one should look at a certain *bad* example of such work from the nineteenth century, such as the last movement of Schumann's Piano Quintet. The feeble combination of themes. Beethoven must have rebelled against this element of musical *language*. Cf. my note on musical stupidity [cf. fr. 140].   [137]

Expression in music is valid within its 'system', and hardly ever unmediated in its own right. The enormous expressive power of dissonance in Beethoven (the semitone step collision between the chord of the diminished seventh and its resolution) is effective only within this tonal complex and with this array of chords. With more extensive chromaticism it would be rendered impotent. Expression is mediated by the language and its historical stage of development. In this way, the whole is contained in each of Beethoven's chords. And precisely this makes possible the final *emancipation* of the individual element in the late style.   [138]

The category of the pseudo-vernacular[136] might well be studied with reference to Mahler. It is an idiosyncratic idiom – one in which the senses speak their own dialect, free from the language to which Mahler inclined. Mahler's banality is a means of making the great alien language of music, as it decays, speak as closely to us as if it were our mother's. This false vernacular is a closeness remote from all meaning. – Is not such idiom always associated with the dissolution of the organic? – Consider Schubert's 'dialect without a soil'.[137] Mahler composed many songs in the (Swabian [*sic*]) dialect. This is a first stammering.   [139]*

There is an element of musical stupidity, in a primary sense not derived from psychology – for example, certain repeated figures in violin solo cadenzas, or certain repetitions of a note instead of a sustained melodic tone, as in the 'Virgin's Prayer'.[138] This moment is always associated with repetition. It is one of those eccentric moments which throw light on a much wider context – tonality itself. Seen from outside, it has the same inane tendency that is displayed by these formulae within it. Beethoven's work is an attempt

* [Marginal note:] Beethoven's *Pastoral* as a model of this.

to overcome precisely this moment – a kind of mimetic naivety – within tonality, just as he was especially allergic to formulae of this kind.[139] They occur only, and in damaged form, in his last works, whereas the 'mimetic' Schubert was insensitive to them: his variation movements, often a spinning-out of themes, are riddled with them. (NB: In this connection, the idiosyncratic element in, and against, Wagner.) – This is one of the missing links between Beethoven and the *Philosophy of Modern Music*. That is, the new music is not merely an expression of a changed spiritual situation, a quest for novelty as such, and so on, but actually represents a *critique* of tonality, a negation of its untruth, so that it has indeed a decomposing effect; and that is its best feature (followers of Schoenberg do not advance their cause by denying it – the reactionaries know better). This idea must be related to that of the objective untruth in Beethoven.   [140][140]

The real difference between our music and that of Viennese classicism is that, in the latter, within a largely pre-given and bindingly structured material, each minimal nuance, through standing out against it, takes on decisive significance, whereas in our music the language itself is constantly the problem, and not the turn of phrase. In this we are, in one sense, coarser and even more impoverished. Some quite radical implications of this can be traced: in tonality, in the cadence with the chord of the Neapolitan sixth in C major, the D^b–B interval is perceived as a diminished third, with the distinct character of a third; we might be able to hear it *only* as a second, since it becomes a third only with reference to the tonal system. Romanticism is the history of the decay of musical language and its replacement by 'material'. That tonality lost its binding character; that its linguistic nature kept any transcendence of this form within narrow limits and always, in a sense, revoked it; and that there was much to which it denied expression: all these are different aspects of the same situation. But what if the expressive urge were finally to turn against the possibility of expression itself?   [141]

FIVE

FORM AND THE RECONSTRUCTION OF FORM

A main concern of an interpretation of Beethoven is to understand his forms as the product of a combining of pre-ordained schemata with the specific formal idea of each particular work. This is a true synthesis. The schema is not just an abstract framework 'within' which the specific formal concept is realized; the latter arises from the collision between the act of composing and the pre-existing schema. It both stems from the schema and alters, abolishes or 'cancels' it. In this precise sense, Beethoven is dialectical, as can be seen most clearly in the first movement of the 'Appassionata'. Through the articulation of the development in terms of the two thematic groups of the exposition, the expansion of the coda, also polarized between these two groups, and the addition of a second coda which integrates both thematic forms while, as it were, abolishing itself, an entirely new form emerges from the bi-thematic sonata while strictly preserving the schema. This new form is itself developed from the dualistic schema, while dramatically remodelling it. Dramatically and not – despite the work's 'strophic' character – epically, because of the identity of the two themes. It is, however, precisely this identity – the moment of strictest unity – which is new in relation to the schema, whereas its remodelling into dramatic stages, which might be called 'acts' – that is, what seems most boldly innovative – itself emerges from the schema. [142]

The uniqueness of Mozart, from the point of view of the philosophy of history, is that the ceremonial, courtly, 'absolutist' character of the music finds itself at one with bourgeois subjectivity. This probably accounts for the success of Mozart's music.[141] A close relationship to Goethe (*Wilhelm Meister*). By contrast, in Beethoven the traditional forms are reconstructed out of freedom.[142]   [143]

Study the pieces in which he first dared to do this;[143] their crucial role: the C minor sonata op. 30 no. 2, the D minor sonata 31, 2, the 'Kreutzer' Sonata and the *Eroica* (the last two simultaneously). On these latter works: the problem of the *absolute* dimension. Later it falls by the wayside. – NB: The conclusion of the Variations in op. 47 ['Kreutzer' Sonata].   [144]

There is a passage in Wagner where he says that Beethoven left the existing forms intact and introduced no 'new' ones. Where?[144] [145]

The view I adhered to more or less up to the *Philosophy of Modern Music*, that a subject–object dialectic exists between the composer and the traditional form,[145] is still too one-sided and undiscriminating. In reality, the great traditional musical forms already shape this dialectic in itself, leaving to the subject a certain *hollow space* (for the philosophy of history, this is of utmost relevance to the very late Beethoven, who turned precisely this hollowness outwards). The schema of the sonata contains parts – the thematic and developmental parts – which are already *aimed at* the subject and which can accommodate the particular, and others in which, by virtue of the schema itself, conventional generalities emerge, like death in tragedy or marriage in comedy. These are fields of tension (for example, the transition in the first movement of *Eine kleine Nachtmusik*) and, especially, fields of dissolution, as in the Mozartian exposition which concludes with a trill on the dominant. However, the dialectic between subject and object in music stems from the relation between these schematic formal moments. The composer has to fill the space set aside for invention in, precisely, an unschematic way in order to do justice to the schema. At the same time, he must so conceive the themes that they do not contradict the objectively prescribed forms[146] – whence the classicist requirement that the invented characters should not be spaced too far apart. And, conversely – and this is the specifically Beethovenian achievement in the inner history of form, which goes beyond Mozart – he must treat the 'confirmed', or prescribed, fields in such a way that they lose the external, conventional, reified, subjectively alien moment – what Wagner called the clatter of crockery on the princely table that is to be heard in Mozart[147] – without forfeiting their objectivity, so that the latter is actually regenerated from the subject (Beethoven's Copernican revolution[148]). This state of affairs might finally explain why the subjectivist Beethoven left the sonata pattern as such intact. But the reconciliation of these demands, in showing up a contradiction *objectively* contained within the form, finally abolishes the pre-scribed order. The subject–object relationship in music, therefore, is a dialectic in the *strictest* sense; it is not a tugging at each end of a rope by subject and object, but an *objective* dialectic disconnected from the logic of form as such. It is the actual movement of the con-cept within the subject matter, which needs the subject only as an agent who complies with necessity out of freedom (but *only* the free subject can perform this function). And that is, at the same time, the supreme confirmation of my conception of the musical process as directed towards the objective.   [146]

In Beethoven's procedures the most profound features of Hegelian philosophy will be discerned, such as the twofold position of 'mind' in the *Phenomenology* as both subject and object. As the latter it is merely 'observed' in its movement; as the former, through observ-ing, it brings the movement about.[149] Something very similar can be seen in Beethoven's most authentic developments, as in the 'Appassionata' and in the Ninth Symphony, and probably in the 'Waldstein' Sonata as well. The theme of the development is mind, that is, the recognition of self in the other. The 'other', the theme, the inspired idea, is, to begin with, left to itself in these develop-ments, and observed; it moves *in itself*. Only later, with the *forte* entry, comes the *intervention* of the subject, as if anticipating an identity as yet unattained. It is only this intervention which creates the actual *model* of the development through a *resolution*, that is, only the subjective moment of spirit brings about its objective move-ment, the actual content of the development. The subject–object dialectic is therefore to be traced in the development. What is meant by the subject here can be defined more closely in the note on the fantasia-like character of the development [cf. fr. 148].   [147]

English terminology for musical forms has a second term for 'devel-opment' which clearly comes from an earlier usage: the 'fantasia sec-tion'. This needs to be investigated in detail. There is clearly a connection between the 'binding', integrating part of the form and its most optional, improvisational, fantasizing, 'off limits' element. Even the irreplaceable development might be seen in this context as *replaceable* – as, indeed, in Mozart, it actually is. The development would thus have two poles: cadenza and fugue. Indeed, in the sonata form the development is the only part which is 'free', not determined by rules governing themes, modulations, harmonic progressions, and so on. And the shaping of the development around a model, which gives this section its true seriousness in Beethoven, also has something about it of a playful 'fantasizing on the model', of freedom. Perhaps this is indeed the mechanism by which, in Beethoven, the objectivity of form becomes palpably embodied in the subject. It is perhaps Beethoven's developments which most closely resemble his free fantasias for pianoforte. Developments in Beethoven which come closest to improvisations need to be studied next – for example, the short E major sonata op. 14; then, look for traces of them in the major developments, as in the 'Waldstein' Sonata. – There is much reason to believe that the analogy between the sonata and the drama, whereby the 'conflict' corresponds to the development, is no more frequently applicable than 'thematic dualism' is to be found in large-scale sonatas. The classical norm is the exception while the high point in this respect, paradoxically, is the *Eroica*. And it contains, precisely, the widest deviation.   [148]

The bipartite nature of the development – first a fantasizing part, then the resolute establishment of a model – is to be found as early as the C major sonata, op. 2, no. 3.   [149]

The bipartite structure of the development – a non-binding fantasia section and a strictly motif-based part brought about by a resolution and usually after sequences on a model – is found in embryonic form in Mozart. Here, however, the latter part usually has the function of a *retransition* (in being derived from the head motif of the main theme). Follow this up historically.   [150]

The curious relationship between development and coda. The latter's relative importance increases with that of the former. It is also related to the development's musical *content*. This is seen in exemplary form in the *Eroica* and in the Ninth, but even in the short Violin Sonata in A minor [op. 23] the coda is a recapitulation of a vivid and autonomous development section. In the 'Kreutzer' Sonata, which, in terms of 'extensive intensity', comes closest to the *Eroica*, it is the coda, not the development, which introduces a new theme [cf. first movement, bars 547ff].

Example 6

This theme has, however – quite unlike the statement of the model in the *Eroica* – the formal character of a close, an *Abgesang*. – In theoretical terms, the relationship between development and coda may well correspond to the non-identical identity of process and result which is found in the dialectic.   [151]

Hölderlin wrote of the 'calculable law' of tragedy.[150] The predetermined object of this theory might well have been the Beethovenian development of the symphonic type. The curve of the development in the decisive works is probably identical. It begins with what in the eighteenth century was called the *fausse reprise*, a recapitulation of the beginning in which the head theme or motif is functionalized by primarily harmonic means. This is followed, after an initial rise, by a descending segment of the curve, customarily associated with a certain dissolution. Then comes the equivalent of Hölderlin's concept of the caesura.[151] This is the moment when subjectivity intervenes in the formal structure. Stated in terms of expressive categories, it is the moment of decision. (The 'Difficult Decision' of the last quartet [op. 135; title of fourth movement] has a technical pre-history running through Beethoven's entire *oeuvre*.) By this decision the actual model of the development is established, often marked *forte* and always with the character of something definitively crucial or serious, or however it may be described. In the 'Waldstein' Sonata this moment comes with the statement of the triplet model [first movement, bars 110ff]. In the 'Appassionata' it occurs at the E minor entry of the main theme under the semiquaver motion ('entry') [first movement, bar 78]; in the Ninth Symphony it is marked by the C minor entry of the concluding motif from the main theme [first movement, bar 217]. The same phenomenon probably also provides the solution to the problem of the new development in the *Eroica*. Its entry comes at precisely the moment of decision. In view of the large scale of the movement and perhaps, also, in order to give pure expression to the principle of the development's caesura, of the 'intervention', Beethoven has resorted here to the extreme device of defining the moment of the new by introducing something unexpectedly new. The development in the *Eroica* is not to be defined in terms of analogies with other developments, of latent thematic relationships, but, in an exact reversal of this, the principle of other Beethovenian developments will be inferred from this extreme. When this is done, the central question of the legitimacy or otherwise of 'mediation' in symphonic logic will arise. Only this approach gives some promise of success in interpreting form in Beethoven. The development of the Ninth Symphony is especially curious, being heavy with allegorical depth. For the working-out and intensification of the closing motif does not lead directly, as in similarly constructed works, to the climax and the beginning of the recapitulation, but ebbs away into a second resolution, which even involves a reintroduction of material from the second subject. Then, suddenly, with a kind of jerk, the main development is resumed and, precipitously, almost as if no further procrastination were tolerable, the climax is reached in a few pages of score. It is almost like Hamlet, who, after infinitely protracted, preparatory 'developments', finally, at the last moment, helplessly compelled by the situation, achieves in an unplanned, gestural way what could not be accomplished as a 'development'. The formal schema of the Gordian knot.   [152]

Furthermore, in the Ninth Symphony a problem already emerges that was to overshadow all else in Wagner and Bruckner: the relation of the important, allegorical, immutable main theme to the functional unity of the movement. Beethoven's solution is one of tact in the Goethean sense. The opening of the development in the Ninth is highly paradoxical: a variation of the invariable. Everything is held in suspension. This will need to be explored in terms of the most precise technical categories. It ought then to be possible to explain the final coda above the chromatic basses with reference to this problem.   [153]

Caesura and turning point in Beethoven: drastically, with the trumpet in the third *Leonore* Overture (bars 272ff), and far more grandly with the turn in the *Adagio* of op. 59, 1 [cf. Text 8, p. 182].   [154]

The turning point in the development of the first movement of the 'Hammerklavier' Sonata, after the passage in B when the main theme is exploded with the low F♯ [bar 212]. This is one of the most magnificent passages in Beethoven. It has something gigantic about it – something by which the sense of proportion in relation to the individual body is entirely suspended.[152]   [155]

NB: The caesura in Beethoven's last works develops very gradually; for example, the close on the dominant and the general pause before the second theme in the slow movement of the 'Hammerklavier' Sonata [bar 27].   [156]

The two-part structure of the major developments, for example, 'Appassionata', 'Waldstein', 'Kreutzer', *Eroica*, op. 59, 1, Ninth Symphony: the first part more vacillating, fantasizing; the second firm, built on a model, objectified, but with the character of a decisive act of *will*, a turning point: it *must* be so. This comes extraordinarily close to Hegel's concept of the subjective moment in truth as the condition of its objectivity. In Beethoven, something like a dialectic of theory and practice manifests itself here – the second part of the development is 'practical' both as an application of theory and as its logical precondition. The whole, Being, can only exist as an act of the subject, that is, as freedom. This principle is raised to a self-conscious level in the new theme of the *Eroica*, which fulfils the form just as it bursts it asunder (being, in this, both a completion and a critique of the bourgeois totality). In Beethoven's compulsion to introduce the new theme here lies the secret of the decomposition of his late style. That is, the deed demanded by the immanence of the totality is no longer immanent in it. This may well be the theoretical basis of the new theme.[153]   [157]

When, in Beethoven, polyphony remains, to an extent, external to the composition, not permeated by the harmonic principle,[154] his composition problem is largely that of compensation, of tact. A splendid example of what I mean is the counterpoint to the recapitulation of the main theme in the *Andante* of the First Symphony. It begins as a true melodic voice, but gradually – and very ingeniously – is turned, from bar 5, into an accompanying, harmonic voice (while it retains a melodic core in quavers, this is resolved into chords by the semiquavers); then it comes to an end. In this way the counterpoint is mediated against the grain of a composition which is really *alien* to it. This would be as unthinkable in Bach as in Schoenberg, but reveals here both an unerring sense of form *and* the antinomy. [158]

The privileged position of the first movement of the *Eroica*. It is really *the* Beethovenian piece, the purest embodiment of principle; the most careful composition, the absolute peak to which all the earlier works lead up. Perhaps one of Beethoven's most fundamental impulses was not to repeat this piece. Dialectical reflections on 'perfection' in art could be attached here.   [159]

Among the most astonishing features of Beethoven's work is that nothing is ever type-cast, fixed, repeated, each work being a unique conception from a very early stage. Even the prototypical *Eroica*, the model *par excellence*, is never repeated. This is the aspect which Bekker, quite inadequately, calls the 'poetic idea'.[155] But what is it in reality? Each work a cosmos, each one the whole – and for that very reason different? Can be studied in, for example, the Violin Concerto and its relationship to the C major Piano Concerto. The only exceptions to this are the last quartets, but in them the *bound-*

ary between one work and another is sublated; they are not works but, as it were, fragments of a concealed music. [160]

On the sketches for the cycle *An die Ferne Geliebte*: the essence of the musical inspiration lies in the realization that it is no such thing. The inspirational idea is a concretization of critique. This is the subjective side of the dialectic objectively carried through within Beethoven's musical logic. [161]

On the connection between idiom – a wide-ranging concept extending from the pre-existing language of music to its forms – and the specific composition: the last movement of the *Eroica*, up to the introduction of the main theme, can only be understood if the bass of the – initially withheld – theme is heard in advance, with a knowledge transcending the movement, as the bass of the still anticipated theme – prospectively. Otherwise the bass on its own, especially after the double bar line, would be completely meaningless. Meaning in music requires the prospective view, which cannot be generated by the piece itself but only by the accumulated musical idiom. [162]

It is necessary to clarify the concept of musical *development* within the text. It is not identical to that of the variation, but *narrower*. A central moment is the irreversibility of *time*. Development is a variation in which a later element presupposes an earlier one as something earlier, and not vice versa. Altogether, musical logic is not simply identity in non-identity, but a meaningful sequence of moments; that is, what comes earlier, and what later, must itself constitute the meaning or result from it. Of course, the possibilities of this are legion, for example: intensity arising from something weaker, complexity from simplicity; but this direction (from simple to complex) by no means defines the concept. It can also *result* in the simple element: the theme; it can simplify the complex, *dissolve* the closed, and so on. Such types could be enumerated; but the concrete composition decides over the logic of what comes before and after. Or are there general laws, after all? One of the most central questions of musical aesthetics.[156] [163]

The following correlations are valid:
   Closed theme – open form (rondo)
   Open theme – closed form (sonata)[157] [164]

The Fantasia for piano op. 77 is especially interesting because it may be assumed to be a retrospective notation of actual fantasizing on

the piano (perhaps at the request of Brunswik[158]). However, two
fundamental points emerge. Firstly, a form is *essentially* inherent in
the fantasia as a rejection of continuous development in principle; it
is the same form that is found in Mozart, a composition made up of
sections which are internally unified but merely juxtaposed, arbitrar-
ily successive. Secondly, this fantasia form is essentially *static*. Just
because of the endless succession of the new, no progress is made.
There is no identical core to be developed. But without such identity
there is no non-identity, and therefore, really, no musical *time*. This
is reflected exactly in the linguistic usage whereby fantasias and preludes are the same (both remaining this side, as it were, of music's
time continuum). Accordingly, consistently a-thematic music would
be, in principle, *timeless*, and the static quality of twelve-tone music
would merely make manifest what is inherent in absolute musical
nominalism: that incessant novelty abolishes progression, experience, the new. – The threshold dividing Beethoven from this static
condition, however, is clearly the *written form* of the music – that is,
precisely its *reification*. There is, therefore, only as much dynamism
as there is fixity – only as much 'subjectivity' as objectification.

[165][159]

The Finale of the very important short A minor sonata op. 23 is like
a preparatory study for the 'Kreutzer' Sonata. – The movement is
extremely loose, a rondo with a main theme recurring in unvaried
form with striking frequency, to which secondary ideas are opposed
in an unconnected way, almost as if filling in spaces. The organizing
principle is located at great depth, so that the first and second subsidiary ideas (in A major [bars 74ff] and F major [bars 114ff and
121ff], respectively) form a relationship of theme and variation,
without this being obvious (harmonies over one bar in both cases):

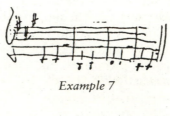

Example 7

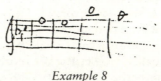

Example 8

The movement is held together, as it were, behind the scenes. But just this loose accumulation allows Beethoven, at the end, to disclose the identity of the two subsidiary sections (that is, to *establish* it as a result); he does so, after a general pause, by suggesting the first, over only eight bars, and then making the second follow directly [bars 268ff]. An example of Beethoven's superb sense of form: the looser a formation, the greater must be its internal economy.   [166]

Theory of the Beethovenian *Variation Form*: to achieve a maximum of different characters with a minimum of compositional means. The theme's treatment is by paraphrase, rather than direct intervention: the bass outline is maintained throughout (all this does *not*, of course, apply to the Diabelli Variations). But the impression is *never* given of a mere change of clothes. The reason for this, apart from the very clear profile of each individual variation, is, above all, that while the harmonic sequence is constant, it does not play 'around' the melody; rather, each of the *corner* notes which coincide with the harmony is retained melodically, while the harmonic line as such is not preserved. Usually, in face of a lyrically melodic theme, the variations are stressed rhythmically, in a symphonically dynamic way. The theme often contains *one* very characteristic element (for example, the momentary modulation into B major [bars 23ff] in the concluding movement of op. 96), which excursion is then maintained, organizing the form through its very conspicuousness. Otherwise, the treatment of form is curiously relaxed, relying, no doubt, on the cohesive strength of the theme, which allows loosely related elements to be juxtaposed. An *adagio* variation often precedes the *allegro* conclusion. In op. 96 thematic ingenuity is confined to one element: the G major *fugato* in the concluding *Allegro* [bars 217ff] is formed from the notes of the theme, made unrecognizable by the rhythm (the serial principle). – The variation form is particularly suited to the late-middle 'epic' style. The incomparable variation movement in the great B♭ major trio [op. 97]. But the principle holds good as far as op. 111.   [167]

The form of the *Abgesang* in large-scale variation movements, as in the B♭ major Trio [op. 97] and in op. 111; also as early as the coda in the C minor Variations [WoO 80]. Its deep meaning? The sublation of the endless sameness of variations.   [168]

In the coda of the first movement of the Fifth Symphony there is a similar *Abgesang* theme to that in the 'Kreutzer' Sonata: fulfilment and, at the same time, an awareness that there is no stopping now. This gesture may be called tragic. Pocket score,[160] pp. 37f, with the crotchets of the violins.   [169]

Regarding some characters in Beethoven; in particular, the closing sections: in the Finale of the first Piano Trio from op. 1. The character of nonchalant exuberance, of jauntiness. There used to be a command 'At ease' after marching on the spot. Likewise, there is a musical 'At ease', a letting go of the static element which is probably inherent in all symmetry. It is the immanent overcoming of the *tectonic* principle of music: perhaps this is the idea of the *Abgesang*. It animates that theme of Beethoven.

The concluding section of the first movement of the *Pastoral*. On the theory of Beethoven's humour. The earthy 'Here we are', with something of the innkeeper's errand boy about it. Humour, that is, a suspension of negativity, is very deep-seated here. The comic narrow-mindedness of that which posits itself; the spuriousness of the 'healthy', the assertion that 'I'm just fine'; what is true and yet, in relation to the whole, untrue and, by that yardstick, comic. Much like the announcement: 'This tastes good.' What is decisive is not just that Beethoven, as a 'Netherlander', *has* this element, but that he has it as something sublated and positively negated.

NB: The comic element in all eating, partly because it is never happiness itself but an Id *mediated* by the Ego.   [170]

Certain expressive configurations in Beethoven have attached to them certain musical symbols – or rather allegories (it is these which become petrified in the late style). But where do these symbols find the almost incomprehensible power to convey such expression in practice? This is one of the most central questions. For the present, the only answer I can imagine is that the origin of meaning in Beethoven lies in purely musical functions, which are then sedimented in the scattered technical means available at the time, to which they accrue as expression. All the same – cannot these functions themselves be traced back to expression?   [171]

One of Beethoven's most splendid formal means is the *shadow*. The *Andante* of the 'Appassionata' begins as if it were bending under the weight of the first movement, and remains beneath it: perhaps it was this sense of form which excluded the *Andante favori* from the 'Waldstein' Sonata: the introduction to the Rondo, which replaces it, holds its breath. – But the first variation of the Arietta from op. 111 is also in shadow. The animated voice hardly dares stir after the compelling appearance of the theme. The moment of 'oppression' has its place here. This expression mark appears in the Arioso [properly: *Adagio*] of the B♭ major String Quartet [op. 130, Cavatina, bar 42], but also applies to the *Arioso* from op. 110 and the E♭ passage in the Arietta Variations [bars 119ff]. The moments of oppression in

Beethoven are those in which subjectivity 'appropriates' a Being alien to it. 'Before you bodies take upon this star',[161] oppression prevails. – Quartet in *Fidelio**   [172]

The *Allegretto* in the Seventh Symphony needs very detailed interpretation. It has often been said that it, too, retains the character of a dance. But this does not do justice to the idea of the movement, which consists rather in the dialectic between rigid objectivity and subjective dynamism. The theme is initially rigid, sustained in the manner of a passacaglia, while being at the same time extremely subjective and even secretive. (NB: The category which mediates between subject and object within the theme itself is that of *fate*. The subjective secret is objective doom.) It counts among the Romantic characters in Beethoven, reminding us of Schubert, especially the counterpoint (cf. the slow movements from op. 59,3 and from the F minor quartet [op. 95], which also recalls the *Allegretto* in the relationship between sombre lyricism and polyphony). The objective rigidity does not stem from the theme itself, but from the unvarying variations. The opening of the Trio which follows, the human sound, the thaw, repeats ontogenetically, as it were, what happened to music as a whole with the advent of Haydn and Mozart. The *Fugato*, as a reversion to the objective intention(?) then leads to the negative triumph of the objective character. At the close this subjectivity persists, but is wholly shattered. All this still very obscure.
                                                                              [173]

The meaning of classicist *gestures* in Beethoven, for example, 'Jupiter rolling his thunder and lightning' at the start of the Violin Sonata in C minor [op. 30,2]. The characters are taken from classicism. A phenomenology – typology – of Beethoven's basic materials needs to be drawn up, on the principle: which gesture is this imitating? Other such characters: furrowing the brow, growling, and so on. But all this is then sublated within the composition.   [174]

Just as there is such a thing as musical stupidity, in the case of Beethoven – in the *Eroica*, for example – I am forced to adopt the idea of musical *intelligence*, both in the procedure itself and in an *expression* it conveys of 'cleverness', adroitness, smartness. For example, the interpolations in the first section of the development in the first movement of the *Eroica*, the model of which first appears

---

* [In margin:] The variations movement of the 'Appassionata' is not quite detached from the rest. Through its link to the Finale and its shortness it has something of the quality of an introduction.

on p. 23.[162] This needs to be investigated. NB: Something *operatic* here; as also, frequently, in *Fidelio*. The intention of leading onwards. 'Intelligence', as a subjective moment, steps in to cancel out the objective gravity, the static quality of the matter itself. 'Wit.' Affinity to the principle of the amusing, the conversational, perhaps even of the gallant.   [175]

The substantive content of music is translated into *syntactic* categories. For example, the dramatic moment in the *Eroica* – the semiquaver theme making its entry above the chord of the diminished seventh [first movement, bars 65ff] – is an interruption of the second subject group, which is then taken up again; this is a conjoining construction resembling a subordinate, concessive clause. Such means are decisive in constructing the musical context.   [176]

Integration in Beethoven is often achieved when the form is 'kept going', as when that which is subsiding, fading away, is made to continue through an intervention, but in such a way that this intervention has the character of objective *necessity*; for example, the first movement of the *Eroica*, p. 16, where the chromatic bass drives the passage onward at the switch to $A^\flat$ V.   [177]

A distinction must be made between manifest and latent – or 'subcutaneous' (Schoenberg) – thematic relationships. Being subjective, the difference is naturally relative; that is, what is *perceived* as thematically related depends on concentration, training, and so on. But *objectively*, functions which are manifestly thematic and those with an organizing function should be identified – for example, the first and second themes of the 'Waldstein' Sonata. There are borderline cases, such as the theme of the closing section of the first movement of op. 59, 2, in its relationship to the main theme. This methodological principle is very important, since it enables us to escape the undifferentiated vagueness of maintaining that 'everything is thematic'. –

There are in Beethoven moments of formal retardation, that is, those which dam the flow of the whole *form* (as is often the case with harmonic details), in order to give greater force to the entry of the fields of dissolution. For example, op. 59, 2, first movement, bars 55–6. The specific character of *continuation* in Beethoven is often attached precisely to such figures. (Also in the Finale of 'Les Adieux'.) Consequent phrases or codas, often with an ineffably peaceful expression, for example, op. 59, 2, *Adagio*, bars 48–51.
                                                                    [178]

In the symphonic *scherzi* the compositional achievement lies primarily in the *metre*, especially at the 'subcutaneous' level, such as the concealed 3/2 in the Fourth Symphony, or in the asymmetries of the *thematic* juxtaposition (*Eroica*).   [179]

Regarding the prospective and the retrospective intentionality of form, a passage from the development of the *Second* Symphony, Eulenburg pocket score, p. 22, is very instructive. It concerns the entry of the theme of the second thematic group after a general pause. Initially, this entry seems formally *'wrong'*, anticlimactic, rhapsodic. It seems wrong, above all, because the listener's sense of form is affronted when, in the development, which is supposed to sublate what has already been stated, the main characters appear in the same sequence as in the exposition. The antecedent phrase seems faithful to the pattern; but instead of the expected consequent phrase, there is a 'residue' which is treated as a new developmental model and leads to a very free, seemingly 'new' variant of the second (march) theme (p. 23, bottom). Through the omission of the consequent phrase, however, the antecedent phrase is 'negated', so that the error of the entry (whether real or feigned) is corrected. Such relationships are an *essential* part of musical form. But they are sedimented *content*; in this case mockery, parody. Cf. the term *fausse reprise*. Something of the dialectical, *non*-linear character of musical form can be demonstrated by this passage; it also provides a concrete example of my thesis concerning formal idiom as a reification of intentional content.   [180]

Analysis of first movement of op. 59,2. The whole movement is the history of the relation between the first and third bars, that is, of their identity. This identity is only realized in the coda, meaning that the beginning is only comprehensible from the vantage point of the coda. Teleology in Beethoven: a force retroacting in time.   [181]

In the 'Kreutzer' Sonata everything simultaneous is immensely simple, lapidary – the density lies in the unfolding in *time*. The piece moves so fast that successive elements appear simultaneous.   [182]

The phrase 'O Freunde, nicht diese Töne' [O friends, no more these sounds][163] sums up the formal law governing all Beethoven's work. It is placed in the Ninth like the players in *Hamlet*. Applies especially to the Fifth Symphony. Cf. 79 [and fr. 339].[164]   [183]

The flagging of energy to be found in Schubert and Schumann is the price exacted for the attempted transcendence of form. More form is less. This flagging – in Schubert the unfinished works, in Schumann the mechanical element – is the first manifestation of the decay of music as an objective language. The language falls breathlessly behind the moment invoked, or is its empty shell.   [184]

On the dialectical relationship of form to content in music: if Beethoven's supremacy over Wagner is seen in his richness of structure, his concrete abundance of relationships as compared to the abstract filling of time with identical entities in motion, this reflects not merely his 'technical' superiority to the more primitive Wagner, but also the precedence of *content*, as plenitude and concreteness, over the *emptiness* of Wagnerian expression in terms of its content.   [185]

Brahms, with incomparable formal tact, faced the consequences of increasing subjectivity as it affected the large-scale form. The critical point in this regard is the finale. (NB: It probably *always was*: the 'happy ending', the finale always gives an impression of embarrassment. Beethoven's great finale movements always have a paradoxical character – perhaps, in the antagonistic world, music was *never* able to close, as has now become obvious. Compare the failure of the concluding movements of Mahler's Fifth and Seventh Symphonies.) Here, Brahms showed a splendid *resignation*: in principle, his best final movements go back to the *Lied*, as if music were returning to the land of childhood. For example, the Finale of the C minor Trio, above all the close in the major, like the last stanza of a *Lied*. Another example is the wholly lyrical Finale of the Violin Sonata in A major. The Finale of the G major Sonata, on the 'Regenlied', acts like a key. – This possibility, too, is already sketched in Beethoven – for example, the Rondo of the Piano Sonata in E minor [op. 90] and, to an extent, the concluding variations from op. 109 and *even* (take care!) op. 111. Also, the Finale of op. 127(?).*   [186]

---

* [At head of text:] Concerning the Beethoven study.

SIX

CRITIQUE

If the autocracy of the recapitulation turns out to be the real barrier confronting Viennese classicism as a whole and, above all, Beethoven – precisely because of his dynamism – the historical origins of this predominance must be traced. It is of recent date. It is not *yet* found in Bach. Or should one just say: not? For it is surely absurd to regard Bach, who died twenty years before Beethoven's birth and belongs essentially to the eighteenth century, as an unquestioning, unwavering master of the old, artisan-like, *pre*-bourgeois school. There is every reason to suppose that all the formal problems concerning us here were already posed, explicitly and consciously, in his work, and that his antiquated features are those of a resolute *harking back*. (That Bach was completely forgotten by 1800 is one of the most momentous facts in musical history. Had it not been so, everything, including 'classicism', would have taken a different course. He was not, however, out of date, but merely too *difficult*. The forgetting of Bach is bound up with bourgeois leisure time, entertainment, and so on. A *precondition* of the whole of 'classicism' is the triumph of the 'gallant' over the 'erudite'.) It can also be said that in Bach the primacy of the recapitulation is not so much undeveloped as negated, or avoided. Bach undoubtedly *knew* about the recapitulation. But in his work it is used not as an *a priori* element of form, but as an artistic means, a device: either in the sense of a refrain in a rondo, of a *rhyme* (for example, in the closing movement of the Italian Concerto, and in the Prelude of the 'English' Suite in G minor), or as marking a clearly felt and affirmative arrival (first movement of Italian Concerto; something similar is to be found only in the most successful recapitulations of Beethoven). Bach was thus entirely familiar with the effects of the recapitulation, but he restricted them with great critical severity. It should also be remembered, above all, that Bach's recapitulations are not *polythematic* complexes but contain only the *thesis*. And that they belong to the concertante style: the *tutti* character of his recapitulations. It is especially illuminating that the avoidance of the recapitulation forms part not only of the archaic fugal form but also of the 'gallant', modern character of the suite, with its symmetrical division into eight-bar periods. This is at its finest in the allemandes and sarabandes, but even a genre piece in almost the nineteenth-century style, such as the Gavotte of the French G major Suite. In such pieces the perfect formal equilibrium, established without any trace of a–b–a rigidity, is perhaps the greatest triumph of Bach's mastery of structure. In this he was more sensitive, less mechanical, more complex than the forthright subjectivism of the classical composers. In the fifty years after Bach's death this ability was entirely lost, and in this very central sense the whole of classicism, including Beethoven, was retrogressive in relation to Bach, much as, from the point of view of construction, Wagner was to mark a step backward from Beethoven. The regression is connected to the *mechanistic* element which spread further and further in bourgeois music and finally imposed its diabolic power even on Schoenberg.   [187]

Postscript: when playing relatively sonata-like pieces by Bach, for example, the last movement of the Italian Concerto, one readily feels that thematic dualism, dynamic modulation, and so on were still *in statu pupillari*; unarticulated, not really developed to the full. But if, immediately afterwards, one plays a piano sonata by Mozart, the form, the separateness of the themes, and so on, seems curiously *crude*, as if already adapted to coarser ears. The dialectic of aesthetic progress. Or rather: in art we can read off clearly the ambivalence of all progress. – In Bach there is more outward, conventional constraint, but at a deeper level more 'freedom' than in the classical composers. There is a question about the substance of the religious element in Bach, which may already have stood for the human and, at any rate, was no longer fully intact. (Where is the truth of Christian art located?) Compare Pascal and Bach. Probably, *ordo* in Bach is really the moment of mechanistic rationalism.   [188]

An expression of *pride*, in that one is allowed to be present at such an event, to be its witness; for example, in the first movements of the E♭ major Piano Concerto and of the *Eroica*. 'Exaltation.' How far this is the *effect* of the composition – a joy which rivets the listener's attention to the dialectical logic – and how far the *expression* creates an illusion of such joy, rests on a knife's edge. Expression is a prefiguration of mass culture, which celebrates its own triumphs. This is the negative moment of Beethoven's 'mastery of the material', his ostentation. This is one of the points which criticism can engage.

[189]

Regarding the *critique* of Beethoven: sometimes, if one listens closely to its idiom, his music has something contrived, a calculation of effects, much as in studio paintings, or effective *tableaux*; and precisely this moment of ham-acting is exposed to obsolescence. It is the reverse side of the mastery of material, and is often to be found in passages of the highest genius, such as the close of the funeral march in the *Eroica* (which, as a whole, is not free of contrivance, perhaps as a result of the work's prescribed, 'imitated' expressive type). Only the late style is entirely exempt from this. What brought it into being? [190]

Beethoven's style of rebelliousness prefigures in certain ways the conformism in that of Wagner: in its gesture of effrontery. The scene in Karlsbad; the lawsuit over 'van'; the 'brain-owner' episode.[165] The music shows traces of this in certain moments of interruption (for example, in the slow movement of the G major Piano Sonata from op. 31), which are intended to present something magnificent but remain simply empty. Even in the *Larghetto* of the Second Symphony there are such moments. Haydn's expression 'the Grand Mogul'.[166] – Some magnificent pieces by Beethoven, above all the overtures, sound from a distance like a mere 'boom boom'. [191]

On the bombastic element:[167] *Plaudite, amici, comoedia est finita.*[168]

[192]

Hitler and the Ninth Symphony: Be encircled, all ye millions.[169] [193]

There are passages in Beethoven where the music seems to take on an envious squint, for example, the start of the development in the first movement of the E♭ major Trio op. 70. [194]

Rage, in Beethoven's music, is bound up with the priority of the whole over the part. As if rejecting the limited, the finite. The melody is growled in anger, because it is never the whole. Rage at the finitude of music itself. Each theme a lost penny. [195]

The connection of the parts to the whole, their annihilation in it, and therefore their relation to something infinite in the movement of

their finitude, is a representation of metaphysical transcendence, not
as its 'image' but as its real enactment, which only partly succeeds –
or is mastered? – because it is *performed* by human beings. This is
where the connection between technique and metaphysics – however
ill formulated at this stage – is located. Beethoven's art achieves its
metaphysical substantiality because he uses technique to manufac-
ture transcendence. This is the deepest meaning of the Promethean,
voluntarist, Fichtean element in him, and also of its untruth: the
manipulation of transcendence, the *coercion*, the violence. This is
probably the deepest insight I have yet achieved into Beethoven. It is
profoundly connected to the nature of art as appearance. For however palpably and non-representationally transcendence may be present in art, nevertheless, art *is* not transcendence, but an artefact,
something human, and ultimately: nature. Aesthetic appearance
means always: nature as the appearance of the supernatural. In this
connection, see I A 3 from the book with Max [Horkheimer] and
The Philosophy of Modern Music, p. 55, footnote.[170]   [196]*[171]

On the previous note, cf. the following remark of Beethoven's
quoted by Bekker [*Beethoven*], p. 189: 'My dear fellow, the surprising effects that many people ascribe to the natural genius of the
composer are often enough achieved quite simply by the correct use
and resolution of chords of the diminished seventh.' Except that,
according to the previous note, precisely this is 'natural genius'. Cf.
the notes on the philosophy of music in the green book between
November 1941 and January 1942.[172]   [197]

The concert *overtures* often represent, in relation to the symphonic
style, a further *simplification*. In Beethoven, the poetic element is
subjected not to a prolific elaboration but, on the contrary, to a
drastic *reduction* at the expense of mediating characters. An antithetical bareness – nowhere is the *classicist* element in Beethoven
more pronounced than here. The overtures of *Coriolan* and *Egmont*
are like movements from symphonies for children. *William Tell* is
somewhat similar. Because of this, despite the striking effects, certain weaknesses of Beethoven, which are splendidly mastered elsewhere, show themselves here. Hence the crucial importance of these
pieces as key to the critical moment in Beethoven. A certain rough-
fistedness, a lack of concern for detail such as is found in Handel,
and thereby an *emptiness*. (The *Egmont* overture in particular,
despite its more lucid articulation, or even because of it, is deeply

---

* [Above the text:] Very important regarding Beethoven.

unsatisfying.) Here, because of the lack of material to work on, the impressive force of the symphonic element takes on something brutal, Germanic, triumphalist. The entanglement of lucidity with pomp, the element of usurpation in the *Empire*, comes to the fore. Cf. in particular the F major 4/4 section of the overture to *Egmont* [*Allegro con brio*; Eulenburg, pocket score, pp. 34ff], where simplification results in a the crudity of a fanfare. This is, furthermore, a triumph without a *conflict*. Such a coda would have presupposed a far more dialectical *development* – which in this piece is merely hinted at.   [198]

Regarding the critique of heroic classicism:

> 'Absorbed in money-making and in the peaceful warfare of competition, it [bourgeois society] forgot that the shades of ancient Rome had sat beside its cradle. Nevertheless, unheroic though bourgeois society may seem, heroism had been needed to bring it into being – heroism, self-sacrifice, the Reign of Terror, civil war, and the slaughter of the battle-fields. In the stern classical tradition of the Roman Republic, its gladiators found the ideals and the forms, the means of self-deception, they needed, that they might hide from themselves the bourgeois limitations of the struggle in which they were engaged, and might sustain their passion at the level appropriate to a great historic tragedy. In like manner, more than a century earlier, and in another phase of development, Cromwell and the English people had borrowed the phraseology, the emotions, and the illusions of the Old Testament as trappings for their own bourgeois revolution. As soon as they had reached the goal, as soon as the bourgeois transformation of English society had been effected, Locke supplanted Habakkuk. (Karl Marx, *The Eighteenth Brumaire of Louis Bonaparte*, transl. by Eden and Cedar Paul, London, 1926, pp. 24–5)

This passage has the most far-reaching implications, not for a critique of the heroic posture but for the category of totality itself – in Beethoven as in Hegel – as a *transfiguration* of mere existence. And just as, from this standpoint, the Hegelian transition to the whole seems questionable in all its stages, so, too, does the superiority of the 'objective' Beethoven over the more 'private' and, as it were, more empirical Schubert. However much more truth there may be in the former, there is as much more untruth as well. The whole as truth is always also a lie. But, were not the 'stern classical traditions' of the Roman Republic *themselves* already a lie – the Roman as a bourgeois in fancy dress? Cicero no less than Cato? Was not Marx, in this part of his construction of history, too *naive*? Cf. the conclusion of the *Philosophy of Modern Music*.[173]   [199][174]

In the light of this note the problem of the late Beethoven would need to be stated as follows: how is it possible for art to divest itself of the 'self-deception' of totality (as the quintessence of classical heroism), *without* thereby falling victim to empiricism, contingency, psychology? Beethoven's last works are *the* objective answer to this objective question.[175]   [200]

Beethoven's Socratic profile. – Lack of feeling for animals, Thomas-San-Galli [*Ludwig van Beethoven*], p. 98.   [201]

On Beethoven – What I find so suspect in Kantian ethics is the 'dignity'* which they attribute to man in the name of autonomy. A capacity for moral self-determination is ascribed to human beings as an absolute advantage – as a moral profit – while being covertly used to legitimize *dominance* – dominance over nature. This is the real aspect of the transcendental claim that man can dictate the laws of nature. Ethical dignity in Kant is a demarcation of differences. It is directed against animals. Implicitly it excludes man from nature, so that its humanity threatens incessantly to revert to the inhuman. It leaves no room for pity. Nothing is more abhorrent to the Kantian than a reminder of man's resemblance to animals. This taboo is always at work when the idealist berates the materialist. Animals play for the idealist system virtually the same role as the Jews for fascism. To revile man as an animal – that is genuine idealism. To deny the possibility of salvation for animals absolutely and at any price is the inviolable boundary of its metaphysics. – And to this the sombre aspects of Beethoven are precisely related.[176]   [202]

---

* [Above the line:] Cf. in this connection, 'effrontery', green book [cf. fr. 191].

SEVEN

THE EARLY AND 'CLASSICAL' PHASES

What is irresistible in the music of the young Beethoven is the
expression of the possibility that all might be well.
Negative Dialectics

In the work of the young Beethoven, op. 18 holds a key position
and should be treated accordingly.   [203]

The first movement of the C minor Violin Sonata op. 30,2 conforms
to the *childhood image* of the sonata as a battle involving a march,
an opposing march, and a collision leading to a catastrophe. It can
be said that this image is *latent* behind very much of Beethoven's
music, but is very seldom made *explicit*. Usually (and this is in keeping with my theory) there is no *outward* clash of themes, the
dynamic residing in their *internal* history. They bring about their
own downfall. ('Appassionata.') Investigate how this might apply to
the *Eroica*. – NB: In this context the two parts of the development,
the fantasizing and the sequence-forming parts.[177]   [204]

In the early Beethoven there is a development from the rhetorically
decorative through the Romantic to the tragic. The stages: first
movement of the 'Pathétique', Finale of the 'Moonlight' Sonata, first
movement of op. 30,2 (which has much in common with the latter,
especially in the modulation in the development section), op. 31,1
(both Romantic and tragic) up to the 'Kreutzer' Sonata as the first
purely tragic symphonic type.   [205]

Towards the end of the so-called first period of Beethoven's work the Romantic element emerges more and more strongly ('Spring' Sonata [op. 24] and the Romantic *Lied*, 'Moonlight' Sonata, *Larghetto* of the Second Symphony, and so on). The transition to the middle period is effected on one hand by the art of the subjective-Romantic element, and on the other by the overcoming of this element through *objectification*. The crucial importance of the D minor Piano Sonata [op. 31,2].   [206]

The Romantic movements in Beethoven include the Finale of op. 31, no. 2 (Schumann).   [207]

The Romantic pieces include the *Andante* of op. 59,3, with its anticipation of Schubert especially in the semiquaver structures (cf. *Scherzo* [properly: *Allegro moderato*] of Schubert's A minor Quartet], but also in the use of the tritone. Study of *differences* especially fruitful here; that is, demonstrate the preservation and abolition of the Romantic moment in the totality. – Then: the 'Harp' Quartet [op. 74], an undervalued but very significant and peculiar piece. The association of chords in the introduction contains the idea of Schumann's 'Der Dichter spricht' even in its details.[178] The slow movement points towards the *late* Schubert in details such as the use of the chord of the sixth as if this were a new, separate stage. Furthermore, the whole quartet is like a premonition of Beethoven's *last* style. A passage from the slow movement quotes the later *Arioso*.[179]   [208][180]

A possible epigraph for a chapter (on the 'classical' phase): 'I had never realized so clearly as when listening to this symphony of Beethoven how perfectly Goethe's dictum applies to music: "Life has value only insofar as it has a consequence"', and so on. Carl Gustav Carus, *Gedanken über grosse Kunst*, ed. Stöcklein, Insel Verlag 1947, p. 50.[181]   [209]

Ibid., p. 52 has the idea I noted very early on, in the green leather-bound notebook, that 'such a work is to be revered more than a work of nature'; quote the passage.[182] – Carus loved the painting of C[aspar] D[avid] Friedrich; *Ferne Geliebte* comes from that landscape, as does much between opp. 90 and 101.   [210]

Regarding Beethoven's last Violin Sonata [op. 96] (and *Ferne Geliebte*), the painting of C[aspar] D[avid] Friedrich and Carus's letters on art.[183] – Similarly with *Sehnsucht*, op. 83, no. 2.   [211]

Not only will the 'classicist' moment in general need to be elaborated, both critically and as a moment of truth – but, at the same time, the difference between Beethoven and the best classicist level achieved by other composers and pianists of his time (*not* Weber and Schubert) must be shown. Only an understanding of this difference will yield decisive insight into Beethoven's meaning and procedure. NB: Eduard [Steuermann] knows about such piano works.

[212]

On the 'Appassionata': Orthography has meaning in Beethoven.*
When, instead of

Example 9

he writes

Example 10

[first movement, bars 1f], this means that the first note must be *drawn out*. At the same time, the semiquaver must never be dropped. This is the dialectical moment of *restlessness* within the quietude of orderly being. No accent on the final note.[184]

The *manner of composing* also has a meaning. In the second part of the theme of the *Andante* (*con moto* and not, therefore, in the style of a prayer), the melody is in the middle voice, the upper voice being a kind of 'cover sheet'. This means that it should *not* be stressed (like a middle voice in Schoenberg, which is marked H; rather, its *character* lies in its veiled quality. Against Schnabel's style of interpretation. In the first movement, the strict sonata form is endowed with speech, and is wholly fused with the dramatic intention. This is achieved not only by unity of motif (*each* of the two primary motifs belongs to *each* of the two thematic groups), but, above all, by the fact that the development treats both main themes, successively, as 'models', and does so in the same sequence as in the exposition, so that the whole development can be seen as a gigantic

---

* [In margin:] NB: Here, pay attention to the expression conveyed by the *visual appearance* of the notes!!!

second stanza to the (NB: *not* repeated) exposition, as its *fully worked-out* repetition, which liberates the dynamic meaning of the original thematic dualism. In this case the coda would be the fourth stanza, but with the two complexes reversed, so that the tragic first one, marked *più allegro*, has the last word. In this way a latent, second, free, 'poetic' form is merged with the manifest, outward, sonata-like one. Thus, the ontological emerges precisely from subjective spontaneity, a key to the whole theory of form.

How the *catastrophe* in the coda of the first movement is brought about. The G♭ [bar 243], as a false progression, *cutting off* the harmonic flow, like a higher authority, but 'the objection is overruled', the G♭ appears a second time [bar 246], and now it is as if the collective were standing behind it.[185]

Regarding the slow movement, Kerr's surprising formulation: chorale of the faithless.[186] (On the *Allegretto* of the Seventh Symphony.)

Moreover, the presto coda of the last movement has something of the Finale of the Seventh – with a negative twist. A 'military' quality. (Russian uniforms in Meyer's *Universal Encyclopedia* looked like this.) The whole Finale is a fully elaborated cadence in F minor, with the Neapolitan sixth as the second degree.

Try to fathom the ineffable character of the syncopated theme in the development of the Finale.

The decisive feature of the development is that the definitive main theme is now drawn into the motion and thus into the immanent form. The overwhelming effect produced through its placing within the form.   [213]

It is worth finding out how Beethoven organizes the first movement he wrote which was of very large scope, inwardly and outwardly – the first movement of the 'Kreutzer' Sonata, which Bekker idiotically underestimates.[187] First of all: the extreme simplicity of composition, the piano writing almost impoverished. Because, given such gigantic dimensions, succession is all-important, the least possible weight is placed on simultaneity. Then: the three main themes, being characters for Beethoven, are spaced very wide apart and form extreme contrasts, above all in rhythm. The first is in crotchets, the second in semibreves, the third essentially in dotted notes. But common to all three is the opening with the minor second, on the upbeat (and thus obvious) in the first and third, and G♯–A in the third. The third, as a rare exception in Beethoven, is not merely a closing section but a self-sufficient main theme – indeed, the most striking 'melody' in the movement. The interval of a second provides abundant links between the first and third themes. However, the movement is held together, above all, by the quavers in the middle section, which have an identical effect, despite their different content in terms of intervals (and above all through their placing and the importance of the octave fingering). After the second theme (*adagio fermata*) there is a direct resumption of the first transition section, the violin marking the *rhythm* of the opening motif of the first theme. Similarly, again, after the third theme, as the real closing section, a link to the first transition section is directly exposed at the end through a quotation of the latter's opening. In this way the exposition is held together. The second theme, a chorale, remains extraneous to it, is not assimilated (even to the development): a chief means of articulation. – The development has three parts. The first, up to the entry in F minor, is an elaboration of the third theme, as often in the symphonies. The F minor section contains the main development model in a highly logical fashion, as the kernel of the diminished second motif common to the first and third themes. The critical point in the movement is reached with D♭ major, for here the momentum of the movement extends beyond the usual end of the development, demanding something more (this passage corresponds formally to the entry of the new theme in the development of the *Eroica*; and there is something similar in op. 59,1). The third theme is taken up again, although here it is not further elaborated but compressed imitatively. When F minor is reached again, the actual third part of the development begins. Its model is based on a motif from the transition section between the second and third themes, and really on the kernel of the 'binding' quavers. The retransition recalls that in the 'Pathétique', just as what in the 'Pathétique' remains a gesture seems here to fill and control the whole movement (a characteristic form of development in Beethoven). The mighty G minor passage (or rather D minor IV) directly before the recapitulation [bar 324]. (Interpret. Incidentally, this is a formal phenomenon [*Gestaltphänomen*] like the opening of the recapitulation in the 'Appassionata'.) The very great harmonic momentum of the development does not permit a simple entry to the recapitulation in A minor; rather, the entry must itself appear, after the immensely dynamic form, as its *result*. Hence:

D minor – F major – D minor – A minor,

the latter appearing as no more than a continuation. The elaboration of the theme by making sequences on its closing cadence, as in the Ninth Symphony. The highly regular recapitulation, compensating for its remoteness to the movement. The coda extremely lapidary, while the *Abgesang* appears to be a new theme, but is really only a resolution, not self-sufficient.

It is incomprehensible that Beethoven did not accept the obligation imposed by the first movement. This was already noticed by Tolstoy.[188] The second movement has a splendid theme, but the first variation is a drawn-out paraphrase, the second positively ludicrous, the third again magnificent (Brahms), the fourth once more a boring paraphrase (we already know all that!); the coda, however, is a stroke of genius, especially the indescribably moving pedal point passage over F [bars 205ff] – The Finale is an excellent, glowing piece – it anticipates Schubert in its shifting modulations and in certain melodic characters – but it simply has not the internal tension to balance the first movement. Its model was probably the Finale of op. 31,3, especially in the dance's growing wildness. Perhaps a first conception of the Seventh Symphony, though the idea of the latter is still rudimentary, an episode. – Whether it was really a concession to virtuosity, or a last shrinking from being Beethoven, is hard to tell. I am inclined to assume the latter. I have learned from Beethoven that whenever something seems to me false, absurd or weak, I should defer entirely to him and seek the fault in myself.   [214]

On some other violin sonatas:

Op. 12, no. 1. The first movement is a textbook case of a piece which stems from the conception of the *whole*: almost devoid of 'ideas', apart from a motif of the main theme and a harmonic figure in the closing section, but with such *élan* in the whole form that its freshness is carried forward even over the empty phrases. The *inward* relationship between the whole and its moments still unresolved. – The second movement has a very charming theme, but gives a curiously abrupt impression, whether because it has too few variations or because the coda, though deeply felt, is out of balance. One of the few movements which gives an impression of failure. At the same time it is highly interesting that the minor variation is shot through with inserted crescendi of the kind sometimes found in the late style. Is the latter a reversion to a gesture from the composer's youth? The Finale sets itself only modest tasks but within this framework is entirely masterful, anticipating the type of the rondo to be found in certain concertos (Violin Concerto). Splendid use of thematic rhythm, wide, vivid intervals, magnificent coda.

Op. 12, no. 2. The first movement stands out in that the entire first theme is developed from *one* motif of two notes, pointing towards the economy of the middle Beethoven. Harmonically, the second subject group is very perspectival, in contrast to the extensive use of A major. It is interesting that the recapitulation, in the modification of the transition, continues the work of the development, the latter seeming to resonate beyond its formal limits as sometimes happens in Mozart. A very interesting start to the coda. The whole movement highly successful. – In view of a certain crudeness in the composition I should like to backdate the second and third movements to Beethoven's youth, perhaps to Bonn; older pieces, perhaps somewhat revised. The slow movement is truly weak. The last, by contrast, is very interesting, as it shows how close to the young Beethoven was the possibility of Schubert[189] (his Grand Duo [C major Piano Sonata for four hands, D 812] is probably derived directly from this movement). This refers not merely to the major–minor element, which is rare in Beethoven, or, especially, to the tone of the middle movement, or even to the modulation within the main theme, but to the undynamic, loosely accumulated form. Not an 'integral' movement. Rather, system and totality in Beethoven are wrung forcibly from a lyrical subject which, itself, is little inclined to hold together. 'Authenticity' is one result.

Op. 12, no. 3. I do not hesitate to count the E♭ major Sonata among the masterpieces, and not merely among those of the early period. The first movement – at full tempo, moreover (*allegro con spirito* can only mean a *fast allegro*, although in crotchets) – is very hard to describe. It has a colourful quality almost unknown in Beethoven, an abounding richness of figures held together by the virtuoso grandeur of the whole. The melody of the second subject group is especially beautiful, as is the *Fidelio*-like, infinitely eloquent theme of the closing section, which seems broken up like an ensemble section of an opera. Everything is extremely well structured, with internal contrasts (antecedent and consequent phrases of the main theme), nothing simply idling along. The close of the development with an entirely new idea in a remote key (C♭ major) is a special stroke of genius. The colourfulness of the thematic material does not allow a linear development: something else must be added (a very Romantic episode which, however, is immediately integrated). – The slow movement is very secure and beautiful, but belongs to a *type* familiar from the younger Beethoven (piano sonatas!). The Rondo, by contrast, is of utmost mastery. It is in sharpest contrast to the first movement (a counterpart to which is to be found, at most, in the first movement of the G major Concerto): extreme precision and concision. Here, literally, not a single note is superfluous. The theme, although speeded up by the tempo of *allegro molto*, seems like a round, a 'convivial song' of the kind written by Goethe.[190] Here the exposition, the thesis represents the objective, while the subject, and a surly subject at that, drives it onward as if grudgingly (and thus comically) fulfilling a duty. A highly characteristic, martial second subject with *sf* on the sixth degree is, altogether, rich in neighbour degrees (contrast to the main theme). Development built up in stanzas over two contrasting models: perhaps the *Lied*-like character of the main theme is echoed in the stanza structure. At the end, and even before the coda itself, the movement expands to fully symphonic breadth in a way very characteristic of Beethoven. *Sforzati* play a major role, though not as much in the form of contrasting accents, as in the middle Beethoven, but directly, as a driving force. Also composed with great virtuosity.   [215]

Pieces like the G major Piano Concerto and the Violin Concerto, and to some extent the 'Pastoral' Sonata [op. 28], belong together. The idea of expressing tranquillity through motion. This plays a major part in the 'epic' pieces of the later middle period, which I have analysed frequently. They are like the female element, the *Shekinah*.[191] Incidentally, within the symphonies, the first movement of the *Pastoral* is probably of this type, being able to combine the type with the symphonic abbreviation of time through the static repetition of motifs (that is, as in the 'epic' type, without a development as such, yet still tautly structured). Is this perhaps the reason for the *dance character* of the piece? Would the Seventh Symphony therefore be the main work of the late middle period, the point of indifference or synthesis between the truly symphonic (*Eroica*, the Fifth, opp. 47, 53, 57) and the epic principle? Would this mean that what I have referred to as the integration of time, the true symphonic idea, had become problematic for Beethoven, and at a relatively *early* stage (op. 59 being, if the Ninth is disregarded, probably its last pure expression)? Problematic in the sense of *illusory*, as no longer capable of being filled with the only kind of musical experience that was now possible for Beethoven; and this feeling of technical fragility was converted in Beethoven into critical categories. For example: the false simplicity, contradicting the substance, which emerged in *weak* pieces of the true symphonic type, especially overtures (*Egmont*, perhaps also *Coriolan*). Or has it to do with pomp and solemnity (the Seventh is ecstatic but not solemn, not to speak of the Eighth)? We touch here on the innermost dynamic law of Beethoven's work, which was to impose the late style. Bekker occasionally betrays some awareness of these questions, without perceiving their full scope, when he talks of the disappearance of the *largo*.[192] As far as I can see, after op. 59, 1 and 2 Beethoven wrote only two more slow movements of this weight and, especially, of this sonata-like density: the *Largo* of the 'Geister' Trio and the *Adagio* of the 'Hammerklavier' Sonata. The slow movements of op. 97 and of the Ninth belong to a different type: the latter to a style of

the nineteenth century. The abbreviation of the very slow movements in the last quartets, or a structural loosening brought about
by self-contained contrasting parts which are hardly 'themes' any
longer (in the A minor Quartet [op. 132] and in the Ninth) and
come closer to being variations (or direct variations movements like
those from opp. 97 and 127, and from the C♯ minor Quartet [op.
131]), is extremely striking. However, Beethoven's experience with
the *adagio* is probably interconnected, in a relationship of polarity,
with his experience of the strictest symphonic idea.   [216]

Beethoven's 'epic' type is perhaps to be derived from the *Pastoral*, in
which, in place of symphonic contraction, a very curious kind of
repetition appears, but in such a way that the relaxed, easy-going
mood of the repetition, the exhalation, bears the expression of *happiness* (as in certain catatonic states?). We find here a motif from
certain modern developments, from Stravinsky.[193] In Beethoven's
last works this element is set free – released, as it were, from the
imprisonment of form, and shows its mythical traits. The key position of the *Scherzo* from the F major Quartet op. 135. Extremely
important.   [217]

Hence, also, the 'maxims':[194] condensed but constantly repeated wisdom.   [218]

A theory of Beethoven's *types* and of his *characters* must be provided. The types are largely independent of formal types. There is an
intensive and an extensive type, in each of which – in the relationship of music to *time* – something fundamentally different is sought.
The intensive type aims at a contraction of time. It is the true symphonic type, that I tried to define in my 'Zweite Nachtmusik'.[195]
This is the true classical type. The extensive type belongs especially
to the later middle period, but also to the classical phase.
Representatives of it are the first movement of op. 59,1 (that of 59,2
is a textbook case of the intensive type, closely related to the first
movement of the 'Appassionata'); the first movement of the Trio op.
97; and that of the last Violin Sonata [op. 96]. This type is
extremely hard to determine. Though outwardly similar to the
Romantic experience of form, especially Schubert's (as is obvious in
the Trio and in Schubert's B♭ major Trio), it is very different to this
experience. Certainly, time is set free: the music takes its time. But,
here too, it does not fill time but controls it. One might perhaps talk
here of a geometrical – instead of a dynamic – relationship to time.
There is scarcely any mediation (aspects of the late style appear
here); for example, the preponderance of modulation through har-

monic shifts (in op. 97, and in the *Ferne Geliebte* – and then in the first movement of the 'Hammerklavier' Sonata). The characters are much further apart. Yet there is unity through a kind of *dividing up* of the whole form. The actual organizing principle of the extensive form is still very obscure to me.[196] The extensive form contains a certain moment of renunciation, an abandonment of the balance of opposites to be found in paradox, so that the fractures already emerge, although they do not yet become, as in the late style, ciphers; rather, they contribute to contingency in the sense that greater weight is given to the moment of abstract time than to construction in the constitution of form. But this temporal moment is itself thematic, perhaps as in the novel, and is the main subject: not an 'idea' which fills time (such ideas are also less prominent here). Abdication before time, and the *shaping* of this abdication, make up the substance of the extensive type. The favouring of very *large* expanses of time (both 59,1 and 97) is very important here. The Ninth is, in a sense, an attempt to interlock the intensive and extensive types. The late style contains both; it is certainly the result of the process of disintegration which the extensive style represents, but, in keeping with the intensive principle, catches up the fragments split from it. The contribution of the concerto form to the extensive type is probably large, and Beethoven's treatment of the concerto may well yield the key to the extensive style. The greatest and most successful example is perhaps the first movement of the G major Concerto. – The absence of smoothness is very characteristic of the extensive type. (NB: Do not restrict this to these types.) Beethoven's *characters* are largely independent of the types, but according to Rudi's [Rudolf Kolisch's] theory[197] each character has its absolute tempo. Characters are probably primal images which are then set free in the late style. Their analysis must be precise. *What is a 'character'?*   [219]

Beethoven's last works are also to be interpreted *historically*, in the sense that it must be shown how the peculiarities, which seem 'personal', all stem from the attempt to resolve certain contradictions, and so on. The theory of the extensive type should be understood as follows: both as a critique of the classical Beethoven, and as a configuration the critique of which gave rise to Beethoven's last phase. The 'origin of the late Beethoven'.   [220]

The style of the late works of Beethoven's middle period – which is so extraordinarily distinct and which I consider here to be represented by the last Violin Sonata [op. 96] and the great B♭ major Trio [op. 97] – seems to me to be characterized especially by a renunciation of the symphonic mastery of time. The gesture of these pieces, especially of their first movements and the variations movement of the Trio, is that of setting time free, as if with an exhalation of breath, and as if it were impossible to linger on the paradoxical peak of the symphonic. Time claims its right: hence, also, the striking dimensions in terms of length. Only against the background of these works can the symphony *par excellence*, the Seventh, be understood. It is, however, this epic moment which, as if over the composer's head, establishes the relationship between Beethoven and Schubert in this period. The closing section of the first movement of the G major Violin Sonata [op. 96] is Schubertian in its major–minor shift as in its willingness to play itself out; *An die ferne Geliebte* is the only song cycle which bears comparison with Schubert's; and the theme of the *Allegretto*, especially its maintenance of counterpoint, might certainly be from the Seventh Symphony of Schubert. On the other hand, Schubert clearly regarded the first movement of Beethoven's B♭ major Trio as his model. [221][198]

On the Piano Trio op. 97: Elements of a Theory of the Extensive Type

1 Contrast – dialectical contradiction – between the character and rendering of the main theme. In its ductus and setting (use of full arm weight [*Vollgriffigkeit*], *sforzati*), the theme is a forte character of a certain epic, affirmative breadth, but is played *piano dolce* (this contradiction points already to the late style). As if someone were beginning to read Homer to himself in a low voice. The mediating 'elaboration' of motifs, is replaced here by the task of resolving the contradiction between the theme and its merely external appearance. The contradiction is left as it is, unmediated.*

2 The drawing out of the cello's F in the eighth and ninth bars (the whole first section, up to the *tutti* entry of the theme, is irregularly constructed, in thirteen bars, with a prosaic, anti-dance quality). The B♭–F step is derived from the first and second bars (NB: the second bar seems in some way to be the first downbeat, the whole first bar having something of an upbeat character). In the drawn-out passage, marked *cantabile*, the *sforzati* return home, so to speak, and are dissolved. The critical notes in the extended passage, F–A–E (and then, correspondingly, in the continuation, E♭–G–D), are the opening intervals of the main theme, which then follows. Thus, as

---

* [Later insertion:] (or: The theme is mediated *within itself*; hence the contingent nature of its appearance.)

also by the accented octaves on the piano, the densest thematic coherence is achieved. At the same time, however, by the disintegrating character of the extension, the immanence of form, the progression of the theme, is dissolved. The piece approaches the character of a *recitative*. A suspension of progression and of unity is achieved while, at the same time, thematic unity is strictly *maintained* (in genuinely dialectical fashion). The form draws breath. This pause is the truly epic moment. But it is a moment when music reflects on itself – it looks around. In the extensive type Beethoven's music attains something resembling self-contemplation. It transcends its own breathless self-containment: the *naivety* that inhabits the rounded, closed masterpiece that purports to have created itself and not to have been 'made'. Perfection in a work of art is an element of illusion, which is opposed by the self-contemplation of the extensive type. 'Actually, I'm not a totality at all.' This looking-around is achieved, however, by using precisely the *means* of totality: music transcends itself.

3 The long holding of some bass notes, though not in the manner of a pedal point. The long waves. A moment not of tension but of *lingering*. The music wants to 'stay here'. This is very characteristic of the whole style of the later middle Beethoven apart from the Seventh and Eighth Symphonies. The earlier tensions, simply by being distributed and maintained over long sections, actually lose the character of tension and are transformed into expressive values (this is a decisive step towards the late style). The proof: the passage analogous to the recitative, after the 'entry'. Here, the recitative character is avoided, while a sense of movement, in contrast to the first occasion, is maintained; the 'speaking' function of recitative is now taken over by the harmonic values. The marking of the passage *pp* points to its finely shaded quality; a crescendo follows only when the pure fourth degree from B♭ major has been reached.

4 A certain simplicity – 'purity' – in the consequent phrase of the main theme, at letter A[199] [bar 29]; this was to become a special characteristic of the late Beethoven. The distinguishing feature is the six–four chord.* It is as if the nature of the cadence were to be displayed as such, abstractly; see above.[200] The expression is that of a soothing, comforting epilogue – that is, of an *afterwards*. Perhaps the deepest reason why the extensive style sets time free is to be found here. Time – as something no longer mastered but depicted – becomes a solace for the suffering represented by expression. Only the older Beethoven discovered this secret of time in music.

* [In margin:] Cf. the six-four chords in the *Adagio* of the last Violin Sonata [op. 96].

5 The transition model, the descending triad in triplets, where the dynamic does not stem from the theme but is 'inserted' by the mordent. Generally, the category of the inserted element in late Beethoven. The essay on the late style[201] in this connection. Examine here the contrast to Schubert, as in the triplet passage in the first movement of the A minor Quartet. – The category of the inserted element in Beethoven must be handled with extreme delicacy. It never involves mere ornamentation or 'filling', or anything naively or ungenuinely extraneous to the material. Rather, the difference between inner and outer becomes a problem and a theme. The passage says that precisely the complete, non-*mediated, unconcealed* externality and abstractness of the ascending triad, the way the material becomes a mere shell, allows subjectivity to make its *unmediated*, expressive intervention in the work of art. This whole point 'on the late style' needs to be substantiated here.

6 The *abrupt shift* – instead of a modulation – from B♭ major to D major in the transition group. Very similar in the 'Hammerklavier' Sonata and the *Ferne Geliebte*. Modulation seems over-ceremonious (NB: the great composers never went in much for modulation – that was left to the harmony teachers and the Regers. Wagner's extremely sparing use of modulation, the 'incorporation' of alien keys in Schoenberg. Correct modulation always has something academic about it – for example, in the close of the first movement of Brahms's Fourth Symphony); modulation's fussiness appears especially as a *veiling*, a tendency which lays it open to criticism by the older Beethoven. The change in the harmonic perspective, the sudden switch, points directly towards Schubert. In Beethoven, it may well have emerged from the dramatic impulse of the technique used in *Fidelio*.

7 The G major passage inserted nine bars before the beginning of the second theme itself. First, a lingering, no haste to get anywhere, the journey is the goal, but as an episode, not a process. Then the floating, suspended character of the passage, which neither moves onward nor emerges, but 'stands still' (the accents being suspended by syncopated ligatures). The whole passage, without thematic contour, is like a blanket or screen beneath which the music continues. An extremely important formal device.

8 On the music's habit of taking its time: the tendency towards thematically unfilled, empty bars, which negate tension rather than producing it: no need to hurry. We find this in the last three bars before the entry of the real second theme (which is very obvious in the works of the extensive type). This is a principle employed very consistently, which returns, for example, at letter D (p. 234 [bar 104], three bars before the introduction of the principal model of

the development. The deliberately over-large retransition to the recapitulation is of this kind, and needs a separate analysis (the real connection to op. 59,1 is located here). The transition is a second development with its own model, the second motif of the main theme. Also point out in this context how long the development takes to gather momentum, eight bars after its main model has been established, at the E^b major entry, p. 235, second staff [bar 115]. On the other hand, the character of a retransition is already present, at least when only the piano remains in D major, p. 236 [bar 132], although the real transition arrives only at letter F [bar 143] on p. 237. The gigantic development actually contains only *seventeen* bars of development; all the rest is introduction and retransition; that is: (including partial close 2,) nineteen bars of introduction and sixty(!!) bars of retransition. Admittedly, the latter is extended as a second development after its model has been established, but gives the impression of a transition – indeed, of a gigantic *cadence* from B^b major, in the form $C \ V - C \ I = B^b \ II = E^b \ VI$ (modulation to E^b; to underline the effect of a cadence the fourth degree from B^b is expanded as an attendant key; harmonic equilibrium requires a strong subdominant element), $E^b \ I = B^b \ IV$; from then on $B^b \ V$ from letter G [bar 168] up to the entry of the recapitulation; before that a brief passage in $B^b \ I$ with a momentary modulation to F major. – The passage is not only harmonically a cadence, but towards the end takes on the character of a (concerto's) cadenza.

What is achieved by this treatment of the development? First, it is stripped of its dynamic quality and tension, the dynamic middle section being reduced to an episode. The power of the development is really established only *retrospectively*, by the long retransition: how far away must one have been to need such exertions to get back. An example of the switch from quantity to quality in Beethoven. The development takes on a certain paradoxical quality decisive for Beethoven's formal intention at this stage: it does not really develop at all; that is, it does not release forces, does not 'produce' unity, yet does not become episodic. This is achieved by minimizing the main element, while, at the same time, what precedes this element seems like its preparation and what follows like its postlude. The extensive type actually has no development, since it lies outside the concept of the Beethovenian development – the contraction of time. Yet it does not abandon unity. It is the paradox of this style that time, having been set free, becomes a means of establishing unity. That is, if the 'classical' development of the type of the *Eroica* or of the 'Appassionata' comes in for criticism, at the same time, by the very scale of the movement – but only retrospectively – the effect of a development which never actually took place is reconstructed. 'After all that, how much must surely have happened.' – The whole orientation of Beethoven's extensive type is that of remembrance: the music does not, like a 'classical' piece, take on its meaning within the contracted present, the moment, but only as something already past. Herein lies the true reason for the *epic* character of this music.

9 It follows that the real critical moment of the extensive type, its 'problem', is the entry of the recapitulation, and it is with this that Beethoven shows himself to be most passionately concerned here. It cannot be a 'culminating' recapitulation, as in the Fifth and Ninth Symphonies, or a 'tectonic' implied reprise. It cannot be the climax, or a mere balancing element. Fundamentally, in the epic style one simply does not know how to start again from the beginning, and every recapitulation is a *tour de force*. The diminuendo is characteristic (in op. 97, as in 96, for example, the recapitulation entry is marked *pp*). The recapitulation must be unobtrusive, since no dynamic progression leads up to it; it must have a certain *irresponsible* quality, yet must be entirely watertight, since otherwise this whole, enormously exposed formal type would ineluctably disintegrate. In op. 97, for example, the (extremely audacious) tonic is introduced one bar *before* the beginning of the recapitulation [bar 190], for the twofold reason that the recapitulation then follows seamlessly, since it does not come as a climax, *and* because it remains inconspicuous, the main harmonic event having already preceded it in the resolved cadence. The *piano* entry of the main theme is *reticent*; it is connected and yet, in contrast to the recapitulation type of the intensive style, it starts from the beginning, as if drawing breath – just as this whole style (see point 2 of this entry) has about it an element of inhalation. *It is a pausing of the narrator within the unity of sustained remembrance.* In this style the recapitulation is a return to something, a calling back to mind. Moreover, the last bar of the recapitulation is related to the famous example in the *Eroica*. For it is not simply the tonic, but an intersection of tonic and dominant, so that, though tightly woven into the structure, the recapitulation can draw breath, not as a fulfilment or as something new, but, as it were, as a *purification*; as the emergence of the tonic which, though already reached, had been obscured, but now frees itself and states retroactively: Yes, that is it and here it is again. It is one of the most artful and fragile passages in Beethoven. – Op. 96 also contains a *tour de force*: the head motif, by exploiting its exclamatory character and by the playful detachment of the trill, is granted a kind of extraneous status; but then, despite its nonchalance, it is interpreted as a beginning after all and, before we have time to think, we are back in the piece again. The subtle deception practised

here points towards the aporia of the extensive type, and this aporia in turn leads forcibly to the late style.

10 The second theme is very far away – too far, for my sense of form. Altogether, the problematic, risky, exposed nature of the extensive type should be strongly emphasized. The risk is proportional to the depth of the question involved. Moreover, the second theme has the effect of the solo in a piano concerto. It seems to me that the extensive style has overreached itself here, although its outsize expansiveness – the far-travelling quality of the epic – constitutes its essence. This is revealed at once in a degree of uncertainty, of stiffness in the response – as if Beethoven were taking cover in a somewhat pedantic imitation (this can be demonstrated in detail). The symmetry of the second and fourth bars, the evenness of the support, and especially the entry of the cello, which repeats the model *literally* and thus gives a mechanical impression, are all disturbing. The diversion introduced by the violin entry is pasted on to the surface and leads nowhere. Only after the eight bars of the theme does Beethoven regain control of the movement, by creating thematic relationships: the *dolce* theme of the cello (with the semi-quavers of the piano) is formed from the close of the main theme and, again eight bars later, the new figure is a variant of the second theme. – The bold caesura (with its 'inserted' ritardando) before the entry of the coda-like closing section is characteristic. It is an integral feature of the extensive type that, in addition to the moment of exertion, it also permits the moment of weariness, of softening, of drawing breath. In Beethoven this is assimilated as a moment to the extensive totality, whereas in Romanticism this moment of subjective fatigue – and hardly of subjective vigour – is the means whereby subjectivity explodes the form. In a certain sense Romanticism represents not an increase but a decrease in subjectivity, a yielding. The extensive type in Beethoven can be understood as an attempt to embody this experience in the constitution of form. – Incidentally, as part of the *critique* of the first movement, the enormous retransition should probably be cited: both to criticize and to vindicate.

NB: The creation of models for sequences, like the whole technique of the development in the middle Beethoven, probably comes from the *fugue* and its use of the theme of the middle section. The term development [*Durchführung*] is common to both the 'integral' forms, the fugue and to the sonata.

11 Regarding the *coda* of the movement, the immensely sparing use of harmonization should be noted. Harmonization is not carried through, being criticized as trivial, in some sense tautological. The tendency in the late style for harmony to wither away is making its appearance here. And at the same time, the tendency to allow har-

mony to emerge in its naked abstractness. A contrast here to the coda of op. 59.1, where precisely the coda is newly and correctly harmonized. (To balance this, in that work the theme had not been fully harmonized.) – The *forte* character of the opening theme, which had been kept secret in both the exposition and the recapitulation – differently in each case – is now stated simply and directly. Directly because the theme is *intrinsically forte,* and had only been *piano* in quotation marks, so that no preparation of its *f*-character is needed, since this would have been pleonastic. The unmediated character of the *forte* is an expression of utmost formal sensitivity.

[222]

Towards a Theory of Beethoven

1 The Ninth Symphony* is not a late work, but a reconstruction of the *classical* Beethoven (with the exception of some parts of the last movement and, above all, of the trio in the third movement). The first movement, with a *stanza-like* structure in which development and coda balance each other, is probably based on the 'Appassionata'. In other words: Beethoven's late style, which elsewhere abandons all this, is essentially critical. That Beethoven was still 'able' to compose in the earlier way – no matter how unimportant in itself for an understanding of the late style – shows the critical intention.

2 The most astonishing feature of the first movement is, perhaps, that in it the idea of the *epic* symphony, which dominates the whole of Romanticism, is paradoxically reconciled with that of the integral symphony, as I described it in 'Zweite Nachtmusik'[202] and in 'Radio Voice'.[203] The epic moment in Beethoven is, precisely, the critical motif, that is, it expresses a dissatisfaction with the totality already achieved and 'finished' – it is, in other words, a realization that time is mightier than its aesthetic syncopation. But this realization, too, is *organized* within the Ninth. What is miraculous is that, for example, after the self-contained – quasi-Brucknerian – first (D minor) stanza, the B♭ major stanza follows, without merely following; but most miraculous of all is that he is able to *continue* the *epically* monumental closing formula of the theme, which later becomes the main model of the development. The last coda of the movement, with the chromatic progression of the basses, was composed over and over again.

* [In margin:] NB: First theme is thought to date back to 1809.

3 On the Trio in E♭ major, op. 70: the first movement contains splendid examples of 'mediation':* the motifs first appear successively in the two string parts, then on the piano. The latter's mechanical character is used to convey the dialectical meaning. The objective and, as it were, smaller sound of the piano presents each theme as a *result*, something attained. – The *detachment*† of the piece: nothing is *immediate* just as it is. Especially the introduction and the second subject group connected to it. This detached, non-literal quality is probably the decisive feature of Beethoven's work as a whole. – Regarding the performance of the third movement: the 'inserted' dynmamics must be *exaggerated*. – In the last movement the canonical passage in the development, where the *coherence* of the piano model, which is interrupted by a pause and overrun by the strings, is established by a minimal detail (chords set first in two voices, then three, providing an implicit crescendo). The question of performance should probably be considered here.   [223]

The passage in the Finale of the E♭ major Trio [op. 70, 2] after the double bar line, where the semiquaver movement breaks off [bar 116], to carry on inaudibly, as it were, behind the scenes. An 'inner intersection'.   [224]

It is necessary to answer the question why, despite the absolute poverty of harmonization and the relative poverty of modulation, the impression *never* arises of harmonic monotony or even of getting stuck. Beethoven accomplishes a *tour de force* at this point. In general, the *paradoxical* nature of everything he does. At the centre of the broad classical totality, something narrow, almost idiosyncratic, from which, precisely, the work derives its power. Extremely important.   [225]

There is a decidedly comic, relatively rare type in the early and middle Beethoven, which deserves utmost attention as 'late style in disguise'. The main examples: the Finale of the G major Violin Sonata op. 30, no. 3 (bear dance) and that of the F♯ Piano Sonata [op. 78]. The absence of important second themes seems characteristic of such movements. In conception, they are *monothematic*. This gives them a stubborn, obsessive, *narrow-minded* character which, however, just because it asserts itself in such exaggerated form, is *cancelled*. The 'Rage over a Lost Penny' is a quintessential example of this

* [In margin] NB: The 'run' and the 'melody' of the main theme are identical. Hence, the run is 'mediated', distanced.
† [In margin:] This must be defined precisely.

type. These movements represent the *negation* of the subject through their exclusive reliance on its contingent aspects, its 'whims'.   [226]

With regard to construction it will be decisive to identify the moment of negativity in the perfection of the middle works, a moment which took the music beyond this perfection.*   [227]

Special attention should be given to certain symphonic passages in the middle Beethoven, for example, in the development of the first movement of the Fourth Symphony and in the *Eroica*, where the music seems to be 'suspended', dangling from some thing to which it is attached. These passages, which are most emphatically distinct from the 'floating' passages to be found in Romanticism, will be easily recognizable from the gestures of a conductor who understands them. In such moments he will turn himself into that to which the suspended music is attached, holding it in his raised hands yet without making any intervention. It is possible that these passages prefigure those in Beethoven's last works, which are formed by irrupting conventions. But in the symphonies they still seem to be generated entirely spontaneously. I should like to characterize them as moments of reification. Their peculiarly playful character stems from the fact that in them what is subjectively produced seems, just as it is about to be dynamically unfolded, to cut itself off from the source of its production. The subjective force, within its 'productive process', that is, technically speaking, in the course of its modulation, becomes alien to itself, confronting itself as a non-human objectivity. These are precisely those passages in which symphonic time seems to stand still: as they swing back and forth, the passages become the pendulum of time itself. The symphonic transformation of time is directly connected to the reification of subjective production, and this may be the deepest point of coincidence between Kant and Beethoven. The incomparable charm of these passages springs, however, from the fact that even in that state of alienation subjectivity smiles in the product, does not entirely forget itself even here. Play: in Beethoven this means that even in its remotest products the memory of the human survives; that in this most central sense all reification is not quite serious, but is appearance, after which its spell can be broken and it can at last be called back to the world of the living.   [228]

Art-works of the highest rank are distinguished from the others not through their success – for in what have they succeeded? – but

---

* [Inserted later at foot of text:] See note of 30 June 49 [cf. fr. 199].

through the manner of their failure. For the problems within them, both the immanent, aesthetic problems and the social ones (and, in the dimension of depth, the two kinds coincide), are so posed that the attempt to solve them must fail, whereas the failure of lesser works is accidental, a matter of mere subjective incapacity. A work of art is great when it registers a failed attempt to reconcile objective antinomies. That is its truth and its 'success': to have come up against its own limit. In these terms, any work of art which succeeds through not reaching this limit is a failure. This theory states the formal law which determines the transition from the 'classical' to the late Beethoven, in such a way that the failure *objectively* implicated by the former is disclosed by the latter, raised to self-awareness, cleansed of the appearance of success and lifted, for just this reason, to the level of philosophical succeeding.   [229]

EIGHT

VERS UNE ANALYSE DES SYMPHONIES

The first movement of the *Eroica*, Beethoven's most 'classical' symphony, is in a certain sense the most Romantic. The exposition closes on a dissonance [bars 150–4], like the *Adagio* of op. 31,1. – The special role of the Schubertian altered chord (G♭ B♭ C E) and of related forms to set the seal on the modulation. The dissonances before the entry of the new theme in the development. Also, the modulation after C♯ minor, quite close to the start of the development [bars 181–4]. Above all, the start of the coda with the nonfunctional parallel descent E♭–D♭–C [bars 555ff], Bruckner's Platonic Idea. The relation between the 'epic' and the symphonic crucial to the first movement of the Ninth, and thus the whole historical tendency, is already contained in this movement. This must be worked out in detail. – Incidentally, the retrospective tendency that I observed in the first movement of the Ninth[204] also applies to the First, which, as Leichtentritt rightly notes,[205] lacks the boldness of many earlier works.   [230]

On the *Eroica*, first movement. Its internal syntax needs to be analysed in its finest details. The ideas include:

1 The introductory chords are schematic (accented chords at the end of the exposition).

2 The extraordinary abundance of figures in the exposition is brought under control by their interrelatedness (develop in detail).

3 Because of the gigantic dimensions, certain *leading* chords are used as connecting means, a situation almost unique in Beethoven. For example, the modulation over the altered four–three chord of

the dominant, and chords of various forms with the collision of the minor second or ninth and the major seventh. This figure, which occurs, for example, at the end of the exposition [bar 150], takes on its full meaning in the extreme tension before the entry of the 'new' theme of the development. The famous collision of seconds at the start of the recapitulation [bars 382ff] may be derivable from this(?).

4 The passage with the C♭ at the end of the exposition [bars 150ff] corresponds to the technical situation as described in the comments on 'peaceful' codas [cf. fr. 178], with a wholly changed expression. (*Abend* [evening]. This tone always makes me think of Matthias Claudius.)

5 The way the music is led on by picking up 'hanging' tied notes is decisive in enabling the form to draw breath. In this connection, analyse especially what happens in [Eulenburg's] pocket score, p. 16, after the syncopated chords. The figure introduced by the *forte* of violas and celli has the character of a concluding coda (the closing section has already been reached on p. 13 with the *forte* entry), but is then drawn back into the dynamic flow by tied notes and modulation to A♭. Here, the immanent requirements of form, of totality, have precedence over all else; where a figure stands out, for reasons of articulation, it has to be withdrawn, 'disclaimed', that is, revealed to be a moment in the flow.

6 The movement is understood only if one is able to determine the role, the syntactic function, of each figure (including the element of polyvalency, as in the doubt over the beginning of the second subject, which is itself a means of creating dynamic tension).

7 There is in Beethoven a dynamic *pp* – that is, one which is stated *immediately* to indicate a coming crescendo. This is an immediacy mediated within itself. Cf. the entry of the minor ninth chord on p. 12 (the dynamic element lies in the dissonance, the crescendo itself beginning only six bars later).   [231]

Further notes on the *Eroica* [first movement]:

1 Regarding the desideratum in point 6 above: according to the modulation scheme, the second subject group is reached on p. 7 with the theme beginning with the tonic of B♭ major (the lower voice of which, incidentally, is related to that of the 'new' theme of the development). But this theme (a) is skilfully kept somewhat non-committal, not being perceived as a main figure; (b) is quite brief, only eight bars long, so that, given the gigantic dimensions of the piece, it 'carries no weight'; (c) through the diminished seventh chord on F♯ it is interrupted by a much more characteristic figure (this is the truly dramatic antithetical moment of the movement). On p. 11 B♭ major is reached once more, and the new figure which starts

here, with the repeated crotchets, is melodically and harmonically much more plastic, much more 'fulfilling' through timbre and much more clearly set off from the movement than the figure on p. 7, and twice as long. But because so much has happened in the interval, it has the character of something coming afterwards – a *consequent phrase*. Thus, there is in the second theme group only one formal gesture which 'points' in a certain direction (cf. especially the $p < >$ on p. 7: only the interpretation, not the subject matter itself, indicates the second theme), and then the *consequent phrase* – the 'theme' being omitted, or replaced by the dramatic moment of the development. However, the formal treatment after p. 11 makes it appear retrospectively as if the theme had been there after all – a consequent phrase to a *non-existent* antecedent phrase, which is yet suggested (the functional character of form). The purpose of the whole, despite the profound way in which the articulation plays on the traditional scheme, is to permit no independent, isolated Being in face of Becoming, just as the dialectic permits no such Being. Beethoven, the dialectician, has no truck with what is crudely called 'thematic dualism'.

2 P. 12, four bars before the *pianissimo* entry, is the critical passage, the caesura of the movement, a dragging or falling which is only retrospectively revoked. *Everything* depends on the understanding of such bars. The immense difficulty of interpreting these four bars.

3 The 'new' theme of the development must perhaps be understood as determined by, precisely, the pure, intrinsic demands of form raised to the highest degree; these require the different element, the new quality, as their result. Immanent form as that which *produces* the transcendence of form. And here the unconnected nature of the second subject group comes into its own. The new theme *is* the song theme which had been omitted, circumvented. As a *thesis* it had been suppressed – now, as a *result*, it is *demanded* – and is at the same time recovered, in accordance with the schema previously suspended. Thus the theme, too, is now absorbed by the immanent form; that is, within the large coda of the whole movement it has its own recapitulation, pp. 67f. But there is an unusual situation here, too, in that the requirements of form are now suspended *beforehand*, by the functionless abrupt parallel fall (as later in Bruckner) of the transition to the coda, pp. 64f, E♭ I, D♭ I, C I.

4 Precisely these moments point to the Romantic element, which is both contained and negated within the *Eroica*. Little in Beethoven is as close to Schubert as the development (for example, 'An Schwager Kronos', the *Scherzo* of the C major Symphony, and prob-

ably that of the String Quintet). Cf., especially, the C♯ minor entry
on p. 21 and the continuation. Such passages probably prepare for
the precipitous descent into the great coda. Clearly, given the
immensely interwoven nature of the movement, the sense of form
calls for a 'lapidary' counterweight as its own contradiction, for perspectives opening up the whole, a restored immediacy.   [232][206]

Further notes on the first movement of the *Eroica*

1 At the very end of the first movement the original – then interrupted – idea of the second subject group reappears as the last thematic event in the movement (apart from the chord syncopations). It
is, as it were, redeemed, vindicated. Cf. Schoenberg's notion of the
obligation once contracted.[207] – Moreover, this theme already contains the kernel of the motif – the repeated crotchets – of the consequent phrase which will follow it in the exposition, after the
dramatic interruption.

2 Given the huge dimensions of the piece, Beethoven needs special means to hold it together – apart from the leading chords and
modulations, he often uses syncopated chords or those forming
pseudo-bars; these serve a double purpose: in contrast to the truly
thematic sections they form 'fields of dissolution', while at the same
time, through accentuation on and off the beat, they carry the tension forward or, as in the middle of the development, drive it to its
highest pitch.

3 The complication introduced by the new theme of the development is balanced by the fact that the second section of the
development, leaving aside the elaboration of the new theme in
double counterpoint, is simplified in construction, is 'lapidary' as
compared to the first part. (For example, the entry of the main
theme in C, pp. 36f). A tendency towards *octaves*, a cursory treatment. This prepares for the sharp harmonic descent at the start of
the great coda.

4 Genius in the treatment of the sonata schema. This is *played
with* in a very profound way; that is, the exposition, immensely rich
in figures and quite unschematic in its intent, nevertheless emphas-
izes the schema by means of certain characters used as if for orientation. For example, p. 5, last bar: 'I am a transition model'; p. 7: 'So
you thought I was a second subject!'; p. 13, *forte*: this is now the
closing section – so there's nothing to interpret. If one immerses oneself single-mindedly in the movement, these formal intentions seem
informed by a curious *humour*.   [233]

The truly magnificent aspect of the slow movement of the *Eroica* is
that the recapitulation is drawn fully into the momentum of the

development. Show at this point what form really means in Beethoven. Also the 'Appassionata', first movement.   [234]

The most characteristic feature of the *Scherzo* of the *Eroica* seems to me to lie in the first six bars, before the entry – emphasized by the doubling of the oboe – of the main theme itself. An attempt needs to be made – as a precondition of any interpretation – to describe the factual situation as exactly as possible. The six bars are not an 'introduction'. The movement 'begins with them' (NB: the tonic!). Nor are they a mere tonal design against the background of which the theme stands out – that would be Romantic, quite un-Beethovenian; the character is too rudimentary and melodic for that. Nor, finally, does the theme 'develop' from the six bars (as at the start of the Ninth Symphony): it emerges fully formed – indeed, as a contrast. Rather, we have here a character kept 'non-committally' vague – it is also tonal through the modulation after the dominant – which precedes a 'binding' or committed character. This interchange dominates the whole movement, the committed character often being drawn into the uncommitted one, so that the whole is kept in suspension. Understanding of form is so important here because, in the late style, such formal subtleties and ambiguities reign supreme. A rebellion against facile formal language – even in the smallest detail, the meaning of the individual characters.   [235]

It seems to me that the comments in the previous entry open up the whole *Scherzo* of the *Eroica*, in that the 'non-committal' aspect of one part of a theme permits ever-changing lengths and thus the joking, the *play*. – According to Bekker, the problematic aspect of the last movement appears to be well known;[208] but where are the problems? They are quite obvious; for example, the padding after the first statement of the (upper voices') main theme. (NB: Bekker does not notice that bass *and* theme provide the main material, just as, in technical matters generally, he spouts nonsense, such as his assertion that from the Second to the Fourth Symphony there are no transition themes, whereas the first movement of the *Eroica* offers the very paradigm of such a theme.) It would be interesting to know *why* the Finale comes to grief. Beethoven clearly wanted to make the ossified variation form more fluid by inserting fugal elements in the manner of a development (as he later did with supreme success in the *Allegretto* of the Seventh), but here is bogged down in outward relationships.   [236]

When undertaking a *critique* of Beethoven, one must no doubt begin by constructing the *problem* that he faced. In the Funeral March and the Finale [of the Third Symphony] he clearly wanted to balance the first movement by providing syntheses of fully developed, closed forms and loose, open ones (song and variations). He succeeded in the Funeral March, but not in the Finale; but he failed here only because he overreached himself. The *means* was to be counterpoint. It can already be doubted in the Funeral March whether the development-like section is fully worked out, or is carried forward in a merely outward way, through arrangement. In the Finale the alternation of variations and counterpoint sections is a fine and novel conception, but is not yet mastered; it fails, not as a composition, but when measured against the problem set (is the same true of the *Missa?*). – There is a clear rupture, for example, in the transition from the real main theme to the first episode, by means of the thematic bass; pocket score, pp. 176–7. Such potpourri-like, patchwork passages occur as late as the Finale of the Ninth. Naturally, Beethoven could have done this more 'skilfully'. If he resorted to such means, the reason can be deduced *a priori* from the antinomies contained in the underlying *formal problem*: the irreconcilability of the open and closed principles. Very important. The B minor entry, p. 185, is a stroke of *genius*, as is the character of the G minor variation, p. 190. – The *proportions* are a very problematic element in this movement (this is somehow connected to the main problem). The *andante* section seems to me relatively too long, whereas the *presto*, in particular, is much too short. – The weakness of the movement seems to have been noticed by every dunce. But what matters is to *explain* the weakness. Cf. the great essay by Schoenberg on this point.[209]   [237][210]

On the Finale of the *Eroica*, again: he sought the characteristic synthesis because, in the deeper formal sense, he needed a contrast to the first movement; but at the same time he wanted to produce something no less committed than that movement. However, the leading *citoyen* and the *Empire* style[211] cannot be reconciled: rupture between bourgeois ideology and reality.[212] Lukács on idealism and realism not irrelevant in this context: the Goethe book.[213] (Evidence!)   [238]

Some comments on the *Fourth Symphony*, a splendid, much underrated work. Regarding harmony and form: the crux of the immensely precise and economical introduction (compare the First and Second) is the reinterpretation of G♭ as F♯ (B minor). By contrast, the turning point of the development interprets F♯ as G♭, as a retransition to B♭. The tension of the introduction is resolved only here: 'functional harmony'. – How unschematically Beethoven thinks: the last four bars of the transition to the second subject group (pocket score, p. 14); the following theme of the second subject group itself and the later melodic idea (canon of clarinet and bassoon), p. 17, are 'too alike', especially the last two, and yet *entirely* compelling. Syncopation *as such* is used thematically in the movement as a linking element, somewhat as chords accented off the beat are used in the first movement of the *Eroica*; cf. p. 13 and the closing section, p. 21. (The *brackets* in Beethoven are identical, even if the content is very diverse. Important.) – The *magnificent* treatment of the development, which (mindful of the *Eroica*?) has a quasi-new theme, though still as a counterpoint, so that it is wholly absorbed into the intrinsic flow of the movement. The development always reminds me of Hegel's *Phenomenology*. It is as if the objective unfolding of the music were steered by the subject, as if the subject were balancing the music. From the bottom of p. 27, the prototype of a symphonic elaboration. – The abbreviation of the motif after the minim passage, p. 16, is a touch of genius ('flashing intention'). I could not get much out of the slow movement when reading the score, but saw it quite differently through a not particularly good recording under Furtwängler (too slow and sentimentalized). Especially the short, development-like section from p. 70 on. I could *not* properly imagine the force of the underlying voice in B♭, or the dynamic contrasts in the last movement (for example, pp. 125 and so on). The danger of *reading*.[214] By contrast, I can effortlessly imagine the harmonic proportions over the longest passages.   [239]

1 In the first movement of the *Fifth Symphony* the *metrics* need to be analysed. The movement is of extreme simplicity as regards melody, counterpoint and harmony. It would lapse into crudity if the treatment of rhythm (in which each bar is only one beat) did not introduce the utmost diversity. One needs to demonstrate:

The purely musical reasons for the irregularity. (Count out the main theme with the pauses – all the irregularity is based on this. It does *not* start on the upbeat!!)
The technique of irregularity (zeugma, constant tendency for the end of one phrase to overlap the beginning of another).
The *function* of the irregularity: a holding of breath (especially the alternating chords in minims in the development with the *ff* interpolations).
The relationship of irregularity to expression. The expressive idea of the movement generates the blockages, or vice versa.

2 The slow movement of the Fifth is a centrepiece for a critique of Beethoven. With one of the most beautiful themes (and because of it??), it is one of the most problematic pieces.

> The over-long and imprecise formation of the consequent phrase of the main theme.
> The failure to continue the march as second idea, which is replaced by mere transposition (weakness = bombast of the expressive element).
> The tediousness of the figurative variations results from the paraphrases' having no corresponding developments. Terseness lapses into a crude rigidity.
> The coda relapses into paraphrase.
> The unmediated contingency, the unrelatedness of the woodwind passage of thirds in contrary motion, magnificent as these are in themselves [bars 131ff].
> The triviality of the *accelerando* passage [bar 205].
> The dubious monumentality. Starting from the pithy bottom C in the theme of the second subject group [bars 32–7].

NB: As a composition, the finale of the Fifth, too, might well contain some very dubious features.

3 Regarding the physiognomy of Beethoven's variants, passages such as the following deserve study:[215]

Example 11

In Beethoven's variants, ornamentation – that which is most remote from humanity in music – becomes the bearer of its humanization.

[240]

Is the slow movement of the Fifth Symphony really good? In face of received opinion, it is hardly possible to raise this question. Yet I have my doubts. Compared to the wonderfully rich articulation of the theme, the variations, which dissolve it in continuous motions, come off badly – a naive ear would say that the theme is mutilated. And the variations remain too *close* to the theme, which is merely paraphrased, instead of engaging with it. – A theme as richly articulated as this calls for a total structure no less articulated: a contradiction between theme and form.* – The banality of the march-like woodwind chorus. – The inability to break away from A♭. – There is much to be said against it – for example, that the movement owes its monumental authenticity to the very crudity of its procedures. Schoenberg to Eduard [Steuermann]: Music is there to be listened to, not criticized. But is this not to condescend? Is this not the talk of philistines who do not want their enjoyment spoiled? Does not Beethoven's grand, lapidary style contain, at the same time, the problem of its *truth*? Was it not for *this* reason that he abandoned his classicism? – This time the last movement, especially the development, seemed to me splendid. But something is not quite right in the entry of the second subject group, perhaps because of the thematic richness preceding it; however, unless my ear deceives me, the same applies to the use of modulation and to the functional harmony. And what impressed one most as a child, the bracketing with the *Scherzo*: is that not a *literary* effect, one which does not arise from the composition itself? This seemed to me particularly the case with the recurring episode which, after this development, was not at all *needed*.   [241][216]

The means of turning an unobtrusive accompanying motif into a decisive development model are already present in the Finale of the Fifth [cf. bars 46–8].

Example 12

[242]

On the *Pastoral*: while the whole piece is dominated by the ideal of rusticity and its technical correlative, simplification, complexity is in no way sacrificed. This is, above all, a static music, yet filled, despite everything, with the utmost symphonic tension. That which is must *become*: the joy of repetition becomes a heightened bliss. I note the following: the theme of the second subject group (pocket score, p. 5), despite its extreme melodic and harmonic simplicity, is ren-

---

* [In margin:] What is magnificent in the theme is the distribution of stresses.

dered expansive through the double counterpoint and through the canonic entries of the counterpoint (repeated at the end where, moreover, its composition is narrowed, not quite pure). (NB: What is theme and what counterpoint is left in abeyance, hence the pleasantly indeterminate quality of the expression.) – The metrical irregularity of the continuation, in which Beethoven wisely, through overlaps, leaves it open to doubt what has three beats and what has four. – The peculiar *harmony* of the whole, with a tendency towards the subdominant (cf. the trio), a shift of harmonic strata instead of progression; 'functionless'. In the closing section the domestic servant is included in the composition. Profound humour, between happiness and apathy, as the exposition ends. – The formulation of the main theme: the timid impulse and the thankful, chorale-like consequent phrase (its character is that of the Finale). – The strophic arrangement of the development: shifts instead of actual modulation. The extreme abbreviation of the polyphony of the development to a mere linking element (NB: that is, no polyphonic obligations are contracted); instead, the onward-gliding of the late part of the development, from p. 17 (model: the consequent phrase of the chorale) until the start of the recapitulation. – The woodwind motif in the concluding section of the exposition, a mere 'filling voice' which is left behind as a residue. – In the coda I do not 'understand', in terms of the inner form, the variation of the theme of the closing section in triplets, that is, its function. I find this passage blurred. How difficult it is to understand music in terms of its deeper logic; how little all this has to do with 'simplicity' (p. 29). But how magnificent, by contrast, is the harmonization of the main theme directly before; a catching up. Even the *non*-harmonized, static part becomes an obligation to think of the music in terms of degrees, but in such a way as to exclude any disruptive logic. – The touch of greatest genius, perhaps, is the theme of the clarinet in the coda, p. 32, formed from the closing element of the antecedent phrase of the theme, but still seeming fresh, above the ticking quavers of the bassoon: time as happiness. The indescribably deep intertwinement of composition and expression in the whole movement. The blissful melancholy of the end, where practically nothing is left.

In the *slow* movement the theme, almost as in Debussy, is a sequence of notes pared to the minimum. Impressionism does not admit the concept of the theme: accompaniment, background are paramount. Even this is realized, prototypically, in Beethoven, and thereby disposed of. Only the refrain-like, repeated, subjectively reflected theme stands out (*dolce*, that is, with expression), bottom of p. 37. Despite Berg's scorn, I do not think Pfitzner's interpretation – 'How beautiful' – stupid at all.[217] – The aimless, timeless, murmuring quality of the movement – also impressionistic,* for example, the return to the principal key on p. 39, the triple repeat of the bassoon motif on p. 42, then again, insatiably, on pp. 44, 45, the refrain theme (including the cadence) almost breaking in. – Of course, a more exact analysis would show how this movement is rendered symphonically dynamic, from the standpoint of expression, of the subject, which seems to become more and more immersed, lost, *moved*, drawing the music, the static element of the mood, with it. (NB: It is a basic feature of Beethoven that the force exerted by the developing symphonic objectification is always, *as such*, the subjective impulse. This is true not only in general for the production or reproduction of form, but *specifically* for the objective elements contributing to the development. Regarding Beethoven's dialectical logic.) – The bird imitation has something mechanical about it, especially through the repetition – it is incomprehensible how he could cause such havoc within his own conception; here the mischief of the 'concession' already begins. At the same time, the fault is so innocently displayed that one is ashamed to criticize.

The *Scherzo* is, no doubt, the model for Bruckner's *scherzi*. NB: The sophisticated relationships of tonality. Trio in the principal key, or with E♭ (mixolydian). – Only the coda redeems the modulatory 'obligation'. – The scherzo itself has two unmediated elements, a form very unusual in Beethoven,[218] that is, the caricatured dance with the famous syncopation is practically as independent of the *Scherzo* itself as a trio, and is also in the same key. The movement is *self-contained* like a suite of three dances.

Even the *programme* of the *Pastoral* is spiritualized; it rises from naivety by way of self-alienation and reification (the humour of the third movement is aimed at convention, which is 'wrong') and an outburst of the elemental which sublates convention, to thanksgiving and humanity. Holidays as a phenomenology of mind.   [243][219]

Pastoral, first movement. The repetition is not, as in Stravinsky, the outcome of a repetition compulsion, but, on the contrary, of relaxation, letting go. The bliss of dawdling. Dillydallying as Utopia.
[244]

The slow movement of the *Pastoral*: blithe regression – to amorphousness; thus without the malevolence of the destructive impulse. How is this possible?   [245]

---

* [In margin:] Like impressionism, the movement combines a dynamic looseness with an aimlessly static quality.

In a grotto in Hellbrunn: hydraulically driven mechanical birds, with a cuckoo. Their last trace at the end of the slow movement of the *Pastoral*.   [246]

How is it possible that in Beethoven – even where antagonistic moments are simply absent, as in the closing movement of the *Pastoral* – symphonic tension is nevertheless created? Through the transition to the general. This happens, however, precisely through an act of subjective will [bars 32f]:

Example 13

etc.

and in this we also find the rupture, the secret negativity.   [247]

The *Pastoral*: the indescribably expansive effect of the organ-like passage in the coda of the last movement [bars 225ff]: not until the bottom C, sixth degree, but especially the chord of the ninth on F, very rare in Beethoven in this form. But – as often with outbursts in Beethoven – the passage becomes even more imposing in the retrospect of the diminuendo. In the Beethovenian form, the present creates the past.   [248]

On the *Eighth Symphony*: the retrospective, stylized, quoting aspect of the work has been noted; nor is its dignity in doubt. How do the two go together? In my view: the *limitation*, the invocation of the *dix-huitième*, is a means of making clear the pioneering, transcendent, ecstatic, frenzied aspect of the work (a sister-piece to the Seventh) all the more emphatically as a consequence of that very restrictedness. From the minuet-like first movement a giant arises – not in an *absolute* dimension (in Beethoven the immanence of style of the sonata is too deeply entrenched for that), but relatively: measured by what is enclosed, it *seems* gigantic. The centring on the finale after two genre-like but very enigmatic middle movements is very closely related to this. The analysis of the Eighth should be carried on along the lines of this dialectic. Cf. the note on coach and moonlight in the *Larghetto* of the Second [cf. fr. 330] – Jean Paul!!!
                                                            [249]

Further to my note on the Eighth Symphony [cf. fr. 249] I need to incorporate my experience of the *Freischütz* in Frankfurt in 1952.[220] In the opera, the expression of the demonic succeeds magnificently whenever it irrupts into Biedermeier narrowness; the waltz, Kaspar's indescribably splendid song of the vale of tears, Agatha's aria, the bridal wreath. But when the music approaches the demonic without reference to the picture-book world of Biedermeier, as in Kaspar's great aria, or when it touches on grace, as in the hermit scene, it is utterly uninspired, idling, an operatic cliché. This wisdom constitutes the idea of the Eighth Symphony – moreover, the finest moments in Beethoven never spring from the thing in itself, but always from a relationship. For the deepest reasons of construction, his dialectical image can never forgo the Biedermeier.   [250]

The gesture of standing firm is nowhere more grandiose than in the 12/8 section of the *Adagio* of the *Ninth Symphony*, where the fanfare of the full orchestra is answered, alone, by the first violins, but *forte* [bar 151]. The weak instruments stand up to the preponderant power, because fate has its limit in the *human being*, whose sound the violins are. The whole temper of Beethoven's music resembles this sixth chord of the violins – and even the single B♭. This is at the same time the metaphysics of the *concerto* form as practised by Beethoven, and perhaps as it always was.

The opening of the recapitulation in the first movement of the Ninth was composed over and over again, on account of its transcendence. But it also represents the utter *immanence* of transcendence, which defeated Brahms, Bruckner and Mahler. While expression is entirely foreign to it, the passage is a strict working-out of the *original bars* of the theme in the exposition – indeed, the transcendence itself is the full working-out of the origin. Music is reduced to its pure becoming: this causes it to pause. And even the *new* element in this passage was everywhere present already.

A standing firm in which[221] one apprehends fate directly. Stretching oneself is both the physical gesture of acceptance of fate, which one resembles, and a withdrawal from it. On waking up, we stretch our limbs. The gestic prehistory of Beethoven's writing. [251]

The theme of the Ninth is static; I have observed the touch of genius, the trick whereby, through the simple device of sequencing in the final two bars, it is, nevertheless, drawn into the dynamic flow. But Beethoven's sense of form is so unerring that he makes up for this at the end of the first movement (homoeostasis!). It ends with the literal theme precisely at the point where it has really come to an end.

[252]

The accented chords used as a transition model in the first movement of op. 30, 2 are, in principle, like a continuation of the main theme of the Ninth Symphony.   [253]

The entry of the recapitulation in the first movement of the Ninth, with the *chiaroscuro*, is one of the passages in music most fertile in consequences. Wagner, Bruckner, Mahler. It is the greatest example of the harnessing of the Romantic moment to construction. In this regard:

  1 The 'extraterritorial' aspect of the introduction is *simultaneously* preserved and abolished. Preserved in that the introduction is repeated, the theme being presented once more *in statu nascendi*. (NB:The static quality of the theme itself corresponds to its *coming into being*, even in the exposition: it is itself a *result*.) The 'colour' of the hollow sound corresponds to that of F♯: firelight to wanness. What was introduction is now climax. In this way the F♯ 'fulfils' the empty fifth in the most literal sense. What existed *before* the symphonic time becomes a standing still of symphonic time. One might almost say: the assumption is proved.

  2 The F♯ becomes F on the weak part of the bar ([bar] 324); the A♭–A relationship reinforces (balances?) that of F♯–F.

  3 The counterpoint to the main theme 317 is taken from the closing section; from 320, from the *continuation* of the main theme of bar 25. In this way the 'paradoxical' problem of continuation posed at the earlier point is resolved differently (the paradox is unrepeatable): the *tour de force* of 21–3 now disappears beneath the impulse of the counterpoint of the basses, and through the repetition of the concluding part, which was the principal model of the development; once the recapitulation of 25 is reached in 329, it has, dynamically, the character of an *response* to the basses. This is underlined by the fact that the semiquaver triplet of that bass counterpoint is taken up by the violins, and imitatively by the woodwind.

  4 In the interest of drawing everything in, of the triumph of immanent form, the music dispenses with the epic stanza form. The theme is dynamically expanded *within itself*, but begins only *once*: as this happens, the B♭ in the exposition, crucial to the second stanza, is, with a stroke of genius, itself made an element of the now continuous thematic complex. There is now 'no stopping', even while the theme pauses.

  The vision, the transcendent aspect, is the moment in which

immanence is apprehended as totality. The idea of the *awed shudder*.   [254]

(Ninth.) The *entire* recapitulation retains the first theme's tendency towards imitative spinning out and 'narrowing'. Consistency. [255]

On the Ninth: the *headlong* quality after the long development before the entry of the recapitulation from [bar] 288 on: almost like the end of *Hamlet*. Time relationships no longer mechanical but determined by meaning. Very important.   [256]

How the gigantic complex of the first movement of the Ninth is really only there for the sake of the few bars at the start of the recapitulation, to show that immensity could not exist without the whole movement – that's how it should be with all good prose.

[257][222]

In the first movement of the Ninth one is struck by the immense economy despite the huge dimensions.*   [258]

In the first movement of the Ninth there are signs of a 'non-committal' style of instrumentation, dissolved into solo voices, which is quite new in Beethoven; these are found at the beginning of the development and in the great coda.   [259]

On the epic character of the Ninth Symphony, cf. Paul Bekker, p. 280.[223]   [260]

Perhaps the urge to make music speak – in the sense defined above [cf. Fr 68] – is the true reason for the choral finale of the Ninth Symphony, the contradictoriness of this urge being the reason for the questionable aspects of that movement.   [261]

Critique: the problematic character of Beethoven's polyphony can be shown, for example, in a passage at the start of the development of the Ninth Symphony, bar 180. It concerns the relations between voices, between the first violins and the solo bassoon. They enter in octaves; then a bassoon G converges on that of the violins; then the two voices lead off in contrary motion (octaval impurities also found, for example, in the canonic passage in the second subject of the Finale of op. 59,1).[224] But one has to decide: either octave

* [Below the line:] (Deliberately spare in form, unlike op. 106 or the first movement of the B♭ major Quartet [op. 130], for example.)

doubling, or independent voices. And yet, the matter is not so simple. For the ambiguous character of the passage, suspended between stasis and development, is emphasized precisely by the 'impurity' of the passage, that is, its *technical* indeterminacy. Beethovenian content is itself a function of technical inconsequentiality – and yet, objectively, this inconsistency remains. This whole dialectic needs to be unfolded if one is to state the truth about Beethoven. – The entry of the principal model (the second main section of the development, as often in Beethoven) in bar 219 has the character of a decision, an abrupt subjective shift. But this decision is not one of subjective expression, but is far more a resolve to look the objective in the face – 'let's face it'. It has the character of alienation – of a subjective, but violent, transition to objectivity. This is no doubt the decisive turning point in Beethoven's dialectic.   [262]

The relationship of the symphony to dance may be defined as follows: if dance appeals to the bodily movements of human beings, the symphony is music which itself becomes a body. The symphony is the musical body – hence the specific nature of symphonic teleology, which does not lead to a 'goal': rather, by virtue of the symphonic process, music is revealed as a body. The symphony stirs 'itself'; stands still, moves on, and the totality of its gestures is the intentionless representation of the body. A relationship to Kafka's death machine in the *Penal Colony*. The corporeal nature of the symphony is its social aspect: it is the giant body, the collective physique of society in the dialectic of its moments. Study this in the first movement of the Ninth Symphony. The music extends or 'stretches' itself, for example, in the unison semiquaver passage in the exposition [bars 15f and 49f]; it 'rears up', collapses; and all this is taken over and misrepresented by programme music, which makes music a representation of the body instead of the body itself.

That it is possible to see the *Pastoral*, but no later 'symphonic poem', as programme music, is very closely connected to this. As a body, the *Pastoral* is still capable of experience. This capability is already lost to Berlioz. If the closing section loses itself in a free-wheeling suggestive of the motion of a coach, the symphonic body is able to feel this motion in itself. The music is drawn along in the coach. Honegger has to imitate the racket of a locomotive[225] because the music is no longer able to apprehend the locomotive's movement within itself.

The contrast between the intensive and the extensive type is perhaps the explanation of the famous duplexity of Beethoven's works. The first movements of the Fifth and Sixth Symphonies are among the purest examples of the two types. The late style is the collision between these types. A prerequisite for understanding the very late Beethoven is therefore an awareness of their divergence. In other words: what did Beethoven *miss* in the integral works, the first movements of the Third, Fifth, Ninth, the 'Appassionata', the entire Seventh? This question takes us to the threshold of Beethoven's secret. It asks what idealism left by the wayside in the triumphal advance of progress. Mahler's whole work is an attempt to answer this question. The *Pastoral* is closest to him. On the question of a specifically symphonic quality – the existence of which Schoenberg is undoubtedly wrong in denying – there is a reference in Strauss to Berlioz's theory of instrumentation, where he recommends a study of string polyphony in Beethoven's quartets, as opposed to his symphonies, and where he touches on the crudeness of the string writing in the latter.[226]

The theme of the disruption of the idyll through its own self-transcendence recurs again and again. It will need to be interpreted as a *question*. The evidence, apart from that already noted:

The close of the *Ferne Geliebte* cycle (cf. early German Romantic painting, Friedrich and Runge).
The Finale of the *Pastoral* (... how can the chalumeau become symphonic?)
and naturally the first movement of the Eighth.   [263]

On the theory of Beethoven and the symphony, Schelling's concept of rhythm in the *Philosophy of Art*.[227]   [264][228]

Text 2a: Beethoven's Symphonies

In principle, Beethoven's symphonies are simpler than his chamber music despite their substantially more lavish apparatus, and this very simplicity showed what effects the many listeners had in the interior of the formal edifice. It was not a matter of adjusting to the market, of course; at most, perhaps, it had to do with Beethoven's intent to 'strike fire in a man's soul'. Objectively, his symphonies were orations to mankind, designed by a demonstration of the law of their life to bring men to an unconscious consciousness of the unity otherwise hidden in the individual's diffuse existence. Chamber music and symphonies were complementary. The first, largely dispensing with pathos in gesture and ideology, helped to express the self-emancipating status of the bourgeois spirit without as yet directly addressing society. The symphony took the consequence, declaring the idea of totality to be aesthetically void as soon as it ceased to communicate with the real totality.

In exchange, however, the symphony developed a decorative as well as a primitive element which spurred the subject to productive criticism. Humanity does not bluster. This may have been what Haydn felt, one of the greatest geniuses among the masters, when he ridiculed young Beethoven as 'The Grand Mogul'. In so drastic a way as could hardly be surpassed in theory, the incompatibility of similar species is the precipitation of the incompatibility of universal and particular in a developed bourgeois society. In a Beethoven symphony the detail work, the latent wealth of interior forms and figures, is eclipsed by the rhythmic-metrical impact; throughout, the symphonies want to be heard simply in their temporal course and organization, with the vertical, the simultaneity, the sound level left wholly unbroken. The one exception remained the wealth of motifs in the first movement of the *Eroica* – which in certain respects, of course, is the highest peak of Beethoven's symphonies as a whole.

It would be inexact, however, to call Beethoven's chamber music polyphonous, and the symphonies homophonous. Polyphony and homophony alternate in the quartets too; in the last ones, homophony tends to a bald unison at the expense of the very ideal of harmony reigning in the highly classicist symphonies, as in the Fifth and Seventh. But how little Beethoven's symphonies and his chamber music are one is evident from the most superficial comparison of the Ninth with the last quartets, or even with the last piano sonatas. Compared with those, the Ninth is backward-looking, takes its bearings from the classicist symphony type of the middle period, and denies admission to the dissociative tendencies of the late style proper. This is hardly independent of the intentions of one who addressed his audiences as 'Friends' and proposed to join them in chanting 'more pleasant tones'.

Extract from Introduction to the Sociology of Music, transl. by E.B. Ashton,
New York 1976, pp. 94–5

Text 2b: Radio and the Destruction of Symphonic Form[229]

Only a crudely realistic view of the work of art, which conceived it in terms of the familiar distinction between the lasting thing and its mere sensuous shadow, could regard the intrusion of radio reproduction into a symphony by Beethoven with indifference. As Paul Bekker was the first to emphasize, the form of a symphony was not that of a sonata for orchestra, which could be conveniently isolated as an abstract scheme.* Specific to this form was intensity and concentration. It was the outcome of a compact, concise, palpable urgency: the technique of motivic and thematic work. Economy of composition conceded nothing to chance, but deduced the whole from the smallest units in a virtual way – something which the serial technique now wishes to accomplish literally. Identical elements were not, however, repeated statically but were, to use the term invented by Schoenberg as the heir to the procedure, varied developmentally. From the basic material, the symphony spins out non-identical elements in time, just as it affirmatively discloses identity in a material which, in itself, is disparate and divergent. Structurally – as Georgiades, too, has stressed – one hears the first bar of a classical symphonic movement only when one hears the last, which redeems the former's pledge. The illusion of pent-up time – so that movements like the first of the Fifth and Seventh Symphonies, or even the very extended one of the *Eroica*, when properly performed, seem to last not seven or fifteen minutes, but only a moment – is produced by that structure, no less than is the feeling of a compulsion which does not exclude the listener: symphonic authority as an immanent property of meaning, and finally of the listener's absorption by the symphony, of the ritual reception of the individual within an evolving whole. The aesthetic integration of the symphonic structure is at the same time the pattern of a social integration. Bekker, since his treatise on the symphony from Beethoven to Mahler, has sought its essence in its 'socio-genetic power'. This theory is undoubtedly wide of the mark in that music, once rationalized and planned in any way, is no longer an immediate sound, but is functionally adapted to social conditions. In general, art is able to posit no real social forms from within itself. Music has not so much been socio-genetic as it has elicited from individuals the ideology that they are linked, has strengthened their identification with it and therefore with each other. Rationalized, this was the disciplinary blessing which Plato and St Augustine already felt. The symphony celebrated the working, antagonistic bourgeois society as a unity of monads, for that society's benefit. The school of Viennese classicism, almost simultaneously with the Industrial Revolution, integrated scattered individuals in the spirit of the age; from their totally socialized relationships a harmonious whole was meant to spring. Aesthetic appearance itself, the autonomy of the work, was at the same time a means within the realm of practical purposes. The totality of life actually reproduces itself through what is divided and in mutual contradiction. This truth authenticated aesthetic success; the

* Cf. Paul Bekker, *Die Sinfonie von Beethoven bis Mahler*, Berlin 1918, pp. 8f.

deception lay in the individual's absorption. This inspired exalted feelings. By so diligently enveloping both the musical detail and the individual listener, it drowned out the awareness of an unreconciled condition. That illusion is dispelled by the radio, which executes the revenge on great music immanent in its role as ideology. No-one listening to a symphony in the bourgeois-individual situation of a private residence can mistake himself as bodily enfolded within the community. To this extent the symphony's destruction by the radio is also an unfolding of truth. The symphony is decomposed: what comes from the loudspeaker contradicts what it has itself been. The memory of a life maintaining itself however painfully within antagonism is replaced by a cast taken from it, in which the individual no longer recognizes either his own impulse or himself as emancipated. At most, it impresses him heteronomously, serving his need for power and glory and thus his consumer psychology. What was once a socially necessary illusion passes over into the individual's socially controlled false consciousness of himself and of the whole, ideology as the pure lie.

This is manifested most obviously in the absolute dynamic of the symphony, sound volume. A chair-sized model of a cathedral is different to the original not only quantitatively but in terms of meaning: if the proportion to the body of the beholder is modified, that which gives the word cathedral its luminosity falls away. Similarly the synthetic power of a Beethoven symphony depends at least in part on the volume of the sound. Only if this is larger, as it were, than the individual is he able to reach the interior of the music through sound's gateway. However, not only sound volume as such but the extent of the range from *fortissimo* to *pianissimo* contributes to the plasticity of the symphonic sound, which constitutes its meaning: the narrower this range, the more precarious the plasticity, and thus the experience supporting the symphonic space. No technical progress can obliterate the loss of all this on the radio. The listening conditions in a private room would not tolerate a sound which, like that in the concert hall, is larger than the individual. Anyone who wanted to experience such a sound with works whose qualities presuppose the categories of a giant orchestra, such as Schoenberg's *Gurrelieder*, would need to travel far from habitation in a car fitted with loudspeakers, in order to achieve something similar, and even then it would probably be distorted. Admittedly, if the radio receiver does not respect the acoustic and social conditions of listening, if it persists in emitting the original dynamics in a private room, then it does still break through the neutralization even today. But in that case the phenomenon is immediately transformed into a wild protest, a barbaric uproar. Not only does it crassly contradict the

existing situation and impel agitated neighbours towards the tele-
phone, but it is as alien to the original as, on the other hand, its
original form is to a house plant. No way out of neutralization.
Even with stereophonic sound it is hard to restore music's spatially
encompassing function. What is left of the symphony is a chamber
symphony, as if the world spirit had taken special care to ensure
that the chamber symphony, and the chamber orchestra in general,
should have evolved in precisely the age of mechanical reproduction.
The modifications to the radio symphony at the sensuous level are a
mortal threat to its structure also.

The classicist type of the symphony from Beethoven's middle
period has given rise to an idealized image of creation out of nothing. This comes into being only to the extent that the initial motif
which, as a derivative of the triad, is largely stripped of qualities, is
at the same time played with such emphasis that, although in itself
quite insignificant, it takes on an aspect of utmost relevance to what
is to follow from it. The first bars of the Fifth Symphony, properly
performed, must be rendered with the character of a thesis, as if they
were a free act over which no material has precedence. Technically,
this requires extreme dynamic intensity: loudness, here, is no mere
sensuous attribute; it is the condition of something spiritual, of
structural meaning. Unless the nothing of the first bars is realized at
once as the everything of the whole movement, the music has
bypassed the movement's idea before it has properly started. The
composition is reduced to inconsequentiality, no tension is accumulated. But the less the listeners – especially those bombastically
invited into music culture by the radio – know about the unmutil-
ated work, the more exclusively they are exposed to the radio's
voice, the more obliviously and powerlessly they succumb to the
effect of neutralization. What had been memory's benign support
becomes its foe, memory-less perception. The structure of the radio
symphony is polarized into contradictory elements, the banal and
the Romantic – elements which then coalesce in the light music
towards which the radio symphony tends. The primal cells in
Beethoven are nothing in themselves, mere concentrates of the tonal
idiom to which only the symphony lends voice. Torn from its context, their artful irrelevance becomes the commonplace which, as the
initial motif of the Fifth, was to be exploited up to the hilt by inter-
national patriotism. Moving intensifications or melodically distinc-
tive second ideas become emotional templates or portentously
beautiful passages. The intensive totality of the symphony deflates,
to become a chronological sequence of episodes. No doubt, symphonic intensity can never be quite eradicated, nor transcendence
towards the whole entirely expunged from the individual detail. But

they are poisoned. The remnants appear like ruins of an absent or obliterated context. In other words: like quotations. For this reason, only the pictorial aspect of the music remains. Not Beethoven's Fifth is heard, but a potpourri of its alleged melodies – at best, musical information on the music, not unlike that of which a visitor to a performance of *William Tell* complained, finding the whole drama reduced to a compilation of apothegms. Yet the Romanticization of as essentially un-Romantic a music as Beethoven's, its translation into a kind of musical popular biography,* plays fast and loose with the very aura which the usual radio transmission of traditional music presumes to safeguard. The exceptional state which music represented up to the dawn of the technological age is levelled down by overstrained glamour to the prose of the barren everyday condition. What is overthrown is the idea of the festive, which Georgiades, in his work on Mozart's 'Jupiter' Symphony, described as essential to Viennese classicism. Perhaps, even in its hour, it was already a subjective performance intended to rescue something objectively vanishing.

[...] No symphony of Beethoven is immune to its depravation. This, however, is to say nothing less than that the works themselves are not self-sufficient, are not indifferent towards the time. Only because they transform themselves historically, unfold and wither in time; because their own truth content is historical and not a pure essence, are they so susceptible to that which is allegedly inflicted on them from outside. This verifies what is taking place within them, the advance of muteness. The phenomena of radio are an index of the general tendency, of the decline of the traditional works themselves and of the approved musical culture. Only as ghosts can the dissociated works survive their downfall.

Extract from *Der getreue Korrepetitor* (GS 15, pp. 375ff) – written 1941/62

---

* Cf. T.W. Adorno, 'Über den Fetischcharakter in der Musik und die Regression des Hörens', in *Dissonanzen*, Göttingen 1958, pp. 9ff [now GS 14, pp. 14ff].

NINE

THE LATE STYLE (I)

Text 3: Beethoven's Late Style

The maturity of the late works of important artists is not like the ripeness of fruit. As a rule, these works are not well rounded, but wrinkled, even fissured. They are apt to lack sweetness, fending off with prickly tartness those interested merely in sampling them. They lack all that harmony which the classicist aesthetic is accustomed to demand from the work of art,[230] showing more traces of history than of growth. The accepted explanation is that they are products of a subjectivity or, still better, of a 'personality' ruthlessly proclaiming itself, which breaks through the roundedness of form for the sake of expression, exchanging harmony for the dissonance of its sorrow and spurning sensuous charm under the dictates of the imperiously emancipated mind. The late work is thereby relegated to the margins of art and brought closer to documentation. Accordingly, references to Beethoven's biography and fate are seldom absent from discussions of his last works. It is as if, in face of the dignity of human death, art theory wanted to forfeit its rights and abdicate before reality.

This alone can explain the fact that the inadequacy of such a viewpoint has hardly ever been seriously argued – an inadequacy which emerges as soon as attention is focused on the works themselves rather than on their psychological origin. For the task is to perceive their formal law, provided one is unwilling to cross over into the field of documentation – where, to be sure, any recorded conversation of Beethoven carries more weight than the C♯ minor

String Quartet. However, the formal law of the late works is such that they cannot be subsumed under the heading of 'expression'. The late Beethoven produced some extremely 'expression-less', dispassionate compositions; for this reason critics are as fond of deducing a new, polyphonically objective construction from his style as they are of invoking the ruthless subjective personality. His inner turmoil is not always associated with a resolve to die or with demonic humour, but is often simply enigmatic, discernible in pieces which have a serene, even idyllic tone. The unsensuous mind does not shun expression marks such as *'Cantabile e compiacevole'* or *'Andante amabile'*. In no way is his attitude straightforwardly covered by the cliché of 'subjectivism'. For originally, in Beethoven's music as a whole, the effect of subjectivity, fully in line with Kant's conception, was not so much to disintegrate form as to produce it. The 'Appassionata' can stand as an example: though certainly denser, more closed in structure and more 'harmonious' than the last quartets, it is to the same degree more subjective, autonomous and spontaneous. Nevertheless, these last works take precedence over it by virtue of their enigma. In what does this consist?

Only a technical study of the works in question could help towards a revision of the accepted view of the late style. This study would concentrate first on a peculiarity which is studiously ignored by the current view: the role of conventions. Their contribution is well known in the works of the old Goethe and the old Stifter; but it is no less to be found in Beethoven, the alleged representative of a radically personal stance. This points up the question still further. For to tolerate no conventions, and to recast the unavoidable ones in keeping with the urge of expression, is the first demand of every 'subjectivist' procedure. In this way the middle Beethoven absorbed the traditional trappings into his subjective dynamic by forming latent middle voices, by rhythm, tension or whatever other means, transforming them in keeping with his intention. Or – as in the first movement of the Fifth Symphony – he even developed them from the thematic substance itself, wresting them from convention through the uniqueness of that substance. Quite different in the late Beethoven. Everywhere in his idiom, even where it uses a syntax as singular as that of the five last piano sonatas, conventional formulae and phraseology are inserted. They are full of decorative trills, cadences and fiorituras. The convention is often made visible in unconcealed, untransformed bareness: the first theme of the Piano Sonata op. 110 has an ingenuously simple semiquaver accompaniment which the middle style would hardly have tolerated. The last of the Bagatelles has introductory and closing bars like the distressed prelude to an aria in an opera – all this in the midst of the hardest rock strata of the multivocal landscape, or the most restrained impulses of a secluded lyricism. No interpretation of Beethoven, and probably of any late style, would be adequate if it were able to provide only a psychological motivation for the disintegration of convention, without regard to the actual phenomena. For the content of art always lies only in phenomena. The relationship between conventions and subjectivity must be understood as the formal law from which the content of the late works springs, if these are really to represent something more than touching relics.

This formal law is manifest, however, precisely in reflection on death. If the legitimacy of art is abolished before death's reality, then death can certainly not be assimilated by the work of art as its 'subject'. It is imposed on creatures alone, and not on their constructions, and thus has always appeared in art in a refracted form: as allegory. Psychological interpretation fails to recognize this. By declaring mortal subjectivity the substance of the late work, it hopes to gain awareness of death directly in the work of art: this remains the deceptive summit of its metaphysics. To be sure, it perceives the disruptive force of subjectivity in the late work of art. But it looks in the opposite direction to that in which this force is acting; it looks for it in the expression of subjectivity itself. But this, as something mortal, and in the name of death, vanishes from the work of art in reality. The force of subjectivity in late works is the irascible gesture with which it leaves them. It bursts them asunder, not in order to express itself but, expressionlessly, to cast off the illusion of art. Of the works it leaves only fragments behind, communicating itself, as if in ciphers, only through the spaces it has violently vacated. Touched by death, the masterly hand sets free the matter it previously formed. The fissures and rifts within it, bearing witness to the ego's finite impotence before Being, are its last work. Hence the surplus of material in the second part of *Faust* and in *Wilhelm Meister's Journeyman Years*; hence the conventions no longer imbued and mastered by subjectivity, but left standing. As subjectivity breaks away from the work, they are split off. As splinters, derelict and abandoned, they finally themselves become expression; expression no longer of the isolated ego but of the mythical nature of the creature and its fall, the stages of which the late works mark out symbolically, as if in moments of pausing.

In this way, in late Beethoven, the conventions become expression in the naked depiction of themselves. This is assisted by the often-noted abbreviation of his style, which aims not so much to purify the musical language of its empty phrases, as to liberate these phrases from the illusion of subjective control: the emancipated phrase, released from the dynamic flow, speaks for itself. It does so, however, only for the moment when subjectivity, escaping, passes through it and harshly illuminates it with its intentions. Hence the crescendi and diminuendi which, seemingly independent of the musical construction, often shake this construction to its foundations in Beethoven's last works.

He no longer draws together the landscape, now deserted and alienated, into an image. He illuminates it with the fire ignited by subjectivity as it strikes the walls of the work in breaking free, true to the idea of its dynamic. His late work still remains a process, but not as a development; its process is an ignition between extremes which no longer tolerate a safe mean or a spontaneous harmony. Extremes in the strictest technical sense: on the one hand, the unison of the empty phrases not endowed with meaning; on the other, polyphony, rising unmediated above that unison. It is subjectivity which forces together the extremes within the moment, charging the compressed polyphony with its tensions, disintegrating and escaping it in the unison, leaving behind the naked note. The empty phrase is set in place as a monument to what has been – a monument in which subjectivity is petrified. The caesurae, however, the abrupt stops which characterize the latest Beethoven more than any other feature, are those moments of breaking free; the work falls silent as it is deserted, turning its hollowness outwards. Only then is the next fragment added, ordered to its place by escaping subjectivity and colluding for better or worse with what has gone before; for a secret is shared between them, and can be exorcized only by the figure they form together. This illuminates the contradiction whereby the very late Beethoven is called both subjective and objective. The fragmented landscape is objective, while the light in which alone it glows is subjective. He does not bring about their harmonious synthesis. As a dissociative force he tears them apart in time, perhaps in order to preserve them for the eternal. In the history of art, late works are the catastrophes.[231]

From *Moments musicaux* (GS 17, pp. 13ff) – written in 1934

After practising the Piano Sonata, op. 101. – Is the first movement the model for the prelude to *Tristan*? Quite different in tone, as if the (incomparably condensed) sonata form had become a lyric poem, entirely subjectivized, spiritualized, stripped of the tectonic. And yet, not only on account of the quavers and 6/8 rhythm, but because of the structural importance of the chromatic (derived from the alternating dominant in bar 1) and an element which is difficult to grasp – sequences of longing – especially in the development after the F♯ minor entry [bar 41]. – The second movement exactly shares

the character (and tempo!) of the introduction to the finale of the A
minor Quartet [op. 132; fourth movement: *Alla marcia, assai
vivace*]. The extraordinary, Schoenbergian passage up to the breaking off over D♭ [cf. bars 19–30] (extremely difficult to perform and
very enigmatic). The equally curious canonic trio in two voices.
Take this in a very *agitated* manner to generate meaning, and under
no circumstances more slowly – despite the enticement to do so.
Take the *adagio* introduction in quavers. A tension with the finale as
in the 'Waldstein' Sonata, only more inward, meditative, prefiguring
the slow movement of the 'Hammerklavier' Sonata. – The *literary*
quality of the reminiscence of the first movement, not inherent in the
form but 'poetic', like the quotation in the introduction to the finale
of the Ninth Symphony. – The Finale is the prototype of the late
style, a kind of primal phenomenon. It has:

A tendency to polyphony (exposition throughout in double counterpoint, preparation for the fugue).
A *bare* quality. Two-part structure in octaves. The simple chords
(derived from the first theme) leading to the theme of the closing
section.
The popular-song banality of this theme itself, which at the same
time is split up by changes of register. It is as if Viennese classicism, *combined* from the 'learned' and the 'gallant', were polarized again into its elements: the spiritualized counterpoint and the
unsublimated, *un*assimilated 'folksiness'.
An extraordinary art, whereby the development does not seem
like a textbook fugue (NB: the irregular responses to the theme:
A, C, D, A) while remaining within the form.
The coda is especially interesting. When the middle section of the
first theme, omitted from the recapitulation, appears in it [bars
325ff], it has the effect of something long *past*, forgotten, entirely
remote from the present, and therefore infinitely *touching* – in
rather the same way as the 'Ach neige' speech in the closing scene
of *Faust*.[232] Such shifts of the musical *present* did not exist before
Beethoven. Wagner then marshalled such effects theatrically in
the 'Ring', above all in the *Götterdämmerung*.
The immense accumulation of force before the entry of the recapitulation (similar to that in the first movement of the
'Hammerklavier' Sonata), which takes on a sombre, threatening
quality.
The close [bars 350ff] with the bottom D [properly: bottom E], a
kind of metaphysical bagpipe effect.

The whole sonata eminently *Hegelian*. The first movement the sub-

ject, the second 'alienated' (at once objective and *stricken*), the third
– were one not ashamed to write it down – the synthesis, sprung
from the force of an objectivity which, in the process, proves identical to the subject, the lyrical core.   [265][233]

An attempt to understand melody formation in the late Beethoven,
from the *Adagio* of the '*Hammerklavier*' Sonata.

1 The melody, judged by traditional notions, lacks plasticity; that
is, it is not obvious, in much the same sense as church music precludes the 'inventions' of secular music. The reasons are: the disappearance of surface articulation (there are no pauses, no sharp
rhythmical contrasts, no 'motifs' and, above all, the harmonic and
tonal basis remains identical throughout the whole theme); and
there is a prevailing tendency to repeat notes, often three times, or
even four. The melody is, as it were, stretched over long arches, pent
up.

2 The first effect is that the melody loses its immediacy, appearing
from the first mediated, and, moreover, 'meaningful'. It is not itself
but what it means. It can hardly be heard and understood as a
'melody' at all, but as a complex of meanings. Nor does it really
move on, but remains, circles around itself, does not develop (only
the consequent phrase character is distinct as such). One might say,
F♯ minor is not fully worked out here, but idiosyncratic peculiarities
of the key are insatiably presented. Instead of being realized, tonality
is portrayed.

3 Development is replaced by a self-transcendence of the tonal
realm: a region formed by the working-out of the Neapolitan sixth.

4 The form of the theme is extremely simple: a two-part song
form, part B being repeated, with a consequent phrase of two bars.
However, through holding fast to the same complexes and through
the non-repetition of part A, this form is not outwardly manifested.
All appears simultaneous, and *yet* is secretly planned.

5 The repeated notes, together with other elements, give rise to
the peculiar *speaking* character of the theme. Melody in very late
Beethoven becomes alienated from melody, and its logic is that of
speech. This must be traced precisely. The allusion to song in opp.
110 and 111 and in the B♭ major Quartet [op. 133].   [266]

On melody formation, and so on, in very late Beethoven (op. 106)

1 The repeated notes contribute to harmonic reinterpretation, frequently with a curious rocking between degrees, especially I and V.
This is connected to suspension effects, and especially to the intention to contrast linked[234] triads as if they were pure, self-contained.

At any rate, to say that the tonal material is ossified into a convention is only a half-truth. In its estrangement from the process and from identity, it juts out bare and cold, like rock. In having become subjectively expressionless, it takes on an objective, allegorical expression. 'Tonality itself speaks.'[235] That is the meaning of the portrayed triads. (The relationship of this expression of the expressionless needs to be precisely clarified.) Example: the coda of the exposition of the 'Hammerklavier' *Adagio*, from the B minor entry to the three sharps [bars 69–73], especially the D major chords within it.

2 On the technical identification of the expression of the 'mystical'. In late Beethoven un-plastic, uncharacteristic motifs are used, invoked, quoted (cf. the same coda to the exposition, *Adagio* op. 106). The *relationship* can be felt, although the model is not manifest. Hence the expression of the mysterious. Extremely important. Note Beethoven's dictum on natural genius and the chord of the diminished seventh. 'Dear boy, the surprising effects which many attribute to the natural genius of the composer alone, are often enough achieved quite simply by the correct use and resolution of chords of the diminished seventh.' Bekker [*Beethoven*] p. 189. This statement is very important for Beethoven's procedure.

3 The recurrent, idiosyncratic harmonic formulae which *intentionally* suspend the surface clarity include, in particular, the chord of the diminished seventh on the anticipated resolving note in the bass.

4 The thesis of the withering of harmony in late Beethoven must be conceived far more dialectically. There is, rather, a *polarization*. While harmony does wither here (most of all, perhaps, in op. 135), at the same time it is nakedly visible, and the change in the melody pattern is precisely a function of this 'nakedness'. That is, the melody line is now only the putting into effect of the pure, intrinsic essence of harmony and is thus *unreal*. To this extent the style of the late Beethoven is the opposite of polyphony, although, on the other hand, all polyphonous melodies, that is, those conceived in true relationships, have something of this unreality.

5 But even where the harmony is nakedly visible, it has nothing to do with fully worked-out tonality, with the aesthetic concept of harmony. Strictly considered, tonality shrinks to the bare chord. Its substantiality passes from the whole to the single chord, which 'signifies' tonality; the chord as allegory replaces the key as process. The term 'functionless harmony', coined for atonality, applies in a certain way to the late Beethoven. Hence the harmonic rocking in these works: a sign of a harmonic shift which is *not* part of a process, does not lead to 'results'. Reference to complementary harmony.[236]   [267]

Text 4: Ludwig Van Beethoven: Six Bagatelles for Piano, op. 126

Unsociably, the very late Beethoven makes no concessions to domestic music-making. Faced with the last quartets the amateur violinist is completely out of his depth, as is the amateur pianist confronted by the five late sonatas and the Diabelli Variations. To play these pieces and even, for that matter, to listen to them is beyond such players. No easy path leads into that petrified landscape. But when Beethoven made the stone speak by carving figures in it with his chisel, the splinters flew under the terrible impact. And as the geologist can discover the true composition of whole strata from tiny, scattered particles of matter, the splinters bear witness to the landscape from which they come: the crystals are the same. Beethoven himself called them bagatelles. Not only are they splinters and documents of the mightiest productive process in music, but their strange brevity reveals at the same time the curious contraction, and the tendency towards the inorganic, which give access to the innermost secret not only of the late Beethoven but perhaps of every great late style. Although generally accessible in collections of Beethoven's 'piano pieces', they are not remotely as well known as the sonatas – as if, in their atmosphere, breathing were difficult. But they reward the laboured breath with immense perspectives for the eye. Pianists should be encouraged to play the second late cycle of bagatelles,[237] the pianistic demands of which are perfectly manageable, provided the musical exigencies are also mastered.

The *first* piece follows the schema of the three-part *Lied* form. A song-like melody, with independent counterparts from the outset, set out over eight bars and repeated with more richness of movement: the middle theme opens very matter-of-factly in the dominant key. A giant hand seems to thrust itself into the peaceful structure. A motif from the fourth bar of the middle theme is taken up, the rhythm being modified according to its law, and is split into ever smaller values. Suddenly it is no more than a cadence: the giant has only been playing, and the recapitulation begins with the final part of the cadence: the theme in the bass, the upper voice formed from the close of the cadence. Then, in a widening counterpoint, the theme appears in the upper part, cadencing to G major: the recapitulation shortened to eight bars. The coda, formed from an inversion of a motif from the middle theme, entirely polyphonic, with very harsh friction between seconds: the voices move apart, giving a view of the abyss between them. At the end the timid, late peace of the first part. – The form of the *second* piece is highly peculiar: it has no reprise or repetition of the beginning. An opening with a univocal, prelude-like semiquaver motion; flowing melodic quavers in contrast to it, both repeated. At the third entry an *fp* in the bass holds back the movement; then the quavers, in extreme registers, suddenly take on a mysterious expression; cadence and trenchant semicadence. The closing motif leads into a *cantabile* middle section, which is repeated irregularly and broken off. As in the first piece, a caesura instead of mediation: the opening motif appears at yawning intervals, is compressed, modulated to G minor. Tempestuous movement: unprepared *sforzato* suspensions threaten the G minor with an apparent F♯ minor, then C minor with D♭ major. A new melodic motif in crotchets detaches itself from the semiquaver motion and, accompanied by triplets, grows more distinct and then self-sufficient: a quotation from the first movement of the 'Hammerklavier' Sonata. It ends with the closing motif of the exposition section. This is taken up, modified polyphonically, a dynamic tremor running through it, then goes out like a light. – The *third* piece is a very simple, three-part song composed in 'harmonic polyphony'. The first part is repeated, the second opens into a small cadenza. The recapitulation contains the opening section and its repetition in figurative variations. Coda from the closing rhythm of the exposition, maintaining a demisemiquaver motion; the four closing bars formed from the opening notes of the melody. – The *fourth* piece, *presto*, very closely related in its motifs to a variation from the Sonata op. 109, its tone pointing clearly towards the last string quartets, is the most important of the cycle. The harshest contrast between polyphony (double counterpoint and *stretto*) and bare, almost monodic simplicity. A tensely polyphonic opening; a response in octaves with wild accents. The middle theme begins with the double counterpoint of the beginning, dissolving lightly into quavers; then, with octaves, the repeated F♯ of the opening intervenes roughly. A new beginning: again the F♯. Then a drawing together in the *stretto*, followed by the main theme over an accompaniment of undisguised crotchet chords, leading directly to the repetition of the first part. The octaves at the close widen and form cadences. The trio: B major, over a bagpipe accompaniment of almost unprecedented crudity a no less simple theme; but this is a deceptive, horrifying simplicity which grows over-distinct in the harsh light of a crescendo and a diminuendo imposed from outside, as a country road shows the ruts and ridges on its surface in the oblique light of nightfall. Then, in solemn semibreves, one of the main motifs of the last string quartets is invoked: minor ninth chord as the most strident dissonance and again the terrible *Pastoral*. Faithful repetition of the *Scherzo*, extended by four bars: caesura. The whole trio once more; but after the caesura, as repetition, nothing but phantasmagoria. Close in the major. – Balanced mastery without terrors in the *fifth* piece. Tender, lyrical polyphony as in the second movement of the C♯ minor Quartet; the middle section very flowing – with a middle voice producing a glorious dissonance; in it, however, as always in Beethoven's lyrical passages, latent symphonic energies, set free by a large, spread-out crescendo. The closing motif creates a relationship to the first part; its recapitulation is much shortened. – The *last* piece begins and ends with six *presto* bars which – with certain passages from the variations of the C♯ minor Quartet – are among the strangest and most enigmatic left behind by the late Beethoven: for the explanation that they are an 'instrumental gesture' cannot satisfy in the case of a master. All that will be said here is that the riddle lies in their *conventionality*. The piece itself is, again, lyrical in nature, its tone recalling the *Ferne Geliebte* cycle. The first theme haltingly composed of motif fragments; then, modulating, a denser melodic fabric, with the fine point of an ornamental triplet motif at the end of the exposition. The middle section is derived from this, and the reprise underpins the triplets as accompaniment. It is extended by six 'free' bars; its second part turns back towards the main key. The coda, like the middle section, takes up the triplet motif and develops it in that the motif takes possession of all voices. Once more, almost like a rondo, the halting main theme. Then the *presto* bars break through the lyrical shell. From his mighty hands the master sheds some scraps. His form itself tends towards the fragment.

(GS 18, pp. 185ff) – written in 1934

The piano and orchestral works form a unity in relation to the chamber music.   [268]

On the first movement of the A minor String Quartet [op. 132]. Extraordinary treatment of the form and its harmonic correlates. The development is hinted at. Its first part corresponds to the main theme, with elements of the introduction. The second intonation, after the general pause, begins (viola + cello in octaves) [bars 92ff] with a model derived from the main theme, which one expects to be elaborated. This, however, does not happen; instead, it closes like the first, followed by play with the introduction and first theme, transition to the reprise. Through anticipation of the theme even before the cadenza, but above all because it takes place in the dominant, not the main key, the development has a non-committal quality, although by and large it proceeds quite regularly. The latent modulatory tension and the indefiniteness of the development affect the coda, seventy bars long. Only here is the principal key restored. But as it must, after all, *close*, it does so as a second reprise, which abbreviates the three main figures but presents them once more in their original sequence and only then (on the re-entry of the theme over the sustained F of the cello [bar 195]) turns into the coda proper, which only now, becoming intensified, *definitively* develops the theme. All this is formed with unimaginable mastery of the irregular. – The introduction is drawn right into the movement, but not in the manner of a quotation; instead (with the long chorale notes and the interval of a second), it provides the cement which *imperceptibly*, as if it were the material itself, holds the movement together (much as does the motif in *Tristan* pointed out by Lorenz[238]).

On the *late style*: the first entry of the main theme in the cello [bar 11] is 'extraterritorial', a 'motto'; only then, on the first violin, is it 'in' the piece [bar 13], while at the same time being concealed through appearing as a mere *continuation* of the recitative melody, not as an *entry* (cf. the tendency of the late Beethoven to avoid the tonic on I!). – The empty octaves of the second violin and the cello in the repetition of the theme [bar 23]. – The broken accompaniment of the first violin to the second subject group on the second [bars 49f]. The music has a shattered quality, added to which is the almost Chinese effect of the analogous passage in the reprise [bars 227ff], where the second subject group begins on the cello, the first violin follows in a seemingly imitative way, but after only three notes turns into a mere duplication of the cello, as if for Beethoven the cleverness of imitation were too stupid, as if he were ashamed of diversity where in truth there is only one thing (see note on the conceptual aspect of the late Beethoven [cf. fr. 27]). – The expression of the chromatic continuation of the second subject group, its ailing quality, at the same time lyrical and empty. – The bare two-part structure in the second intonation of the development. – The analysis of the movement leads me to the technical explanation of the bareness of the late Beethoven, from which the philosophical interpretation must follow. The so-called thematic work, which Beethoven had established, for example, in op. 18, is usually a dividing up and rupturing of something unified – of a melody. Not genuine polyphony, but the *appearance* of it within harmonic-homophonic composition. To the late Beethoven this seems uneconomical, superfluous. Where there is only one thing, where the *essence* is a melody, only one should appear, at the expense of harmonic balance. The late Beethoven is the first great rebellion of music against the ornamental, that which is not necessitated purely by the matter itself. He presents, as it were, the essence always *intended* by diaphonic work, as a phenomenon. No 'beating about the bush'. In this way, through the assertion of the *concept* proper to the music itself, the 'classical' element, fullness, roundness, closedness, are lost. The late style, the splitting up into monody and polyphony, is inherent in the classical Beethoven. To be purely the matter itself, to be 'classical' without adjuncts, classicity burst into fragments. This is one of the decisive tenets of my interpretation.   [269][239]

NB: Last movement of A minor String Quartet *not* late Beethoven. Derived from sketches for the Ninth and Tenth Symphonies.   [270]

The striking divergence between the style of the late string quartets and the finale of the A minor String Quartet seems to me to be explained by the fact that the theme belonged to the complex of the Ninth and Tenth Symphonies and that Beethoven *consciously* exempted the symphonic style from the criticism represented by the late style. In this sense Bekker's remark about the 'backward-looking character' of the Ninth (Beethoven, *Beethoven*, p. 271) is justified. Bekker also sees the epic character of the Ninth (ibid., p. 280).[240]   [271]

In late Beethoven the 'harmonic rhythm' ('Piston') is disrupted, that is, the harmonic stresses are largely separated from the rhythmical. This does not involve a displaced, syncopated use of rhythm as in Brahms (who took over elements, for example, from the slow movement of op. 103, from the late Beethoven, while softening them into something 'organic'), but an intended *rupture*: the accents go largely *with* the metre, the harmonies *against* it. An aversion to the tonic on I. This is initiated in the late middle style and is one of the most important phenomena in the fracturing of tonality.   [272]

Regarding the separation[241] of rhythmical and harmonic accents in the late style: in the trio of the 'Hammerklavier' Sonata harmonic cadences are avoided, the whole harmonic element being in suspension (much III degree as six–four chords), while the metrical-melodic processes suggest cadences. A deliberate paraphrasing fracture. Moreover: the direct taking over of the repeated flat from the scherzo at the start of the trio; it becomes a kind of refrain. A similar procedure in the *Prestissimo* of op. 109.   [273]

The importance of the wide register in late Beethoven.   [274]

In op. 111 there are 'basic shapes'. The following motifs are very closely related: G C E♭ B [1st movement, bars 19f], G C B C F E♭ C [ibid., bars 36f] and the A♭ major motif of the second subject group [ibid., bars 50ff]. Everywhere triads and second neighbour notes, but 'rotated'. (Also the close [of the exposition; ibid., bars 64f].)

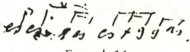

Example 14

[275]

NB: *On octaves in late Beethoven.* The dragging passages in Beethoven, like the closing section of the first movement of the great B♭ major String Quartet [op. 130, 1st movement, bars 183ff],

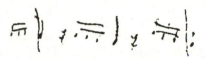

Example 15

passages in the developments of opp. 101 and 111. What do they mean? Link with Beethoven's shadow. Even in early works, for example, the coda of the Finale of the D major Piano Sonata from op. 10 [bars 94ff]. (NB: These have a character of continuation, not statement.)

[276]

The principle of syncopation and accentuation in middle Beethoven is heightened in the late work to the point where torrents rush through convention.

[277]

In late Beethoven, a kind of theme which might seem folkloristic and which I should most like to compare to verse sayings from fairy-tales, such as 'Knusper, knusper Knäuschen, wer knuspert an mei'm Häuschen' [Nibble, nibble mousey, who's nibbling at my housey]. An example from the scherzo of the String Quartet in C♯ minor [op. 131; bars 141–4 and so on.][242]

Example 16

and especially in the last movement of the F major String Quartet [op. 135]. These passages all have something of the ogre about them.   [278]

The moment of distress in late Beethoven, for example, in the second movement of op. 130 after the trio. – Also, the gruff humour as a means of transcending form, of 'smashing things up'. The ogre.[279]

The stereotypes in late Beethoven are in the vein of 'My grandfather used to say'.   [280]

Of relevance to certain themes of late Beethoven is his (canonic) dictum of 1825: 'Doktor sperrt das Tor dem Tod. Note hilft auch aus der Not' [Doctors keep our death at bay. Music too keeps woe away]' (Thomas-San-Galli, *Ludwig van Beethoven*, p. 402).   [281]

A theory of the very late Beethoven must start from the decisive boundary dividing it from the earlier work – the fact that in it nothing is immediate, everything is refracted, significant, withdrawn from appearance and in a sense antithetical to it (my essay in *Der Auftakt*[243]). What is mediated is not necessarily expression, although expression if of utmost importance in late Beethoven. The real problem is to resolve this allegorical element. This complex precedes all technical and stylistic questions, which have to be determined and solved with reference to it. Late Beethoven is at the same time enigmatic and extremely obvious. – The boundary is doubtless marked by the Piano Sonata op. 101, a work of the highest, of inexhaustible beauty.   [282]

The rendering indifferent of the material, the stepping back from appearance which characterizes the late style[244] applies much earlier to the *chamber music* – and only to it. The String Quartets op. 18, which, incidentally, were probably intended as a companion-piece to the six dedicated to Haydn by Mozart, which acted as a kind of pattern and masterpiece (cf. letter to Amenda), are already 'much better quartet-writing',[245] more suited to each instrument, with themes more split between voices, than op. 59, which still belongs entirely to the *classical* Beethoven; they often have an angular, unpolished element running counter to sensuous balance (No. 3 is a virtuoso piece for quartet ensemble rather than a quartet). This observation supplements my comment that the Ninth Symphony is *excluded* from the late style [cf. fr. 223]. A strict separation of categories in Beethoven, contrary to Schoenberg's opinion.   [283]

To understand the late style, see what the late Beethoven found *superfluous* in his earlier work, for example, by comparing op. 18 with the last string quartets. Not only do the empty phrases disappear, but even categories such as *durchbrochene Arbeit* [phrases fragmented between different instruments] take on, under the saturnine gaze, an ornamental, superfluous aspect and are eliminated. The unfolding of essence makes essence itself inessential. Very important. NB: A turning away from bustle. 'Accomplishment' as vanity. [284]

In late Beethoven there is no longer any 'fabric'. Instead of *durchbrochene Arbeit* there is frequently a mere division of the melody, for example, in the first movement of op. 135. At the very place once occupied by dynamic totality, there is now fragmentation.[285]

TEN

LATE WORK WITHOUT
LATE STYLE

The extraordinary difficulty which the *Missa Solemnis* presents
even to straightforward understanding should not deter us from
interpretation. Beethoven called it the best of his works.[246] For all
his diplomacy towards the Archduke, he would not have done this
without an objective reason. – What first strikes us is that the
Missa holds a place entirely apart from the rest of Beethoven's
oeuvre. From it there are *hardly* any connections to his other
works, even the late ones – neither formally, nor thematically, nor
in the characters, nor – above all – in the treatment of musical surfaces, in the composing itself. The sole exception, perhaps, is the
variations movement from op. 127 – itself extremely obscure –
which is reminiscent of the 'Benedictus' – but the 'Benedictus' is
itself the exception in the *Missa*, the most accessible piece, the only
one with a 'character' in the traditional sense; it might be called
the mediation between the *Missa* and music. The obvious explanation for the remoteness of the *Missa* from Beethoven's other music
is its use of the church style, which in principle precludes the
dynamic-dialectical character essential to his style. In Mozart, too,
the sacred compositions are infinitely removed from the secular
ones (not in Bach). But the question still remains why the late
Beethoven, who must have stood very aloof from organized religion, devoted many years of his most mature period to a sacred
work and – at the time of his most extreme subjective emancipation – experimented with the rigidly bound style. The answer
seems to me to lie in direct line with Beethoven's critique of the
'classical' symphonic ideal. The bound style *allows* him a develop-

ment which was hardly permitted by instrumental music:

1 There are no tangible 'themes' – and therefore no development.
2 The entire music is conceived in terms of undynamic, but *not* pre-classical *surfaces*. Its organizing principle must be sought.
3 It is *not* essentially polyphonic, but not melodic either. The curious indifference of the style.
4 Thoroughly opposed to the sonata, but *not* traditionally sacred.
5 The indirectness, the element of avoidance, significant through the avoidance. *Omission* as a means of style and expression.
6 The refracted, 'stylized' relationship to sacred music. Much as the Eighth Symphony is related to the earlier symphonic style. A complete absence of the influence of Bach, or of real counterpoint.
7 The expressive characters. The mediated, muted, distanced quality despite major outbursts in the 'Credo' (which is doubtless the centre of the work). Most peculiar the 'Agnus'.

This is the first formulation of the *problems* posed by the *Missa*, which are entirely obscured by the habitual mixture of respect and incomprehension. Be careful of over-easy answers (deduced from the total concept of my work). The question of the *Missa*'s *formal law* is central. – NB: It lacks all unmistakably Beethovenian characteristics. He has, as it were, eliminated himself.   [286]

To Gretel's question what was actually so incomprehensible about the *Missa Solemnis*, I answered first of all with the very simple observation that hardly anyone who did not know could tell by listening to the work that it was by Beethoven.   [287]

It is advisable when considering the problem of the *Missa* to look at other works of a related genre by Beethoven. It is highly characteristic that they are all entirely forgotten: I have not even succeeded in finding a copy of *Christus am Ölberg*. But I have looked closely at the C major Mass. It has in common with the *Missa* its unfamiliar style – no one could guess that it was by Beethoven. The indescribably tame 'Kyrie' is like very weak Mendelssohn. Also the episodic character, disintegrating into small details. The whole an entirely uninspired, 'nice' work in which Beethoven tries by force to feel his way into an entirely alien genre, in which – to his honour – he does not succeed. There would be no need to discuss this at all if these same traits did not reappear in the extremely ambitious *Missa Solemnis*, which does give much food for thought. – Probably decisive for the *Missa* was the (unquestionably intentional) omission of any developmental principle; a mere succession of formal elements, with endless simple repetition. Even in the 'Benedictus'. This could be compared to the variations from op. 127. – Rudi [that is, Rudolf Kolisch] attaches great importance to the theme of the 'Dona nobis pacem'.   [288]

On the *Missa*. Avoidance of plastic themes, and of negativity, the music paying no attention to the 'Kyrie' and the 'Crucifixus'. By contrast, the 'Dona'.   [289]

Missa Solemnis. A damming up of expressive means. Expression through archaism; modal elements.   [290]

The division into short sections. Question of form attained not by development but by balance.   [291]

No dynamic structure, but built up in sections, entirely different formal principles than elsewhere in Beethoven. Articulation through vocal entries, reiteration of components of motifs. A different kind of *peinture*.   [292]

Erosion of harmonic steps, avoidance of dynamics even in harmonic progression.   [293]

The difficulty of the *Missa* is not that of complexity. Most of it is simple on the surface. Even the fugal sections are homophonic in spirit, with the exception of 'Et vitam venturi'. ('Credo' probably the crux.)   [294]

The outward difficulties are merely vocal, exposed upper register, not unduly complicated.   [295]

A liking for pomp, doubling of brasses.   [296]

The intentionally non-committal themes.   [297]

Humanization and stylization. The sacred receding in favour of the human. Thus in the 'Kyrie' of the 'Homo'; the centre of gravity in the idea of the *future*; of the 'Dona'. – Is the aesthetic problem of the *Missa* that of the levelling down to the universally human? Totality as levelling.   [298]

The archaistic features of the harmony, unique in Beethoven, match the formal archaism. [299]

Missa, continued. Empty talk about the expansive, novel aspect of the thematic work. [300]

It might appear after all this that the *Missa* has been understood. But to recognize the obscure as obscure is not necessarily to understand it; the given characteristics may be confirmed by listening, but do not yet allow us to listen correctly. [301][247]

NB: Instead of motivic work a puzzle-like procedure. Succession, grouping around, unvaried motifs. [302]

The *aesthetic* fragmentariness of the *Missa* corresponds, despite the closed surface, to the cracks and fissures in the texture of the last string quartets. [303]

The tendency to hark back in the late phase of *all* great composers = limit of the bourgeois mind? [304]

Repetition of the word Credo, as if he had to convince himself of it. [305][248]

Text 5: The Alienated *Magnum Opus*: On the *Missa Solemnis*[249]

The neutralization of culture – the phrase has the ring of a philosophical concept. It indicates a more or less general reflection on the fact that intellectual formations have lost their bindingness, because they have detached themselves from any possible relationship to social praxis and become what aesthetics has retrospectively credited them with being – objects of purely mental apprehension, of mere contemplation. As such they finally lose their intrinsic, their aesthetic seriousness; with the tension between them and reality their artistic truth also vanishes. They become cultural commodities exhibited in a secular pantheon in which contradictory entities – works that would like to strike each other dead – are given space side-by-side in a false pacification: Kant and Nietzsche, Bismarck and Marx, Clemens Brentano and Büchner. This waxworks of great men then finally confesses its desolation in the uncounted and unconsidered images in every museum, in the editions of classics in covetously locked bookcases. Yet however far awareness of this has spread by now, it is as difficult as ever – if we disregard the fashion for biography which reserves a niche for every queen and every microbe chaser – to define the phenomenon conclusively. For there is no superfluous Rubens whose flesh tints the connoisseur could abstain from admiring, and no poet of the publisher Cotta whose verses, ahead of their time, do not await resurrection. From time to time, however, one can name a work in which the neutralization of culture becomes irrefutable. There is even one which enjoys the highest fame, has its undisputed place in the repertoire, while remaining enigmatic and incomprehensible and, whatever it may conceal within itself, offering no support for the popular acclaim lavished upon it. Such a work is Beethoven's *Missa Solemnis*. To speak seriously of it can be nothing other than, in Brecht's phrase, to alienate it; to rupture the aura of unfocused veneration protectively surrounding it, and thereby perhaps to contribute something to an authentic experience of it beyond the paralysing respect of the culture sphere. The attempt to do so must necessarily use criticism as its medium; qualities which traditional awareness uncritically ascribe to the *Missa Solemnis* must be tested, to prepare for a perception of its content – a task which quite certainly no one has yet performed. The aim is not to debunk, to topple approved greatness for the sake of doing so. The disillusioning gesture which sustains itself on the prominence against which it is directed is enslaved by that very prominence. But criticism, in face of a work of such stature and of Beethoven's entire *oeuvre*, can be nothing other than a means of unfolding the work, fulfilment of a duty towards the matter itself, not the gratified sneer at finding one thing less to respect in the world. To point this out is necessary because neutralized culture itself ensures that, while the works are not perceived in an original way but are merely consumed as something socially approved, the names of their authors are taboo. Rage is automatically aroused when reflection on the work threatens to touch on the authority of the person.

Such a reaction must be disarmed at the outset if one plans to say something heretical about a composer of the highest standing, comparable in power only to the philosophy of Hegel and no less great in an age which had irrecoverably lost its historical preconditions. Beethoven's power, however, which is founded on humanity and demythologization, demands, on its own terms, the destruction of mythical taboos. Moreover, critical reflections on the *Missa* are very much alive among musicians as an underground tradition. Just as they always knew that Handel was no Bach, or that some questions surround Gluck's qualities as a composer, while only timidity before established public opinion kept them silent, they also know that the situation regarding the *Missa Solemnis* is a peculiar one. Little criticism of a penetrating nature has therefore been written about this work. Most of it is content with general professions of reverence for an immortal *chef d'oeuvre*, and is embarrassed when called upon to say in what its greatness consists; such criticism mirrors, but does not breach, the neutralization of the *Missa* as a cultural commodity. Hermann Kretschmar, who belongs to a generation of musical historians who did not yet repress the experiences of the nineteenth century, came nearest to allowing himself to be astonished by the *Missa*. According to his reports, earlier performances of the work, before it was elevated to the official Valhalla, left no lasting impression. He sees the difficulty above all in the 'Gloria' and the 'Credo', explaining it by the abundance of short musical images which need to be unified by the listener. Here Kretschmar at least names one of the alienating symptoms displayed by the *Missa*; admittedly he overlooks its connection to the essential qualities of the composition, and therefore believes that the clamping effect of powerful main themes in the two large sections is enough to dispose of the difficulty. That, however, is no more the case than that the listener masters the *Missa* simply by concentrating at each moment, as one does with the great symphonic movements by Beethoven, on calling to mind what has gone before and thus following the emergence of unity from multiplicity. Its unity is of a wholly different kind to that engendered by the productive imagination in the *Eroica* and Ninth Symphony. One hardly commits a crime in doubting whether this unity is, as it stands, comprehensible at all.

The historical fate of the work does indeed appear strange. In Beethoven's lifetime it is thought to have been performed only twice: once in 1824 in Vienna, together with the Ninth Symphony, but incomplete; then, in the same year, complete in St Petersburg. Up to the early 1860s there were only isolated performances; not until more than thirty years after the composer's death did it attain its present standing. Difficulties of interpretation are hardly sufficient to explain this; while there are some problems in the treatment of voices, in most parts there is no special musical complexity. Contrary to legend, the last string quartets, far more exposed and demanding, were appropriately received from the outset. Moreover, Beethoven, in contrast to his custom, put his authority directly behind the *Missa*. When he offered it for subscription, he called it '*l'oeuvre le plus accompli*' – his most successful work. Over the 'Kyrie' he placed the words: 'From the heart – and may it reach the heart' – a confession one looks for in vain in all the other printed editions of Beethoven. His attitude towards his own work should not be underestimated, nor blindly accepted. Those utterances have an admonitory tone, as if Beethoven had sensed something of the

Missa's unfathomable, elusive, enigmatic quality and were trying to use the force of his will, which otherwise shaped the flow of his music itself, to impose the work from outside on those on whom it could not impose itself. Admittedly, this would be inconceivable if the work did not truly contain a secret which in Beethoven's eyes legitimized such an intervention in its history. But when it did really find acceptance, the by now unquestioned prestige of its composer is likely to have helped. His main sacred work was praised as the companion-piece to the Ninth Symphony, on the model of the emperor's new clothes, without anyone daring to voice questions by which they would merely have displayed their own lack of depth.

The *Missa* could hardly have become established if – like *Tristan*, for example – it had shocked the audience by its difficulty. That was not the case. If we disregard the occasionally unusual demands on the singers' voices, which it has in common with the Ninth Symphony, it contains little which does not remain within the confines of traditional musical idiom. Very large sections are homophonic, and the fugues and *fugati* also merge without friction into the thorough bass schema. The harmonic progressions, and thus the surface cohesion, are hardly ever problematic; the *Missa Solemnis* is composed far less against the grain than the last string quartets or the Diabelli Variations. It does not fall within the stylistic category of the late Beethoven, as derived from those quartets and variations, the five late piano sonatas and the last Bagatelle cycles. The *Missa* is distinguished by certain archaic moments in its harmony, an ecclesiastical tone, rather than by daringly advanced techniques as in the *Grosse Fuge*. Beethoven not only always kept the musical genres far more strictly separate than is supposed, but within them he embodied temporally distinct stages of his *oeuvre*. If the symphonies, despite or because of their rich orchestral apparatus, are in many respects simpler than the great chamber music, the Ninth Symphony falls outside the late style altogether, turning retrospectively towards the classical, symphonic Beethoven, without the edges and fissures of the last string quartets. In his late period he did not, as might be thought, blindly follow the dictates of his inner ear and compulsively neglect the sensuous aspect of his work, but made masterful use of all the possibilities which had grown up during the history of his composing; suppression of the sensuous was only one of them. The *Missa* has occasional abrupt moments, the omission of transitions, in common with the last quartets, but little else. In general, it displays a sensuous aspect diametrically opposed to the spiritualized late style, a tendency towards pomp and monumentality of sound that is usually absent from Beethoven's works. Technically, this aspect is embodied in the procedure reserved for moments of ecstasy in the Ninth, when vocal parts are doubled by brass, especially trombones but also horns, which lead the melody. The frequent terse octaves, coupled with deep harmonic effects, have a similar purpose. These are seen typically in the well-known 'Die Himmel rühmen des Ewigen Ehre', and decisively in 'Ihr stürzt nieder' in the Ninth Symphony – later to become an important ingredient of Bruckner. It was certainly not least these sensuous highlights, a liking for overwhelming sound effects, which gave the *Missa* its authority and allowed its listeners to disregard their own incomprehension.

The difficulty is of a higher order – it concerns the content, the meaning of the music. It is perhaps easiest to picture what is at issue if we ask whether an uninformed listener could recognize the *Missa* – leaving aside a few parts – as a work of Beethoven. If it were played to such listeners who had not previously heard anything from it, and they were asked to guess the composer, one could expect surprises. Little as the so-called handwriting of a composer constitutes a central criterion, nevertheless, its absence indicates that something is slightly amiss. If we pursue this question by looking around at Beethoven's other sacred works, the absence of Beethoven's handwriting is found again. It is revealing how forgotten these other works are now, and how difficult it is to track down a copy of *Christus am Ölberg* or the by no means early Mass in C major, op. 86. The latter, unlike the *Missa*, could hardly be attributed to Beethoven even in individual passages or phrases. Its indescribably tame 'Kyrie' suggests, at best, a weak Mendelssohn. However, it has many features which recur in the much more ambitious and fully formed *Missa*, which is conceived on a far larger scale: dissolution into often short parts which are not symphonically integrated; a lack of the striking thematic 'inventions' which every other work by Beethoven makes use of; and an absence of long, dynamic elaborations. The Mass in C major reads as if Beethoven had had difficulty in deciding to feel his way into an alien genre; as if his humanism had bridled at the heteronomy of the traditional liturgical text and had delegated its composition to a routine devoid of genius. In groping towards a solution to the riddle of the *Missa*, one will have to keep in mind this aspect of his earlier sacred music. Certainly, it became a problem which wore down his strength; but it helps somewhat in defining the invocatory nature of the *Missa*. It cannot be separated from the paradox that Beethoven composed a mass at all; if we understood why he did this, we would no doubt understand the *Missa*.

It is commonplace to assert that the work went far beyond the traditional form of the mass, importing into it the full riches of secular composing. Even in the volume of the *Fischer-Lexikon* devoted to music, recently edited by Rudolf Stephan, which disposes of many other conventional views, the work is praised for its 'extraordinarily ingenious thematic work'. As far as one can speak of any such work in the *Missa*, it uses a method exceptional in Beethoven of shaking the contents about as in a kaleidoscope and subsequent recombining. The motifs are not altered in the dynamic flow of the composition – it has none – but constantly re-emerge in a changed lighting, yet identical. The idea of a disintegrated form applies at most to the outward dimensions. Beethoven will have thought of this when he considered performance of the work at a concert. However, the *Missa* does not break through the pre-ordained objectivity of the schema by means of subjective dynamics, nor does it generate totality from within itself as happens in the symphony – precisely by thematic work. Rather, the consistent renunciation of all those things disconnects the *Missa* from all Beethoven's other output with the exception of his earlier sacred works. The inner composition of this music, its fibre, is radically different to anything bearing the stamp of Beethoven's style. It is itself archaistic. The form is not attained through the evolving variation of core motifs, but accumulated additively from sections usually imitative among themselves, in a similar practice to that of Netherlandish composers of the mid-fifteenth century, although it is uncertain whether Beethoven knew of them. The formal organization of the whole is not that of a process with its own momentum, not dialectical, but seeks to be induced by the balance of the individual sections, and finally by contrapuntal clamping. All the strange characteristics are directed towards this. That Beethoven could do without Beethovenian themes in the *Missa* – for who could quote from it by singing, as from any of his symphonies or *Fidelio*? – is explained by the exclusion of the principle of development: only where a stated theme is developed, and must therefore remain recognizable in its alteration, is the plastic form needed; the idea of plastic form is alien to the *Missa* as to medieval music. One need only compare Bach's 'Kyrie' to Beethoven's: in Bach's fugue we find an incomparably memorable melody suggesting the image of humanity as a procession dragging itself along, bent under a colossal weight; in Beethoven, complexes with hardly any melodic profile, which trace out the harmony and preclude expression by the gesture of monumentality. The comparison leads to a real paradox. According to a widespread if questionable belief, Bach, summarizing the closed, objective musical world of the Middle Ages, had, if not created the fugue, then at least given it its pure, authentic form. It was as much his product as he was a product of its spirit. He had a direct relationship to it. Hence, many of the themes of his fugues, perhaps with the exception of the speculative late works, have a kind of freshness and spontaneity that is found only in the *cantabile* inventions of later subjective composers. At Beethoven's historical hour that musical order had passed away; its lustre had afforded Bach the *a priori* basis of his composition, and thus a harmony between musical subject and forms which permitted something like a naivety in Schiller's sense. For Beethoven the objectivity of the musical forms with which the *Missa* operates is indirect, problematic, a subject of reflection. The first part of his 'Kyrie' adopts Beethoven's own standpoint of harmonious subjectivity; but by being moved immediately within the horizon of sacred objectivity, it, too, takes on a mediated character detached from musical spontaneity: it is stylized. For this reason the simple harmonic opening section of the *Missa* is more remote, less eloquent that its eruditely contrapuntal counterpart in Bach. This is still more true of the themes of the fugues and *fugati* in the *Missa*. They have a quality peculiarly suggestive of quotations, of something based on a model. By analogy with a literary custom widespread in antiquity, one could speak of compositional *topoi*, of the treatment of the musical moment in terms of latent patterns intended to reinforce the work's objective claims. This is probably responsible for the strangely intangible quality of these fugal themes, which denies primary fulfilment and also affects their continuation. The first fugal section of the *Missa*, the 'Christe eleison' in B minor, is an example both of this and of the archaistic tone.

The work is altogether as distanced from expression as it is from all subjective dynamism. The 'Credo' seems to hurry past the 'Crucifixus' – in Bach a main expressive part – although marking it by an extremely striking rhythm. Only at the words 'Et sepultus est', that is, at the end of the Passion itself, is an expressive emphasis reached, as if the thought of the frailty of human beings had brought attention back to the Passion of Christ, although the following 'Et resurrexit' is not endowed with the pathos which is raised to an extreme pitch in the analogous passage in Bach. Only one passage, which accordingly has become the most famous of the work, forms an exception, the 'Benedictus', the main melody of which suspends the stylization. The prelude to it has a depth of harmonic proportions matched only by the twentieth Diabelli Variation. However, the 'Benedictus' melody itself, which has been praised not without reason as inspired, recalls the variation theme of the E♭ major Quartet op. 127. The whole 'Benedictus' calls to mind the custom attributed to late medieval artists, who included their own image somewhere on their tabernacle so that they would not be forgotten. But even the 'Benedictus' remains true to the style of the whole. Like the other pieces it is articulated in sections, or 'intonations', and the ungenuine polyphony merely paraphrases the chords. This in turn is connected to the deliberately secondary role of themes in the method of composition; this allows the themes to be treated imitatively and yet to be conceived principally in harmonic terms, as suited the basically homophonic consciousness of Beethoven and his age: the archaic style had to respect the boundaries of the musical experience open to Beethoven. The great exception is the 'Et vitam venturi' of the 'Credo', in which Paul Bekker has rightly seen the core of the whole, a fully developed polyphonic fugue, related in its details and its harmonic shifts to the finale of the 'Hammerklavier' Sonata, and aimed at large-scale development. For this reason it is melodically quite explicit and is heightened to the utmost in intensity and strength. This piece is probably the only one which could be said to disrupt the general pattern, being the most difficult both in complexity and for performance; but through the directness of its effect it is, with the 'Benedictus', the easiest to apprehend.

It is no accident that the transcendent moment in the *Missa Solemnis* relates not to the mystical aspects of transubstantiation, but to the hope of eternal life for humanity. The puzzle posed by the *Missa Solemnis* is the deadlock between an archaic procedure which implacably sacrifices Beethoven's achieved techniques, and a humane tone which seems to mock these archaic means. This puzzle, the linking of the idea of humanity to a sombre aversion to expression, might be deciphered by assuming that the taboo which later marked its reception is already detectable in the *Missa* itself. This taboo concerned the negativity of existence, which is the only deduction to be drawn from Beethoven's despairing desire for salvation. The *Missa* is expressive whenever it addresses salvation, where it pleads in a literal sense; the expression is cut off mainly where evil and death are mentioned in the text of the Mass, and through this silence the work bears witness to the impending preponderance of the negative; despair through reluctance to give voice to negativity. The 'Dona nobis pacem' takes over the burden of the 'Crucifixus'. Accordingly, the means carrying expression are held back. What carries expression is not dissonance, or only very seldom, as in the 'Sanctus', before the *allegro* entry of 'Pleni sunt coeli'; expression is attached, rather, to the archaic, the sequences of scale steps [*Stufenfolgen*] characteristic of the old church music, the shudder at what has been, as if suffering were to be transported into the past; what is expressive in the *Missa* is not the modern, but the very ancient. In it the idea of humanity is asserted, as in late Goethe, only through a desperate, mythical denial of the mythical abyss. It calls to positive religion for help, as if the lonely subject no longer felt able, on its own merits as a purely human being, to calm the rising chaos of the dominance of nature and nature's rebellion against such dominance. To explain why the highly emancipated Beethoven, who relied entirely on his own intellect, should have felt drawn to the traditional form, it is no more adequate to cite his subjective piety than, conversely, to resort to the vacuous assertion that in the work, which subjects itself to the liturgical purpose with zealous discipline, his religious impulse had broadened beyond dogma to a kind of general religiosity, and that his was a Mass for Unitarians. However, the work suppresses professions of subjective piety in relation to Christology. At the point where the liturgy immovably dictates the words 'I believe', Beethoven, as Steuermann has strikingly observed, betrays the opposite of such certainty, repeating the word 'credo' in the theme of the fugue, as if the solitary person had to convince himself by the repeated invocation that he really did believe. Nor is the religiosity of the *Missa*, if we can use that term as it stands, that of someone safely ensconced in the faith, or a world religion of such idealistic nature that it does not require the subject to believe anything. What is at issue for him, expressed in later terminology, is whether ontology, the subjective spiritual order of Being, is still possible at all. He is concerned with saving ontology musically in a state of subjectivism, and his recourse to liturgy is meant to achieve this in the same way as invocation of the ideas of God, freedom and immortality was to do for the critic Kant. In its aesthetic form the work asks what can be sung without deception about the Absolute, and how it can be sung. This gives rise to the shrunken quality which alienates the work and makes it almost incomprehensible – probably because the question it poses is not amenable to a concise answer even in musical terms. The subject in its finitude is still exiled, while the objective cosmos can no longer be imagined as a binding authority; thus the *Missa* is balanced on an indifference point which approaches nothingness.

Its humanistic aspect is defined by the richness of harmony in the 'Kyrie', and extends up to the construction of the closing piece, the 'Agnus Dei', which is based on the design of the 'Dona nobis pacem', the plea for inward and outward peace, as Beethoven again writes in German above the piece; this breaks out expressively once more after the threat of war allegorically represented by bass drums and trumpets. As early as the words 'Et homo factus est' the music is warmed as if by a breath. But these are exceptions: usually the style and tone, despite all the stylization, withdraw towards something unexpressed, undefined. This aspect, the resultant of mutually contradictory forces, is probably the main obstacle to comprehension. Though conceived in terms of undynamic areas, the *Missa* is not

articulated in pre-classical 'terraces', but frequently blurs the out-
lines; often, brief insertions neither emerge into the whole nor do
they stand alone; they rely on their proportions to other parts. The
style is contrary to the spirit of the sonata, and yet is less traditionally sacred than secular, couched in a rudimentary church idiom
retrieved from memory. The relationship to this idiom is as refracted
as is that to Beethoven's own style, in a distant analogy to the standpoint of the Eighth Symphony with regard to Haydn and Mozart.
Except in the 'Et vitam venturi' fugue, even the fugal parts are not
genuinely polyphonic, but neither is a single bar homophonically
melodic in the manner of the nineteenth century. While the category
of totality, which always has primacy in Beethoven, otherwise
results from the inherent motion of the individual moments, in the
Missa it is maintained only at the cost of a kind of levelling. The
omnipresent principle of stylization tolerates nothing truly particular, wearing down the characters in blank conformity to the rules;
these motifs and themes lack the power of the name. The absence of
dialectical contrasts, which are replaced by the mere opposition
between closed sections, therefore sometimes weakens the totality.
This is seen especially in the close of sections. Because no path has
been travelled, no resistance of the particular overcome, the trace of
arbitrariness is transferred to the whole, and the sections, which no
longer lead to a goal that the urge to the particular might have
imposed, often end dully, stopping without the warranty of a conclusion. All this, despite the outward vigour, not only creates an
impression of something mediated, which is equally remote from
liturgical obligation and from free fantasy, but also gives rise to the
enigmatic quality which sometimes, as in the short *allegro* and
presto passages of the 'Agnus', verges on the absurd.

After all that it might seem that the nature of the *Missa*, characterized in its peculiarities, has been identified. But darkness is not light-
ened simply by being perceived as dark. To understand that one
does not understand is the first step towards understanding, but not
understanding itself. The characteristics indicated may be confirmed
by hearing the work, and the attention concentrated on them may
prevent disorientated listening, but they alone by no means allow
the ear spontaneously to perceive a musical meaning in the *Missa* – a
meaning which, if it exists at all, is constituted precisely by a refusal
of such spontaneity. So much, at least, has been established, that the
strangeness of the work is not dispelled by the formula that the
autonomous composer selected a heteronomous form remote to his
inclination and fantasy, and that this prevented the specific unfolding of his music. For clearly Beethoven was not seeking in the *Missa*,

as sometimes happens in the history of music, to legitimize himself in an out-of-the-way genre in addition to his real works, while making no special demands on that genre. Rather, each bar of the work, as well as the unusual duration of the process of composition, bears witness to the most insistent concentration. However, this was directed not at asserting his subjective intention, as in his other works, but at eliminating it. The *Missa Solemnis* is a work of omission, of permanent renunciation. It already forms part of the efforts of the later bourgeois spirit, which no longer hoped to conceive and express the universally human in the concrete form of particular people and relationships, but by abstraction, by excising the fortuitous, by holding fast a generality which had become insane through reconciliation with the particular. In this work metaphysical truth becomes a residue much as the contentless purity of 'I think' does in Kant's philosophy. This residual character of truth, which abstains from penetrating the particular, not only condemns the *Missa Solemnis* to being enigmatic but also imparts to it, in the highest sense, a trace of impotence – an impotence less of the mighty composer than of a historical state of the spirit which can no longer or cannot yet say what it here sets out to say.

But what drove Beethoven, the composer of unfathomable richness in whom the powers of subjective production were heightened to the point of hubris, to the point where man becomes Creator, towards the opposite tendency, of self-curtailment? Certainly not his personal psychology which, at the same time as he was writing the *Missa*, was exploring the opposite tendency to its furthest limit, but a compulsion residing in the music itself which, though resistingly, he obeyed with utmost exertion. Here we come upon a common feature of the *Missa* and of the last quartets in their spiritual constitution – something which all in common avoid. To the musical experience of the late Beethoven the unity of subjectivity and objectivity, the roundedness of the successful symphony, the totality arising from the motion of all particulars, in short, that which gives the works of his middle period their authenticity, must have become suspect. He saw through the classic as classicism. He rebelled against the affirmative element, the uncritical approbation of Being, inherent in the idea of the classical symphony, the trait which Georgiades called 'festive' in his study of the finale of the 'Jupiter' Symphony. He must have felt the untruth in the highest aspirations of classicist music: that the quintessence of the opposed motions of all particulars, which are annulled in that quintessence, is positivity itself. At this point he raised himself above the bourgeois spirit, of which his own *oeuvre* is the highest musical manifestation.

Something in his genius, probably the deepest thing, refused to reconcile in the image what is unreconciled in reality. Musically, this may well have expressed itself in an increasing resistance to splitting themes between voices and to the principle of the development. This is related to the distaste which affected the advanced literary sensorium, especially in Germany, with regard to dramatic imbroglios and intrigue – a sublimely plebeian distaste, hostile to the courtly world, which first entered German music through Beethoven. Intrigue in the theatre always has something fatuous about it. Its bustle seems to have been set in motion from above, by the author and his idea, but never quite motivated from below, by the *dramatis personae*. The bustle of thematic work may have evoked to the mature Beethoven's ear the machinations of courtiers in plays by Schiller, disguised wives, forced caskets and intercepted letters. It is, in the proper sense of the word, a realistic trait in him which is dissatisfied with tenuously motivated conflicts, manipulated antitheses of the kind which in all classicism generate a totality which is supposed to transcend the particular but in reality is imposed on it as if by a dictate of power. Traces of this arbitrariness are detectable in the resolute shifts occurring in the developments of works as late as the Ninth Symphony. The late Beethoven's demand for truth rejects the illusion of such identity of subjective and objective, which is almost the same thing as the classicist idea. A polarization results. Unity is transcended, yielding fragmentariness. In the last quartets this is achieved by the abrupt, unmediated juxtaposing of bare axiomatic motifs and polyphonic complexes. The rift between the two, which proclaims itself, turns the impossibility of aesthetic harmony into aesthetic content, failure in the highest sense into a yardstick of success. In its way the *Missa*, too, sacrifices the idea of synthesis, but it does so by peremptorily debarring from the music a subject which is no longer ensconced in the objectivity of the form but is also unable to generate this form intact from within itself. For its human universality it is willing to pay with the silence, perhaps even the subjection, of the individual soul. That, and not a concession to church tradition or a desire to please his pupil, Archduke Rudolph, is likely to lead us towards an explanation of the *Missa Solemnis*. Out of freedom the autonomous subject, which knows itself to be capable of objectivity in no other way, cedes to heteronomy. Pseudomorphosis to the alienated form, at one with the expression of alienation itself, is to achieve what is otherwise no longer achievable. The composer experiments with the rigidly bound style because formal bourgeois freedom does not suffice as a principle of stylization. The composition tirelessly checks what can still be filled by the subject, what is possible for him, under a stylizing principle imposed in this way from outside. Rigorous criticism is applied not only to each impulse which might contest the principle, but also to each concrete embodiment of objectivity itself which has degenerated into a Romantic fiction, whereas it should be, even as a skeleton, real, sturdy, devoid of illusion. This twofold criticism, a kind of permanent selection, imposes on the *Missa* its distanced, silhouettish character: despite the replete sound, it places the work in opposition to sensuous appearance no less rigorously than does the asceticism of the last quartets. The aesthetically fractured quality of the *Missa Solemnis*, its renunciation of clear structure in favour of a question, of almost Kantian severity, as to what is still possible at all, corresponds, despite the deceptively closed surface, to the open rifts displayed by the fabric of the last quartets. However, the *Missa* shares the archaizing tendency, which is kept in check even here, with the late style of almost all great composers from Bach to Schoenberg. All of them, as exponents of the bourgeois spirit, reached its limit, without being able to transcend it while using the resources of the bourgeois world; the suffering inflicted by the present forced each of them to fall back on something from the past as a sacrifice to the future. Whether this sacrifice bore fruit in Beethoven, whether the quintessence of omission is indeed the cipher for a fulfilled cosmos, or whether, like the attempts at reconstructing objectivity which followed it, the *Missa* itself failed, can only be judged once historical and philosophical reflection has advanced, through the structure of the work, into the innermost cells of its composition. However, now that the principle of the musical development has run its course historically and has been overturned, the fact that composition now finds itself obliged to accumulate sections, to articulate 'fields' without any thought for the procedure of the *Missa*, encourages us to treat Beethoven's admonitory claim that it was the greatest of his works as more than mere admonition.

From *Moments musicaux* (GS 17, pp. 145ff) – written in 1957

ELEVEN

THE LATE STYLE (II)

After reading the E♭ major String Quartet, op. 127, one of the most difficult and mysterious works. The late Beethoven *covers its traces*. But which? That is no doubt the riddle. For, on the other hand, the musical language is displayed here nakedly and – as compared to the middle style – *directly*. Does he, in order to enable tonality, and so on, to emerge in this way, obliterate the traces of *composition*? Is this supposed to sound as if it had not been composed? Has the subject passed over into the production, so that it is *eliminated* as the producer? An image of *autonomous motion*? And does this give rise to an impression of something written against the grain? To me, *everything* seems to depend on this – perhaps even the deciphering of the *Missa*. But I am not yet able to give an answer.   [306]

The late Beethoven's uniqueness is that in him the spirit remains master of itself in experiences which are otherwise inevitably purchased with madness. These experiences, however, are not those of subjectivity but of language, that is, of the collective. Beethoven looks the bare language of music, purified of all individual expression, in the eye. Relevant here is the curious statement of Grillparzer, quoted by Thomas-San-Galli, *Ludwig van Beethoven*, p. 374: '. . . I did not want to give Beethoven cause, misled by a half-diabolic subject,[250] to step still closer to the extreme limits of music, which were there in any case, like a threatening abyss.' (About 1822.)   [307]

The bareness of the very late Beethoven's music is connected to the *inorganic* element. What does not grow, does not luxuriate. Unadornedness and *death*. – Allegorical rather than symbolic. [308]

What otherwise merely functions in music, its essence – as determined by function – is made thematic in late Beethoven. In this way he divests himself of the bad individuality which merely disguises.

[309]

The truly characteristic element of Schumann – and then of Mahler and Alban Berg – is the inability to hold themselves back, the tendency to give, to throw themselves away. Here the Romantic principle means to give up the ownership aspect of experience, indeed the self. The nobility in this has an un-ideological content: weariness with the privation[251] implicit in the private. One senses exploitation extending even into the *principium individuationis* and turns away. In Schumann consciousness came very close to this. For example, in the words 'sollte mir das Herz auch brechen, brich o Herz, was liegt daran' [Even if my heart should break, break O heart, it matters not].[252] (The choice of the text of *Frauenliebe und -leben*, which provokes the mockery of the bourgeois, has a deep meaning. 'Masochism' does not say enough. The identification with woman aims at an attitude which declares war on the appropriation implicit in the male, patriarchal order. Hölderlin has such traits. Perhaps the idea of the *Biedermeier* is located precisely here.) Or stated directly in Schumann's writings, [*Schriften*, I, ed. Simon, p. 30]: '*Richness of youth*. What I know, I throw away – what I have, I give away. – Fl.' This motif is purest, however, in the C major Fantasia, the last movement of which entirely resembles allowing oneself to be carried out to sea. In the distinction between this gesture and the so similar one in Wagner, of drowning, sinking, of 'unbewusst, höchste Lust' [void of thought/highest bliss],[253] almost, philosophical truth is contained. The difference between inwardness and sensual intoxication is too conventional to do justice to the distinction. Schumann is much better than inward. The gesture is very modest: I commend myself. I do not wish to disturb (bourgeois: Schumann is as much better than Wagner as he is more bourgeois). Death is the throwing off of a burden (in Schubert also), a self-abandonment because one can no longer bear the injustice of life, but not a self-identification with the injustice of death. There is much rather an element of trust in it, though this has nothing to do with trust in the power of the existing order – of fate – but has its homeland in theology.

Precisely this trait marks out one border of Beethoven, or an aspect in which Romanticism actually goes beyond him. The work represented by Beethoven is the one which supports itself. In its totality resides the positivity of possession, which cancels the negativity of all individual aspects. The expressive seal of this is defiance – which yet has a quality of humanity. The human in Beethoven is linked to *tact*, as it is in the old Goethe. 'O dass ich dir nicht lohnen kann.'[254] Schumann is tactless; if he cannot reward, he gives himself instead. And still falls short of Beethoven by making things too easy between himself and the world. – This dialectical approach provides a basis for understanding very late Beethoven.   [310]

In late Beethoven it is not polyphony which seems to me technically decisive; this is kept well within limits and by no means forms the entire style, being, rather, episodic in character. It is really the splitting into extremes: between polyphony and monody. It is a dissociation of the middle. In other words: the withering of harmony. This refers not merely to harmonic fullness and decorative harmonic counterpoint, or even to the simplification ('Ever more simple, and all piano music likewise', quoted by Thomas-San-Galli, *Ludwig van Beethoven*, p. 359). But harmony itself, which survives in many areas, takes on something mask-like or husk-like. It becomes a convention keeping things upright, but largely drained of substance. In the last string quartets at least, one can hardly speak any longer of the construction of tonality. It no longer has an autonomous law of motion, but remains behind as a sound veil, and it is not harmonic proportion but the individual harmonic effect which counts in this dimension. An index of how harmony is becoming illusory is the tendency to stand still, and for harmony to stretch and expand, for example, in the *Adagio* of op. 106. – To be sure, this must be said with great reservations, since even the late Beethoven achieves magnificent effects of harmonic perspective, for example, in the first movement of op. 111, in the slow 6/4 Diabelli Variation (perhaps the finest example of the construction of tonality), sometimes in the C♯ minor String Quartet and, of course, in the Ninth Symphony. But all that is not really late style. The main examples of the withering of harmony are probably in the B♭ major and F major string Quartets [opp. 130 and 135], the Quartet Fugue [op. 133] and the late Bagatelles [opp. 119 and 126]. Harmonic, by contrast, the Finale of the A minor String Quartet [op. 132]. – In the late style harmony shrivels.

To make clear the importance of this process one must look back at the construction of tonality. This means in essence that, through the way music is formed, its precondition is raised to a result. Clearly, an experience which can be repeated rebels against this. The precondition raised to a result is sedimented as material. It thereby ceases to constitute the problem of music: one already knows all about it. Through Beethoven's process tonality became universally established. Everything is related to its function: it no longer needs to prove itself. The precondition has become so substantial through the process that it no longer needs its confirmation as result. But precisely thereby it loses its substantiality and becomes a discarded convention, alienated from music in its concreteness.

As this happens, however, the critical movement takes hold of the true centre of middle, classical Beethoven. His 'harmony' is the identity of precondition and result. Criticism is directed against this identity, which is, really, that of subject and object. The precondition is no longer mediated: as something attained once and for all it stands abstractly still and is, as it were, shot through by the subjective intentions. The compulsion of identity is broken and the conventions are its fragments. The music speaks the language of the archaic, of children, of savages and of God, but not of the individual. All the categories of the late Beethoven are challenges to idealism – almost to 'spirit'. Autonomy is no more. [311]

Perhaps the split between polyphony and monody in the late style is explained by the non-fulfilment of the obligations of polyphony (cf. the Schoenberg memorial essay[255]). Harmony is avoided because it produces an *illusion* of the unity of many voices. Bare monody expresses their irreconcilability within tonality. [312]

Beethoven's polyphony is in the most literal sense an expression of the waning of belief in harmony. It presents the totality of the alienated world. – Much music by the late Beethoven sounds as if someone, alone, were gesticulating and mumbling to himself. The episode with the runaway oxen.[256] [313]

One can perhaps come close to understanding the 'polarization' in late Beethoven as follows: tonality is rendered indifferent because the same chords say the same thing over and over again. Beethoven's stepping back from appearance, the withering of harmony in the widest sense, stems from resistance to subsumption by the unchanging. Instead of stating the unchanging in its aesthetic mediations – which are experienced as illusory since it is always the same thing – it must be expressed as such, unmediated, in its abstractness and thus its *truth*. The concreteness of the aesthetic *Gestalt* itself is burst asunder as a mere façade, in face of the identical core of the language. This is probably behind the 'abstractness' of the late Beethoven. Because the triads have the same function in all works, they must themselves be forced to utter the secret of this function. This is the key passage in my social interpretation. [314]

NB: Wherein lies the illusory character of harmony in late Beethoven – this needs to be formulated exactly.

Harmony suffers the same fate in late Beethoven as religion in bourgeois society: it continues to exist, but is forgotten.   [315]

On the sedimenting of tonality and the formation of the late style: 'Religion and *basso continuo* are both closed subjects that need no further discussion', Bekker, *Beethoven*, p. 70. To Schindler, therefore rather late. Earlier he certainly 'discussed' these matters.   [316]

At the repeat of the theme at the end of op. 109 [third movement, bars 188ff] an eminently cadential effect is produced by adding very few octaves, giving the melody the character of something objectively confirmed, collective. This is an example of the increasing power and significance of allegorical features inserted from 'outside', a process connected to the dissociation of organic unity in late Beethoven.   [317]

All the commentaries on late Beethoven – that is, strictly *only* the last string quartets, perhaps the Diabelli Variations and the last Bagatelles [op. 126] – have not quite hit the mark. One must start from the 'allegorical', and in an important sense fractured, nature of these pieces, from the fact that they dispense with unity of sensuous appearance and content, whatever that may be (cf. the essay on Beethoven's late style [see above, pp. 123ff]. That, however, is not a reflection derived freely from the works, but is made necessary by their appearance itself. One must therefore ask two questions: in which of their sensuous aspects do these pieces point beyond their appearance, and what kind of meaning does their cipher-like character constitute? The first question must be clearly distinguished from symphonic transcendence in the 'classical' sense, which cannot be accepted as an immediate, 'symbolic' unity either. The late Beethoven is distinguished from the classical one by the fact that meaning is no longer mediated by appearance as a *totality*. If we now come to the question about the appearance of non-appearance, we are first drawn to the themes and melodies. In late Beethoven these are always so constituted – whether by their curious inauthenticity, or through excessive simplicity – that they appear not as themselves but as signs of something else. The phenomenon itself is refracted. The themes are not actually concrete, but in a sense the accidental representatives of the universal. They are as if pruned, disrupted, both below and above the theme; they say: that is not it at all. (In classical Beethoven precisely this was said by the totality.

Here, the individual is the negativity which, in the earlier period, was mediation by the whole.) Technically this is linked to the predominance of counterpoint. Insofar as all themes are adapted to counterpoint, they are no longer 'melodies', self-sufficient formations. Through the concern for possible counterpointing they are both restricted ('unfree', cannot live for themselves, economy with notes, and so on) and more general, more formulaic (which is connected to their very restrictedness). In addition, the element of 'conventionality' from the essay [that is, 'Beethoven's Late Style'], and the shrinking of themes to a few basic motifs (the thematic interrelationships of the last string quartets). The latest Beethoven represents an attempt to reconstruct the *cantus firmus* from subjectivity. The starting point of the entire late style is connected to this. All else can be derived from the problem of this *cantus firmus* and from the question of the compulsion towards counterpoint. A neutralization of the thematic takes place. The themes are neither melodies which stand on their own, nor motivic units which pass over into the totality – which is itself suspended. They are possibilities or ideas of themes.   [318]

The tendency towards *compression* in late Beethoven; that is, mere indications often stand for groups in the formal schema. The music does not 'live out its life'; this at the expense of the classical 'dynamic' form. The prototype is the first movement of op. 101, which, in its two pages and with its lyrical tone, carries the weight of a major piece. Something similar in opp. 109 and 110, and probably in the first movement of 111. But there is also an opposing tendency, which allows the schema to emerge barely, and very long movements as in the String Quartets in A minor and B♭ major [opp. 132 and 130].   [319]

If asked for the true reason for Beethoven's greatness I would probably answer first of all (in contrast to Rudi's [Rudolf Kolisch's] theory of tempi[257]): that he did not simply produce one good Beethoven piece after another, but he incessantly – virtually infinitely – produced new characters, types, *categories* of music (compared to them, certain characteristics of the *details*, in which the spontaneity of other composers resides, are rather hackneyed). In Beethoven there is no reification of forms. It often seems that his imagination does not engage at all with the level of the immediate, the musical inspiration, but with that of the *concept* – an imagination of a second and higher order, comparable to the post-Kantian doctrine of the everlasting production of categories. If he repeats characters, it is usually in order to crystallize out their Platonic ideas purely; for example, the B♭ major Piano Sonata op. 22 prefigures the 'Waldstein' Sonata. Then it is abandoned. It is positively a miracle that after the *Eroica*, in which he had found what for *every* other composer would have been 'his' form, he incessantly created entirely new categories, in a secularized application of the theological concept of the creator – not rhapsodically, but as a consequence of his musical thinking. This, however, is connected at the deepest level to the *content* of Beethoven's music. It is the truly *human* element, something not ossified but genuinely dialectical – the exact opposite of the para-noiac. This ability has such importance in Beethoven because it is entirely without anything accidental, irresponsible, *aperçu*-like – because in him, philosophically speaking, the power of the system (the sonata is the system as music) equals that of experience, each reciprocally producing the other. In this he is really more Hegelian than Hegel, who, in applying the *concept* of the dialectic, proceeds far more rigidly, in the manner of all-embracing logic, than the theory itself teaches (even in the *Phenomenology*, where some categories really just *rush through*). Beethoven is implacable and yielding at once. It must be so, but the prisoner is granted bread and water. One can no longer compose like Beethoven, but one must *think* as he composed.   [320]

The production of categories instead of individuations, once released, is perhaps the key to the late style as a kind of vision in terms of categories.   [321]

Perhaps the last notes [cf. frs 319–21] contain the 'key' to the late style as mediated, in the precise sense that here each individual part stands not for itself but as a representative of its type, its category, a situation which indeed comes very close to the allegorical. Here, *only* types are invented, everything singular being set down as a sign for them; and, conversely, the force of each individual element lies in the fact that it is replete with its type, is no longer itself. Everything individual is both shrunken and saturated with the ideal unity of its species. It is probably this which establishes the late Beethoven's relationship to axiomatic wisdom. Moreover, the style of every great artist's old age has something of this, especially the 'Art of Fugue'. Note in this connection the much-observed predilection of the late Goethe for the typical. Technically, therefore, the 'typicality' of the themes, and so on, of the late Beethoven needs to be demonstrated. His characters are like *models* of everything which is possible in this direction. But what are the musical correlatives of this intellectual relationship? That is now the problem posed by an adequate theory.
[322][258]

The ideas set down here need to be related to the Hegelian notion of bad individuality, the conception that only the universal is substantial. The purpose of the *fractured* quality of late Beethoven would then be to express the fact that such substantiality of the universal represents *alienation*, violence, privation – that is, it does not raise the individual positively to a higher level. Beethoven becomes 'inorganic', fractured, at the point where Hegel becomes ideological. He is led by a dissatisfaction, a disgust with the individual in its fortuitousness; it seems to him too little, too insignificant, and this is profoundly related to his tragic, idealistic streak. Here, too, the motif of wanting not to move the listener but to 'strike fire from the soul'.[259] But there is also a strictly dialectical movement in the music itself. For the individual element in Beethoven is, indeed, 'insignificant'; and whereas the 'classical' style sublates this element within the totality and gives it the *appearance* of significance (NB: appearance as a decisive category in middle Beethoven), now the insignificance of the individual element emerges as such and makes it the 'accidental' bearer of the universal. In other words, the late style is the self-awareness of the insignificance of the individual, existent. Herein lies the relationship of the late style to *death*. [323]

TWELVE

HUMANITY AND DEMYTHOLOGIZATION

Possible epigraph for a chapter:

> Und Freude schwebt wie Sternenklang
> Uns nur im Traume vor.
> [And joy is glimpsed in dreams alone, like music of the stars.]

Goethe, *Skizzen zu Faust I*, 81, ed. Witkowski, I, p. 414.[260]   [324]

Possible epigraph for the last chapter of the study of Beethoven:

> Die letzte Hand klopft an die Wand,
> die wird mich nicht verlassen.
> [On the wall taps the last hand, and will not leave me.]

From *Des Knaben Wunderhorn*.[261]   [325]

On Beethoven and music as language see Hofmannsthal, 'Beethoven', in *Reden und Aufsätze*, Leipzig 1921, p. 6:

From an unbroken spirit, pious(!) despite its rebellion, he became the creator of a language above language. In this language he is present entirely: more than sound and tone, more than symphony, more than hymn, more than prayer: it is something inexpressible: in it is the gesture of a man who stands before God. Here was a word, but not the profane word of language; here was the living word and the living deed, and they were one.

This quotation, in which some of the most profound insights (reconstruction of language, gesture of someone standing firm – cf. this notebook, expression of the theme of the Ninth [cf. fr. 31]) are engulfed in a flood of cultural claptrap, should be introduced with utmost care. – Beethoven's work in its entirety as an *attempt at reconstruction.* [326]

If Benjamin, in his early study on language, supposes that in painting and sculpture the mute language of things is translated into a higher but related language,[262] it might be supposed of music that it saves the name as pure sound, but at the cost of separating it from things. Relationship to prayer.   [327]

The unique nature of music, to be not an image standing *for* another reality, but a reality *sui generis.* Not subject to the ban on images, and *yet* magical as a ritual of assuagement. Thus, at the level of mythology, both demythologization and myth *at the same time.* Therefore, in its innermost composition, identical to Christianity – it could be said that there is only as much music as there is Christianity in the world and that all the forces of music communicate those of Christianity. Music and the 'Passion', the incomparable pre-eminence of Bach.[263] This imageless magic is, however, a demonstration: this is how the cosmos *should* be: Pythagoreans. Music says: Thy will be done. It is the pure language of prayer as devoted entreaty. Beethoven is deeply connected to this through the element of *rhetoric.* His music is the this-worldly prayer of the bourgeois class, the rhetorical music of the secularization of the Christian liturgy. The elements of language and humanity in his music will have to be demonstrated from this standpoint.   [328]

From a comparison with any instrumental piece by Schubert (I was struck by this in childhood, listening to the A minor Piano Sonata[264]) we can conclude that Beethoven's music is *imageless.* Romanticism reacted against this. But this is not simply an Enlightenment tendency in Beethoven, but a sublation [*Aufheben*] in the Hegelian sense. Where his music contains images, they are images of the imageless, of demythologization, of reconciliation, never those which lay claim to unmediated truth within themselves.   [329]

The *Larghetto* of Beethoven's Second Symphony belongs to the world of Jean Paul. The infinite moonlit night speaks only to the finite coach driving through it. Its confined cosiness reinforces the expression of the unconfined.   [330]

This element is very important for the whole of Beethoven. I am thinking of the contingent and idyllic exposition of *Fidelio*. But above all of the Eighth Symphony. This is, in a sense, the negative of *Hermann und Dorothea*. If the historical process is reflected in the idyll of that work, in the Eighth the idyll is burst asunder by its own latent driving forces. The smallest detail can become the whole, because it is already the whole. This gives access to the late Beethoven, who no longer mediates between these extremes but makes one switch abruptly into the other. – The strength of the early Beethoven is exactly measurable by the ability to juxtapose heterogeneous or widely separated shapes *and* to bind them together as a unity – as 'simultaneous'. To be sure, certain limits are set to this – moments of 'intermission' [*Aussetzen*] – such as the accented chords in the overloaded *Larghetto* of the Second, which threatens to disintegrate. Perhaps the attempt either to transcend these limits or to mark them in the work itself is the true motor driving Beethoven's 'development'.   [331]

Fidelio has a hieratic, cultic quality.* In it the Revolution is not depicted but re-enacted as in a ritual. It could have been written to celebrate the anniversary of the Bastille. No tension, just the 'transformation'† in Leonore's moment in gaol.‡ Decided in advance. An eccentric, 'stylized' simplicity of means. It is a correct instinct to play the Third *Leonore* Overture after the gaol scene. – Here, too, a bad Wagnerian element is held in good suspension.   [332]

On the hieratic element in *Fidelio*, cf. 'secular awe' (over 'O Isis') and the *Magic Flute* in general. Einstein, *Mozart*, p. 466.[265]   [333]

When, in *Fidelio,* the words 'Der Gouverneur' are heard for the first time, suspended, on the *fermata*, it is as if an oblique sunbeam had entered the gaoler's gloomy dwelling, in which light it recognizes itself as part of the world.   [334]

In what does the expression of the human manifest itself in Beethoven? I would say, in the fact that his music has the gift of sight. The human is its gaze. But this must be expressed in technical concepts.   [335]

---

* [In margin:] The unity of the hieratic and the bourgeois in Beethoven is his *Empire* quality.
† [Below the line:] (Sacrifice!)
‡ [In margin:] No 'conflict'. Action as mere working-out.

Benjamin's idea of the 'conditions of humanity', that is, of indigence (in the collection of letters, in connection with the letter by Kant's brother[266]), should be taken up in the Beethoven study and traced in relation to my subject, the bareness of the material. Beethoven as one of the few who *knew* about this condition: hence the cult of Handel, of whose modest qualities as a composer Beethoven cannot possibly have been unaware. The *Missa* is decisively connected to this. On Beethoven's horizon – as on Goethe's – the idea of false opulence already appears, of goods abounding for profit, and he reacts against it (false opulence was represented for him on one hand by Romanticism and on the other by opera). He opposed progress out of radicalism: hence the retrospective tendency of his late phase. Expressed technically: only against the meagre, the most limited material, is the mighty effect of the divergent possible: it vanishes as soon as the divergent becomes universal (since Berlioz). But this also applies, in a way still to be worked out, to expression and content. The bareness guarantees, as it were, the universal, the human in Goethe's sense (as the abstract aspect of death?). Through it Beethoven stands opposed to the nominalism of progress, like Hegel. Take this further.   [336]

'Poor instrumentation.' It is easy to demonstrate that Beethoven was weak at instrumentation. As the arrangement of the score seemed to suggest, he always placed the oboes above the clarinets, without thinking of their specific registers. He used the brass to make a noise; the wretched natural tones of the horns protrude, without ever really forming independent parts. He did not consider the proportions of strings to woodwind: one woodwind player is treated as equivalent to a combined string voice, and in a dialogue the woodwind section is completely eclipsed. Specific colours are heard only as exceptions, as 'effects' – like the muted horn at the end of the *Pastoral*. But what does that matter? Is not precisely the meagre, impoverished sound of this orchestra, always slightly shrill, with over-prominent oboes and bassoon humming along in attendance, inaudible stationary woodwind voices, the grunt of the horn, the inordinately simplified string writing (compared to the chamber music), deeply intertwined with the music itself? Is not poverty a leaven of its humanity – as it were, the timbre of abstraction striking on humanity – for which this orchestra provides the convention? Is this not the poverty of Goethe's death chamber, the sobriety of the greatest prose of the period? That the forces of production were not more highly developed instrumentally is, at least, not *only* a defect. This very absence, due to fettered productive forces, is in secret communication with the substance. What is banished is that which must stay away in order to survive, and only against this lack does the voice of the instrument become an overwhelming sound. Here we can see clearly the questionable nature of artistic progress. The path leading from this orchestra to that of *Salome* is the same one which has so levelled musical expression through *embarras de richesse* that the utmost ecstasy of the violins, filtered through the radio, hardly compels us to listen any longer.

Webern has revealed something of the double character of 'poor instrumentation' in the dances of Schubert.[267] 'The classical orchestra.' Nothing in great music, moreover, is as near to classicism as this sound.   [337]

The idea of the totality mediated within itself will need to be brought together with the stratum of the chthonic[268] (NB: the chthonic element in Mörike's 'Märchen vom sicheren Mann', which comes very close to an interpretation of Beethoven[269]). Probably the mediation lies in the Beethovenian moment. In terms of formal analysis this moment – and this is the core of my theory of the symphony – would be defined as the point where the individual in Beethoven becomes aware of itself as the whole, as more than itself ('gaining momentum'). But this is always at the same time the moment of awe when nature becomes aware of itself as totality and therefore as more than nature. '*Mana.*' Cf. the passage from the mythology study.[270] The 'spirit' in Beethoven, the Hegelian element, the totality, is nothing other than nature becoming aware of itself, the chthonic element. Development of this insight is one of the main problems of my study. The anti-mythological tendency lies, however, in the music's equating itself with myth precisely *as* spirit, totality, representation. Music withstands doom by being it. 'That is the sound of fate knocking at the door.'[271]   [338]

'The sound of fate knocking at the door.' But those are only the first two bars. A movement emerges from them, not to demonstrate fate but to cancel, preseve and elevate [*aufheben*] those portentous beats.   [339]

Mörike's legend of the 'sicherer Mann', the giant Suckelborst, belongs in the context of the legends of Rübezahl [Spirit of the Mountains] recorded by Musäus, of the intertwinement of the chthonic with humanity;[272] a detailed interpretation will probably be needed in this study. Some verses in Mörike's prose fairy-tale call to mind the adage-like themes of the last quartets.   [340]

The constellation of the chthonic and the Biedermeier is one of the innermost problems in Beethoven.   [341]

An essential trait of Beethoven's physiognomy is the coexistence of the great 'humane' individual with the subterranean goblin or gnome. The humanistic element in Beethoven is the chthonic which has gained mastery of itself in breaking through the surface. In *Volksmärchen der Deutschen* (Meyers Groschenbibliothek, Hild-burghausen and New York, undated, Part Two, p. 85), Musäus gives a description of *Rübezahl*, which seems to fit Beethoven exactly and is highly revealing with regard to the historical and philosophical constellation:

> For Friend Rübezahl, you should know, has the make-up of a titanic spirit, moody, impetuous, odd; rascally, crude, immodest; proud, vain, fickle, today the warmest friend, tomorrow distant and cold; sometimes kind, noble and sensitive; but in constant contradiction to himself; foolish and wise, often soft and hard in two consecutive moments, like an egg which has fallen into boiling water; mischievous and strait-laced, stubborn and pliable; according to the mood brought upon him by his humour (! the chthonic disposition) and his inner urge to grab whatever catches his eye.[273]

Insight into Beethoven depends finally on an interpretation of this complexion – the dialectic of the mythical. – The fairy-tale concerned is the one in which Rübezahl tears up the promissory note – a very Beethovenian gesture, which must be seen in conjunction with 'Wut um den verlorenen Groschen'. – The relationship of Musäus to Jean Paul, for example, the 'woodland misanthropist'.[274] – In the world of fate and domination only the demon in the human being is human.[275]   [342]

The symphonic widening at the end of *Ferne Geliebte* – 'und ein liebend Herz erreichet' – has something almost of the character of *rage*. The chthonic element in Beethoven cannot be separated from the symphonic. As imprecation. For whether 'a loving heart attains' its goal is highly uncertain in the state of alienation. It *should* do so, just as a dear Father *must* dwell above;[276] and the music is not content to state this but *enacts* the invocation of absent transcendence out of subjectivity. Not from abstract but from mythical subjectivity – the subject as nature. The demonic and the ideal are thus intertwined in Beethoven. The gesture of invocation can, however, remain impotent, and that is the case in the *Missa Solemnis*. Then it becomes abstract. Beethoven's assertion that the *Missa* was his best work is such an invocation. (Take care in this very important note with the concept of the abstract. In a sense everything mythical is abstract; and in a sense Kantian transcendental subjectivity is, precisely, *not* abstract!)   [343]

Beethoven's character – the boorish, aggressive, repellent trait – has become a kind of model for musicians (Brahms, probably Mahler). The connection with Schopenhauer. – The element of tomfoolery in their humour (as early as Mozart). Here, in the nonsense, may lie one of the deepest approaches to Beethoven.   [344]

The legend of Nöck will need to be included in the Beethoven study – indeed, the dialectical schema of the whole construction – myth and humanity – might perhaps be modelled on it. It can be quoted from Jacob Grimm l.c. [*Deutsche Mythologie*, 4th edition, Berlin 1876],[277] I, pp. 408f:

> Here we should tell the touching legend in which, for his music teaching, the river spirit, 'Strömkarl' or 'Neck', did not merely sacrifice himself, but also promised himself resurrection and redemption. Two boys were playing by a stream, Neck sat playing his harp. The children called to him: 'Why do you sit here playing, Neck? You won't be blessed for that!' Then Neck began to weep bitterly, threw away his harp and sank into the depths. When the boys got home they told their father, who was a priest, what had happened. Their father said: 'You have sinned against Neck. Go back, comfort him and promise him redemption'. When they got back to the river, Neck was sitting on the bank, grieving and weeping. The children said: 'Don't cry like that, Neck, our father told us that you, too, have a Redeemer.' Then Neck happily picked up his harp and played sweetly until long past sunset.

The last words of the Grimm version should perhaps be included in the treatment of late Beethoven. – On the 'river' my idea that Eichendorff's poetry (for example, from Schumann's *Lied* cycle) seems to echo not an object but the subterranean, incessant murmur [*Rauschen*] of language itself.[278] Similarly, the *Adagio* of the 'Hammerklavier' Sonata listens to the murmur of music itself, which at the end seems to sound back into the music. NB: What is this *murmur*? One of the basic questions concerning Beethoven. – NB: The dialectical counterpoint of sacrifice and promised redemption for Neck. – Beethoven's anger: that is how Neck scolds the children. The throwing away of the harp as the gesture of the late Beethoven. – The return, the granting of grace as a revocation. – Neck's sinking into the depths: humanity resides precisely in submersion in the chthonic. – Neck's mourning is mute.   [345]

On my theory about humanism and the demonic, p. 72 in this notebook [cf. fr. 342]. *Imitation* as a way of casting out demons. Beethoven like certain processions with the *Butzemann* [bogeyman] in German villages. The relationship of human being and demon is at the centre of the theory. Relate this to the survival of the matriarchal in the 'Reason' study.[279] Beethoven transcends culture to the exact extent that it has not comprehended him. The human in the inhuman world as the barbaric. – Precisely here, Beethoven's superiority to 'classical idealism'.   [346]

Bring together the idea of music's *standing fast* with that of its *becoming corporeal* [cf. fr. 263]. Does not music perhaps stand firm against fate precisely in *becoming* fate? Is not imitation the canon of resistance? I have said[280] that the Fifth and Ninth stand firm through looking-in-the-eye. Is that not still too little? Does not the Fifth stand firm through taking-into-itself? Does not gaining-power-over-oneself, freedom, lie only in imitation, in making-oneself-similar? Is not that the meaning of the Fifth, rather than the feeble *per aspera ad astra*? Is this not altogether the theory of the 'poetic idea',[281] and at the same time the law of the connection between *technique* and idea? Is not new light shed from here on programme music? To explain why the first movement of the Fifth is better than the rest.   [347]

Where the theory of standing firm is developed I should refer to Hegel's *Ästhetik*, for example, I, 62–4.[282] – Also cf. Hölderlin's xenium on Sophocles.[283]   [348]

Kant's concept of the dynamically sublime in the *Critique of Judgment*, Beethoven and the category of standing firm. Quote.[284]
                                                                           [349]

One of the major categories in Beethoven is that of serious significance [*der Ernstfall*], of being no longer mere play. This tone – which almost always results from a rising to the level of form – did not exist before him. He is at his mightiest where the traditional form still holds good and seriousness breaks through – for example, the close of the slow movement of the G major Concerto, the opening motif below the stationary E [bars 64–7]. Also the great G minor chord in the first movement of the 'Kreutzer' Sonata, before the start of the recapitulation [bar 324].[285]   [350]

On the category of seriousness, apart from the passage in the slow movement of the G major Piano Concerto, the G minor triad (rather: the fourth degree of the subdominant key) before the recapitulation in the first movement of the 'Kreutzer' Sonata. Necessity arising *from below*.   [351]

On the category of seriousness, the shrouding in clouds, the darkening of the stationary chords below the violin part in the first movement of op. 59,1. – This long and important movement is very close to the formal idea of the *Eroica*: the second development contains a new theme which is conceived from the outset as a *counterpoint*. But it is probably related more to the opening material. This may help an understanding of the *Eroica*. – The coda, the weightless floating away, one of the most magnificent characters in Beethoven. – The changing interpretation of the theme as on and off the upbeat. The whole quartet is one of the most central pieces in Beethoven, the slow movement the absolute *Adagio*, one of the key pieces. NB: In the D♭ major passage of its development, the extra bar before the entry of D♭ major *before* the new melody begins; also the E♭ of the second violin over its cadencing [bars 70f], the *immanence* of protest.   [352]

It will be necessary in identifying expression in Beethoven to interpret minute variants like that in the second theme of the *Adagio* of op. 31,2, where the syncopation appears [bar 36]. It causes the theme to 'speak', in just the same way as something extra-human – starlight – seems to bend towards the human being as solace. It is the sign of *yieldingness* – just as transcendence is presented as something invoked (but then demonically entreated) in Beethoven. The expression 'humanized star' in a poem by Däubler[286] comes very close to this. This sphere, and its symbols, are especially relevant to the great *Leonore* Overture.   [353]

Example 17

The connection of the ethical to natural beauty (cf. note on music as natural beauty in the green leather-bound notebook[287]). That the solace and assuagement of a natural expression appears as a promise of goodness. The gesture of nature as good; the remoteness of nature, sensuous infinity, as idea. The decisive dialectical category which is relevant here is that of *hope*, the key to the image of humanity. On the E major *adagio* of the Fidelio aria.   [354]

Hope and star:[288] *Fidelio* aria and second theme from the slow movement of the D minor Piano Sonata op. 31.   [355]

Hope and star. Nohl, vol. I, p. 354 (as reported by Schindler), where a comment by Beethoven on the funeral march in the *Eroica* after

Napoleon's death is recorded: 'Yes, in interpreting this movement he went further, claiming to see in the motif of the middle theme in C major the shining of a star of hope on Napoleon's adverse fate, his reappearance on the political stage in 1815, and the mighty decision in the hero's soul to oppose the fates' (NB: Star, hope *against* fate!), 'until the moment of capitulation comes, the hero sinks to the ground and is buried like any mortal.'[289]   [356]

The character of the 'star': in the second theme of the *Adagio* of op. 31,2; in the D♭ major passage in the *Adagio* of op. 59,1;[290] at the start of the trio in the funeral march of the *Eroica*, and in *Fidelio*. This character then disappears. Are its heirs the short song-like themes in the A♭ major Piano Sonata op. 110, in the B♭ major and F major Quartets [opp. 130 and 135], and the Arietta [of op. 111]?
[357]

Text 6: The Truth Content of Beethoven's Music

The claim that the metaphysical content of the slow movement of Beethoven's Quartet op. 59, no. 1, must be true provokes the objection that what is true in it is the longing, but that that fades powerlessly into nothingness. If, in response, it were insisted that there is no yearning expressed in that D♭ passage, the assertion would have an obviously apologetic ring that could well be met by the objection that precisely because it appears as if it were true it must be a work of longing, and art as a whole must be nothing but this. The rejoinder would be to reject the argument as drawn from the arsenal of vulgar subjective reason. The automatic *reductio ad hominem* is too pat, too easy, to be an adequate explanation of what objectively appears. It is cheap to present these too facile measures, simply because they have rigorous negativity on their side, as illusionless depth, whereas capitulation vis-à-vis evil implies identification with it. For it is deaf to the phenomenon. The power of the passage in Beethoven is precisely its distance from the subject; it is this that bestows on those measures the stamp of truth. What was once called the 'authentic' [*echt*] in art – a word still used by Nietzsche though now unsalvageable – sought to indicate this distance.[291]

The spirit of artworks is not their meaning and not their intention, but rather their truth content, or, in other words, the truth that is revealed through them. The second theme of the Adagio of Beethoven's D-minor Sonata, op. 31, no. 2, is not simply a beautiful melody – there are certainly more buoyant, better formed, and even more original melodies than this one – nor is it distinguished by exceptional expressivity. Nevertheless, the introduction of this theme belongs to what is overwhelming in Beethoven's music and that could be called the spirit of his music: hope, with an authenticity [*Authentizität*] that – as something that appears aesthetically – it bears even beyond aesthetic semblance. What is beyond the semblance of what appears is the aesthetic truth content: that aspect of semblance that is not semblance. The truth content is no more the factual reality of an artwork, no more one fact among others in an artwork, than it is independent from its appearance. The first thematic complex of that movement, which is of extraordinary, eloquent beauty, is a masterfully wrought mosaic of contrasting shapes that are motivically coherent even when they are registrally distant. The atmosphere of this thematic complex, which earlier would have been called mood, awaits – as indeed all mood probably does – an event that only becomes an event against the foil of this mood. The F major theme follows with a rising thirty-second-note gesture. Against the dark, diffuse backdrop of what preceded, the accompanied upper voice that characterizes the second theme acquires its dual character of reconciliation and promise. Nothing transcends without that which it transcends. The truth content is mediated by way of, not outside of, the configuration, but it is not immanent to the configuration and its elements. This is probably what crystallized as the idea of all aesthetic mediation. It is that in artworks by which they participate in their truth content. The pathway of mediation is construable in the structure of artworks, that is, in their technique. Knowledge of this leads to the objectivity of the work itself, which is so to speak vouched for by the coherence of the work's configuration. This objectivity, however, can ultimately be nothing other than the truth content. It is the task of aesthetics to trace the topography of these elements. In the authentic artwork, what is dominated – which finds expression by way of the dominating principle – is the counterpoint to the domination of what is natural or material. This dialectical relationship results in the truth content of artworks.

Paralipomena to *Aesthetic Theory*, transl. by R. Hullot-Kentor, London,
Athlone Press, 1997, pp. 284–5

Music is name in the state of absolute impotence; it is also the remoteness of name to meaning, and both are the same thing. The holiness of music is its purity from dominance over nature; but its history is the inevitable development of that dominance as it became master of itself; its instrumentalization cannot be separated from its assumption of meaning.[292] – Benjamin speaks of song, which may possibly rescue the language of birds as visual art rescues that of things.[293] But this seems to me the achievement of *instruments* much rather than of song; for instruments are far more like the voices of birds than are human voices. The instrument *is* animation: just as there is always equivalence between subjectification and reification. This is the primal phenomenon of all musical dialectics.   [358]

Gretel asked me why composers, almost without exception, cling to vocal composition despite the spiritualization of music. I tried to answer: firstly, because the transition from the vocal to the instrumental, the true spiritualization ('subjectification') of music through its reification, was infinitely difficult for humanity, so that composers have repeatedly, and tentatively, reversed this form of Enlightenment. But then, this is not a pure regression, for the vocal is inalienably *preserved* in all instrumental music. Here we should not think only of the 'vocal' flow of the instrumental melody, which in turn determines the vocal flow in the *Lied*, but of something much more primitive, almost anthropological. For the imagination of *all* music, and especially of instrumental music, is vocal. To imagine music is always to sing it inwardly: imagining it is inseparable from the physical sensation of the vocal cords, and composers take account of the 'vocal limit'. Only angels could make music freely. These ideas must be related to Beethoven. In musical terms, humanity means: the permeation of the instrumental with spirit, reconciliation of the alienated means with the end, the subject, within the process, instead of mere humane immediacy. That is one of the innermost dialectical moments in Beethoven. The cult of the vocal against the instrumental today points precisely to the *end* of humanity in music.   [359]

Soul is not an invariant, not an anthropological category. It is a historical gesture. Nature, having become the ego, opens its eyes *as* ego (not *in* the ego, as its regressive part) and becomes aware of itself *qua* ego as nature. This moment – that is, not the breakthrough of nature but its awareness of differentness – is closest to reconciliation as also to lamentation. It is, however, re-enacted by all music. It represents the act of animation, of being endowed with soul, over and over again, and the differences in the content of music are really always differences in the way this animation is meant. In the case of Beethoven, therefore, one will have to ask: What, in this sense, is meant by soul in his music?   [360]

Beethoven was furious if anyone cried while listening to his music[294] – even Goethe. [361]

'Les Adieux': the clatter of horses' hooves moving away into the distance carries a greater guarantee of hope than the four Gospels.[295]

[362]

The sonata 'Les Adieux', a kind of stepchild, seems to me a work of the *highest* rank. Its simple, crude design in terms of programme music has yet provided an impulse for extreme humanization and subjectification, as if to be human were actually to be able to read the language of post-horn, hoof clatter, heartbeat. The outward is a means of inwardness. The question how the formula can come alive, a problem very closely related to the late style (in which it is inverted: How can the living become a formula, its own concept? The late style corresponds to Hegel's subjective logic[296]). Above all, the first movement, in which the simplicity of tone painting shifts suddenly into metaphysics. The deceptive cadence as early as bar 2 of the indescribable introduction, which turns the fifths of the horn towards seriousness and humanity, and then especially the transition to A major, one of the most magnificent allegories of hope in Beethoven, comparable only to *Fidelio* (to which the whole sonata is closely related), and to the great passage from the *Adagio* of op. 59,1. The modulation conveys the unreality, the non-being of hope. Hope is always *secret*, because it is not 'there' – it is the basic category of mysticism and the highest category of Beethoven's metaphysics. – The introduction, as in the late style, is incorporated as material into the main movement. In the latter, above all the airborne, pulsing character of the transition, of unparalleled subjective eloquence. A wise abbreviation of the development. The lyrical nature of the movement precludes dialectical work. By contrast, the coda, in every respect one of the most enormous passages in Beethoven. The harmonic collision of the horn chords; the indescribable moving away of the coach with the fourth (the eternal attaches itself precisely to this most transient moment), and then the last cadence of all, where hope disappears as into a gateway, one of Beethoven's greatest theological intentions, comparable only to certain moments in Bach. (As in Goethe, hope in Beethoven is decisive as a secularized though not a neutralized mystical category – this phenomenon, for which in my haste I can find only the most inadequate words here, must be *exactly* grasped and depicted, as it is of central importance. An image of hope without the lie of religion. NB: Hope is one of the imageless images which are conveyed specifically, directly by music; that is, it is a part of music's very language.) – The second movement is interesting for its early-Romantic, eloquent quality, anticipating *Tristan*, as well as for its rhythmical relationship to the introduction, and for the two double stanzas, but it suffers from a weak and conventional transition to the Finale. If this had been as successful as in the E♭ major Concerto, the sonata would have been the equal of the 'Waldstein' and the 'Appassionata'. – The Finale is perhaps the first of those movements which seem to last for only a moment: prototype for the Seventh Symphony, intensive totality. [363]

Today the experience of *leavetaking* no longer exists. It lies in the depths of the humane: the presence of the not-present. Humaneness as a function of traffic conditions. And: is there still *hope* without leavetaking? [364]

The meaning of the Beethovenian coda is no doubt that work, activity, is not everything, and that the spontaneous totality does not contain its whole meaning within itself but merely as something pointing beyond it. Movement is directed towards repose. That is one of the primal motifs of transcendence in early Beethoven. Music – spread illumined before us. Often the expression of *thanks*. Thanks are one of Beethoven's great humane categories ('Euch werde Lohn'[297] and the prayer of thanksgiving in the A minor Quartet [op. 132, 3rd movement]). In its thanking lies the turning backwards of music – that which most deeply distinguishes it from brisk efficiency. Beethoven's thanking is always related to leavetaking ('Les Adieux', close of first movement, is one of Beethoven's decisive metaphysical figures). – In early Beethoven the expression of thanks is quite pure at the close of the 'Spring' Sonata [op. 24]./ Cf. Hegel, *Phänomenologie des Geistes*, p. 146. Thanks and unhappy consciousness.[298] [365]

The close of the Arietta variations [of op. 111] has such a force of backward-looking, of leavetaking, that, as if over-illuminated by this departure, what has gone before is immeasurably enlarged. This despite the fact that the variations themselves, up to the symphonic conclusion of the last, contain scarcely a moment which could counterbalance that of leavetaking as fulfilled present – and such a moment may well be denied to music, which exists in illusion. But the true power of illusion in Beethoven's music – of the 'dream in stars eternal'[299] – is that it can invoke what has not been as something past and non-existent. Utopia is heard only as what has already been. The music's inherent sense of form changes what has preceded the leavetaking in such a way that it takes on a greatness, a presence in the past which, within music, it could never achieve in the present.*   [366]

If Rudi's [Rudolph Kolisch's] theory[300] were correct, Beethoven's work would be a gigantic puzzle composed of the same characters in kaleidoscopic permutations. That sounds mechanical and blasphemous, but Rudi's verdict carries far too much weight to allow the possibility to be dismissed without serious thought, and the statement about the seventh chords and Beethoven's 'stenography'[301] point in the same direction. But is it not the case that the finite mind has only a limited, countable number of ideas open to it – and was it not Beethoven's whole art to *conceal* this very fact? Was the inexhaustibility of his ideas finally one with aesthetic illusion? Is not, perhaps, the infinite – metaphysics – precisely that which is contrived in art, and therefore *not*, as I always would like to think, the guarantor of truth but a phantasm, and all the more so the higher the art-work is? Perhaps only an irrationalist aesthetic would answer Rudi's theory[302] – but in truth it touches on the frontiers of art itself. Also in this connection, Max [Horkheimer]'s criticism of Rembrandt, the element of the 'posed', of the studio, in his work, too.   [367]

Beethoven. If one can speak of the middle phase as the metaphysics of tragedy – the totality of negations as a position, the affirmation of what is, in its recurrence, as meaning – then the late phase is a critique of tragedy as *illusion*. However, this moment is teleologically prepared in the middle phase, in that the meaning is not present but is *invoked* by the emphatic nature of the music; and just this is the mythical stratum in Beethoven. The centrepiece of his construction.   [368]

Beethoven and the doctrine of the Cabbala, according to which evil arose from the excess of divine power. (Gnostic motif.)[303]   [369]

On the metaphysics of musical time. Relate the end of my study to the teaching of Jewish mysticism about the grass angels, who are created for an instant only to perish in the sacred fire. Music – modelled on the glorification of God, even, and especially, when it opposes the world – resembles these angels. Their very transience,

---

* [In margin:] A closely related effect, though not as piercing as in the Arietta, at the end of the variations in the great B♭ major Trio [op. 97]. – Extreme contrast to Pfitzner's aesthetics.

their ephemerality, is glorification. That is, the incessant destruction
of nature. Beethoven raised this figure to musical self-consciousness.
His truth is the destruction of the particular. He composed to its end
the absolute transience of music. The fire which, according to his
stricture against weeping, is to be struck from a man's soul,[304] is 'the
fire which consumes [nature]' (Scholem, chapter on the Zohar,
p. 86). Cf. Scholem, 85f.[305]   [370]

APPENDIX I

Text 7: Rudolph Kolisch's Theory of Tempo and Characters in Beethoven

Los Angeles, 16 November 1943

Dear Rudi,

I have read your study on Beethoven[306] with the greatest interest. It is, of course, by far the most important and penetrating contribution that has ever been made on these matters. Apart from its extraordinary practical implications in enabling a true restoration of Beethoven interpretation, it has, for me, the very special practical value of showing, in an extremely specific and concrete way, an aspect which has been totally repressed by the conventional view but is of central importance to an understanding of Beethoven. This might be called the Enlightenment aspect or, if you will, the 'rationalist' aspect. When I finally set about writing my long-planned book on Beethoven (I think it ought to be the first thing I do after the war, if there is a break in our collaborative work here[307]), I will work out this aspect as energetically as possible, in the quite different context of Hegelian logic. The metronome-loving Beethoven is the same man who, as I discovered to my astonishment in the manuscript of the 'Geister' Trio [cf. fr. 20], noted his ideas in a kind of shorthand, and who stated that much of what lay-people attribute to the 'natural genius' of a composer is in fact due to the skilful use of the diminished seventh chord.[308]

Aside from this, the thesis of your study is the relationship of tempo to 'character'. This, too, has enormous implications, and reading your examples one is aware of countless connections one had not thought of before. But I see a certain danger here. I would call it – if you will excuse the banal expression – the danger of the mechanistic or positivistic. Do not misunderstand me – I am the last person to uphold intuitionism as a means of understanding music. And, like you, I believe in the strict knowability of music – because music is itself knowledge, and in its way very strict knowledge. But in my opinion this knowledge must be concrete and must yield over-arching connections through the movement from one particular moment to another, and not through establishing general features. I believe that it is not possible to construct Beethovenian 'types' on the basis of an isolated aspect such as tempo, and that this often brings together heterogeneous elements (though often surprisingly related ones as well). You yourself make a cautious comment to this effect, admitting that the tempo-character relation is only *one*, arbit-rarily isolated, consideration.[309] But in the end this is the one on which all the light of your study is shed, and I would ask if such an isolating procedure is appropriate to music, and especially to Beethoven. Could it not lead to schematizations which are external to the concrete, immanent law of his music – in rather the same way, to overstate the case, as Lorenz's schemata are external to forms in Wagner.[310]

I do not come to this view on the basis of general reflections on the philosophy of music, but through considerations relating specif-ically to Beethoven. We have always been in agreement that the motif, the individual element, the definite, finite thing composed, while being certainly 'there' in Beethoven, at the same time is not there, is nothing, insignificant. And I would say that the sense of form in his music consists very largely in revealing this insignificance through the whole. But if that is so, how can one assign to the indi-vidual element, the motivic figure (which is the measure of the char-acteristic of tempo to which, in constructing types, you must constantly return), the power so to decide over the whole that the nature of an entire movement is measured in terms of the ('insignific-ant') motif, the role of a quaver followed by two semiquavers, and so on. Such similarities can be an *index* of typical relations, but they are not a criterion for them, for the criterion is the relevant whole, or, more precisely, the relation of this whole to the detail. For ex-ample, you relate the first movement of the little B♭ major Quartet op. 18, no. 6, very closely to the first movement of the Fourth Symphony because of the indeed very striking metronome setting of whole bars = 80, and because of the basic type of the main figure, which moves in extremely quick crotchets and dissected triads. But have these movements, in terms of their musical *essence*, really any-thing in common? Is not the quartet movement really a compressed game, whereas the symphony movement, through the splendid sus-pension in the development, takes this game into the realm of ser-iousness? Forgive me if I am talking like a literary historian, but do not musical eras – *divertissement* and 'serious significance' – lie between these two movements? And is a typology adequate if it flat-tens out the really decisive differences for the sake of the 'factual situation'? I believe it will be our task to define these differences of *essence* in terms of concrete musical (not stylistic) categories. But not to level them out through classification.

I am sure you will have understood me even though I have only managed to stammer, and I am very eager for your reply.[311]

Typewritten letter; from a carbon copy in the Theodor W. Adorno Archiv,
Frankfurt/Main

APPENDIX II

Text 8: 'Beautiful Passages' in Beethoven

Integration, the longed-for reconciliation of general and particular in the aesthetic *Gestalt*, will probably be impossible as long as reality outside art persists in remaining unreconciled. Any art-work which raises itself above society is immediately brought to earth by reality and its distress. As long as reconciliation is confined to an image, it has an impotent, invalid quality even as an image. Accordingly, tension in great works of art would need to be not only resolved within their scope – and even Schoenberg demanded no more than this – but also preserved within that same scope. But this means nothing less than that precisely in legitimate works the whole and the parts cannot coincide in the way demanded by an aesthetic ideal by no means confined to classicism. A correct hearing of music requires no less a spontaneous awareness of the non-identity of whole and parts than the synthesis which unifies them. Even in Beethoven the resolution of the tension – a resolution in which he was unequalled, since nowhere else was the tension so powerful – required an element of contrivance. Only because the parts are already fitted to the whole in his work, preformed by it, are identity and equilibrium achieved. The price of this is paid on the one hand by the decorative solemnity with which the identity is proclaimed, and on the other by the deliberately planned insignificance of the individual element, an insignificance which from the outset drives that element beyond itself so that it may become something, awaiting the whole which the individual element becomes while being abolished by it. The medium which made this contrivance possible was tonality, the general principle whose typical manifestations in Beethoven coincide with the particular elements, the themes. With the irrevocable demise of tonality this possibility has gone; nor, once its principle has become transparent, it is to be desired.

[. . .]

I spoke earlier of the preformed and relatively subordinate quality of many musical ideas in Beethoven, to which Paul Bekker also drew attention. This statement must now be qualified by conceding that Beethoven was supremely capable of producing the so-called melodic invention whenever this was needed. Much that his fastidious severity passed over because he wanted to keep his distance from rising Romanticism for the sake of objectification nevertheless is preserved as an aspect of his work. For example, the first movement of what became popular as the 'Moonlight' Sonata from op. 27 can be seen as a prototype of the nocturne later to be cultivated by Chopin. But there are also passages in Beethoven in which beauty of melody is just as intrinsic as in Schubert. I shall play such a passage from the slow movement of Beethoven's Third 'Razumovsky' Quartet of 1806, written when Schubert was still a small child.

> String Quartet op. 59,3, Eulenburg score, p. 15, second-lowest staff, after the double bar line, beginning with cadence 2, up to lowest staff, bar 2, closing with the A minor chord.

In utmost contrast to this type, and peculiar to Beethoven, are those beautiful passages – if we wish to call them that – whose beauty is generated only by relationships. I should like to give you two extreme examples. The theme of the variations in the 'Appassionata' begins:

> Piano Sonata op. 57, *Andante con moto*, first eight bars.

However, this theme only becomes really eloquent if it is heard directly after the coda of the first movement, a fully worked-out catastrophe.

> The same Sonata, close of first movement, from *più Allegro* onwards, then the variations theme.

After that explosion and collapse, the theme of the variations sounds as if it were bowing under a gigantic shadow, a crushing weight. The veiled quality of the sound seems to consolidate this sense of a heavy burden.

The Piano Trio in D major, op. 70, no. 1, is commonly known as the 'Geister' Trio, because of the *Largo assai ed espressivo*, one of Beethoven's conceptions in which he comes closest to the Romantic imago. Now allow yourselves to feel the effect, in direct succession, of the close of this movement and the beginning of the *presto* finale which follows it:

> Piano Trio in D major, op. 70,1, Peters edition, p. 170, last staff, from letter S to the fermata over the fourth bar of the *Presto*.

In isolation, the start of the *Presto* might not sound very striking; but after the close of the *Largo*, which is darkened beyond any classicist measure, the opening has something of the palely comforting dawn of a day which promises to put right all the havoc that has gone before; the expression of early bird-calls, without Beethoven's having in any way imitated birdsong.

The consoling passages in Beethoven are those in which, beyond the densely woven internal relationships of the musical structure which seem to leave no way out, something nevertheless dawns which is exempt from that structure, and does so with a power that makes it difficult to believe that what such passages say cannot be the truth and is subject to the relativity of art as something made by human beings. They are passages like the sentence from Goethe's *Elective Affinities*: 'Hope descended from the heavens like a star',[312] perhaps the highest which were ever granted to the language of music, and never to its individual works. Beethoven wrote such passages from a very early stage. The Piano Sonata in D minor, op. 31, no. 2, after a few transitional bars, sets out a theme expressing their essence.

> Piano Sonata op. 31,2, *Adagio*, bars 27–38, closing with the *piano* F major chord.

I would also draw your attention to the fact that, when this theme is repeated, a variant is inserted.

> From the same passage play successively bars 31 and 32 and then bars 35 and 36, upper voice only.

Through the addition of the song-like second step downwards from C to B♭ the seemingly extra-human theme is humanized, answered by the tears of one whom the earth has reclaimed.[313]

Beethoven's music fashions the character of dawning hope most perfectly in the retransition to the recapitulation of the *Adagio* from the First 'Razumovsky' Quartet, one of the greatest works of chamber music in the whole literature. As the simplicity of the passage, for which language offers no other term than that of the sublime, is equal to its perfection, one must experience the preceding development to feel its full effect. The passage will be played to you without any commentary from me.

> String Quartet op. 59,1, *Adagio*, Eulenburg score, p. 36, 3rd staff, last bar (46), up to p. 40, bar 84, closing with the F minor entry.

The antagonist of the character of hope in Beethoven is that of absolute seriousness, when music seems to throw off the last vestige of play. I shall show you two models of this, too. One is the truly implacable close of the short, intermezzo-like *Andante* from the Piano Concerto in G major.

> Fourth Piano Concerto, G major, the last eleven bars of the *Andante*, beginning with the arpeggio chord at *a tempo*.

While this passage speaks for itself, although the characteristic motif of the basses articulates the whole piece, the context of the following one needs to be explained. It comes from the first movement of the 'Kreutzer' Sonata and, like that from op. 59, no. 1, it is taken from the retransition to the recapitulation. Perhaps it may be said that, in many cases in Beethoven, all his powers of artistic shaping are concentrated on the preparation for the repetition, since this is the schematic aspect of the sonata form which, from the standpoint of autonomous composition, needs to be justified each time it occurs. As if to compensate for the schematic residue of the structure, he deploys his productive imagination to the utmost. After the development has ended in a kind of cadenza and the belief has been aroused that the music can start again from the beginning without further ado, Beethoven, with a chord of the fourth degree of the subdominant key, placed most threateningly in the bass register, lays open for a second the abyss of the passion which the sonata had unleashed earlier. The retransition, then the moment of seriousness and thus the start of the recapitulation are as follows:

> 'Kreutzer' Sonata, op. 47, Peters edition of the Violin Sonatas, p. 189, seven bars after letter I (begin with E on violin and left hand), up to p. 190, fermata before letter M.

Extract from the radio talk *'Schöne Stellen'* (GS 18, pp. 698ff) – written in 1965

APPENDIX III

Text 9: Beethoven's Late Style

In introducing a discussion[314] on late style in art with a few impromptu remarks on the late style of Beethoven, one cannot help thinking it slightly impertinent to adopt so casual an approach to this least casual of subjects. Perhaps one may seek an excuse in the fact that in the Beethoven literature, as far as I know, there is very little serious discussion of Beethoven's late style. To be sure, there is agreement on the fact that the works from about the Piano Sonata in A major op. 101 onwards – and the borderline can be drawn quite clearly – constitute an essentially different style – the late style of Beethoven. But if we then try to find out of what this style consists, we receive little help from the literature. One reason for this – I cannot avoid saying – lies in the current state of musicology, which up to now has been more interested in historical and biographical questions that in music itself. But another reason is a certain timidity towards Beethoven's late style which now prevails, and which is explainable. In my few words of introduction to this discussion I should like to take this timidity as my starting point.

In face of the late works of Beethoven – I am thinking primarily of the five last Quartets, and especially the *Grosse Fuge* with which this evening is to close – one has the feeling of something extraordinary, and of an extreme seriousness of a kind hardly to be found in any other music. At the same time, one feels an uncommon difficulty in saying precisely – I mean, in terms of the composition – in what this extraordinariness and seriousness actually consist. One therefore escapes into biography, trying to explain the sense of the extraordinary by the life of the old Beethoven, his illness, his difficulties with his nephew and all those things. In the sphere of music, at any rate, there is as yet no equivalent to studies of the problem of late style of the kind to be found in the essay by the Lenz editor Ernst Lewy on the language of the old Goethe,[315] for example.

I should like to demonstrate how much nonsense has been talked about the style of the late Beethoven by examining two characteristic attitudes, not in order to criticize but because they pinpoint complexes of problems which may enable something serious to be said. One of these highly problematic clichés, these *topoi*, is the blanket reference to the polyphony, the contrapuntal structure of Beethoven's last works. Now there are a number of very polyphonic movements and there are polyphonic passages in all the late works, at least to a greater extent than in the early and middle phases, the period of Beethoven's classicist style. But it would be fundamentally wrong to sum up the late style of Beethoven as essentially polyphonic. The polyphony is not wholly predominant. The polyphonic pieces are matched by numerous homophonic, indeed almost univocal, monodic parts. The great exception is the B♭ major Fugue, which was originally the Finale of the String Quartet op. 130 but was then separated by Beethoven, and which has now quite rightly been restored to its place at the end of the great cyclical work it was intended to close. There are two other such great fugues: one is the 'Et vitam venturi' of the *Missa Solemnis*, and the other is the Finale of the 'Hammerklavier' Sonata. In addition, there is a long fugal insertion in the Finale of op. 101, and the A♭ major Sonata op. 110 has a fugue at the end. But all this is not enough to characterize the style of late Beethoven as polyphonic. Critics have agreed to do this because they have told themselves that difficult and obscure is the same thing as complex and complicated, complicated is polyphonic, therefore late style equals polyphony, whether that is actually true or not.

But Beethoven's late style cannot be characterized either, as is often done, by the element of expressivity. Undoubtedly, there are some unusually expressive pieces. I would mention the theme of the variations of the E♭ major Quartet op. 127 and other very expressive details such as the start of the String Quartet op. 131. But there are also very distanced pieces, which avoid expression and, to put it paradoxically, take on their expression through leaving it out. If it can be said, therefore, that the late Beethoven cannot be characterized by the objectivity of a thoroughgoing polyphonic style, it is also true that he cannot be typified by the element of subjectivity in the sense of expression.

I should like to try to start out from what, in purely musical terms, motivates the timidity towards the late Beethoven, the feeling of extreme seriousness conveyed by his work. Listen, for example, to the opening of the B♭ major Quartet op. 130.

String Quartet in B♭ major, op. 130; 1st movement, bars 1–4.

Another example of this character of seriousness is the start of the C♯ minor Quartet: the exposition of a fugue at a slow tempo which is, at the same time, as I have indicated, of a highly expressive character.

String Quartet in C♯ minor, op. 131; 1st movement, bars 1–8.

And finally, another such instance is the start of the very last string quartet, the F major Quartet, that may also be used as an example here.

String Quartet in F major, op. 135; 1st movement, bars 1–17.

If I may characterize straight away what, for me at least, constitutes this element of seriousness, I would say that its basis is something almost overloaded with content, although this content itself is as if veiled. It is thus very difficult to indicate what it consists of and, above all, to find out how the content is communicated within the composition. One thing can be said: the passages you have heard have something in common, which is also common to most of the pieces included in Beethoven's late style. There is a statement by Goethe to the effect that ageing is a gradual stepping back from appearances.[316] These passages conform entirely to Goethe's dictum. There is in them something like a paring away of the sensuous, a spiritualization, as if the whole world of sensuous appearance were reduced in advance to the appearance of something spiritual. This is done in such a way that the appearance is no longer incorporated with the spiritual in an immediate unity, as something at once sensuous and spiritual, as the traditional aesthetic concept of the symbol teaches. In the opening bars of the B♭ major Quartet which you have heard, you can detect this spiritualized element asserting itself in a curious way against the musical material, if you pay attention to the crescendo, which here is not so much derived from the line of the music as inserted into it, as meanings are inserted into allegories, and which does not then lead to a *forte* but vanishes again in a *piano* – a device, incidentally, which was widely used by Beethoven. A similar crescendo is also found at the start of the C♯ minor

Quartet, where there is also an accent which disturbs the flow of the melody, which for its own purposes seems by no means to call for such an accent. Likewise, in the opening section of the F major Quartet, there are accents added from outside, not immanent in the music. It is as if the composer's hand were intervening with a certain violence in his composition. And a melody, in itself almost innocuous and thus all the more disconcerting, is divided up between different successive instruments, taking on a fragmented quality, as if it were internally fractured. Here, in the opening of the very last quartet, that in F major, you can also hear very clearly the tendency I spoke about earlier, towards single- or bare two-part writing, a tendency which is connected to the late Beethoven's rejection of all ornamentation, of everything in music which is mere beautiful illusion. It can be said that in the latest Beethoven the fabric, the interweaving of voices to form something harmoniously rounded, is deliberately cut back. In Beethoven's late style there is altogether something like a tendency towards dissociation, decay, dissolution, but not in the sense of a process of composition which no longer holds things together: the dissociation and disintegration themselves become artistic means, and works which have been brought to a rounded conclusion take on through these means, despite their roundedness, something spiritually fragmentary. Thus, in the works which are typical of the true late style of Beethoven, the closed acoustic surface which is otherwise so characteristic of the sound of the string quartet with its perfect balance, also disintegrates. In saying this I refer predominantly to Beethoven's last string quartets, since I find the late style crystallized in them most purely – more purely, for example, than in the late piano sonatas.

Now, I should like to stress that the spiritualization I am referring to is not simply a permeation of appearance by spirit, but something like a polarization. It is as if the subject were stepping back from his music and, in leaving appearance to itself, were allowing appearance to speak all the more eloquently. This is probably the reason why the late Beethoven has been seen, not without justification, both as extremely subjective and as objective in a constructivist sense. The late Beethoven dismissed the ideal of harmony. By this I do not mean harmony in the literal musical sense, for tonality and the predominance of the triad remain in place; I mean harmony in the sense of aesthetic harmony, or balance, roundedness, identity of the composing subject with his language. The language of music or the material of music speaks by itself in these late works, and only through the gaps in this language does the composing subject really speak at all, in a way perhaps not quite dissimilar to what took place with poetic language in the late style of Hölderlin.[317] It might be said that for this

reason Beethoven's late works, which are undoubtedly the most substantial and serious to be found anywhere in music, have at the same
time an element of the unauthentic, in that nothing which occurs in
them is simply that which it appears to be.

We need now to ask how this has come about. This aesthetic harmony, this wholeness in which unity exists between all the particip-
ating elements and which Beethoven brought into being in a manner
which had not existed before him, now becomes suspect to him as
illusion. This illusion is revealed by an element of the fictitious and
contrived, a decorativeness, in all classicism; and Beethoven becomes
aware of this in his artistic genius if not in his conscious reflections.
Beethoven's late works can therefore be understood as a critique of
his classicist works, using the word critique in its proper sense to
refer to an immanent logic of composition. In this connection I
should like to read a quotation from Marx, from the *Eighteenth
Brumaire*, which, it seems to me, throws extraordinarily penetrating
light on the situation I am concerned with here.

'Absorbed in money-making and in the peaceful warfare of competition, it' – that is, bourgeois society –

> forgot that the shades of ancient Rome had sat beside its cradle.
> Nevertheless, unheroic though bourgeois society may seem, heroism
> had been needed to bring it into being – heroism, self-sacrifice, the
> Reign of Terror, civil war, and the slaughter of the battle-fields. In the
> stern classical tradition of the Roman Republic, its gladiators found
> the ideals and the forms, the means of self-deception, they needed,
> that they might hide from themselves the bourgeois limitations of the
> struggle in which they were engaged, and might sustain their passion
> at the level appropriate to a great historic tragedy. In like manner,
> more than a century earlier, and in another phase of development,
> Cromwell and the English people had borrowed the phraseology, the
> emotions, and the illusions of the Old Testament as trappings for
> their own bourgeois revolution. As soon as they had reached the goal,
> as soon as the bourgeois transformation of English society had been
> effected, Locke supplanted Habakkuk.[318]

Thus Marx. Beethoven's development gave expression to this feeling of dissatisfaction with the drapery, with the claim to classical
totality. Critique here means simply to obey in the work the ideal
inherent in the problem posed by the work; it is an objective critique
arising from the compulsion of the subject matter, not from subjective reflection. Nevertheless, there is subjective, biographical support
for the idea that the development leading to the late work, and the
constitution of this work, were critical in nature. And this takes me
to a point which, I suspect, has been given far too little attention.

Beethoven's late style is not simply a reaction of a person who has grown old, or even of one who, having gone deaf, no longer has full mastery of the sensuous material. Beethoven *was* still fully able to write works conforming to the classicist ideal of his middle phase, and he *did* so in some of the most famous works of precisely this late phase. The first movement and the *Scherzo* of the Ninth Symphony are not late style but middle Beethoven, although they fall within the late period – just as, in general, Beethoven's symphonies are always less experimental and exposed than the piano and chamber music. The *Missa Solemnis*, too, although for different reasons, can hardly be counted among the works in the late style proper. And even in the last quartets there are individual movements – I would mention the Finale of the C♯ minor Quartet and, to a certain extent, that of the A minor Quartet – which show none of the tendencies of dissociation and alienation which I consider essential to the late style. Now I have already said that all this is carried on within the language of tonality. And it would be entirely to misunderstand the late Beethoven to equate the tendency towards alienation which he practised with the tendency of a later historical development to transcend tonality altogether. He does not do that. But he polarizes tonality. The tendency, I have said, is towards the single voice or towards polyphony, and not towards a midway harmony in the aesthetic sense; there is no balancing, no homoeostasis, no mediation of any sort as a middle term between the extremes, but, as in Hegel, only a mediation passing through the extremes. The music has, as it were, holes, artistically contrived fissures. This puts an end to the affirmative, hedonistic element otherwise always inherent in music, and in *this* respect there is a relationship between Beethoven and certain phenomena of modern music, as exemplified by Arnold Schoenberg's statement: 'My music is not lovely.' It probably also gives rise to the feeling of seriousness, a feeling which, in the last quartets, has been experienced as their relationship to death. The last quartet, with its wild, unbounded second movement and the fiddle tone of its last, is, indeed, something like a *danse macabre*.

I said that tonality is retained in these works, but it is also broken. This is done in many cases by the manner of composition and by the empty sound. As an example, listen to a few bars from the second theme of the first movement of the A minor Quartet op. 132, with the somewhat broken, imitative counterpoint.

String Quartet in A minor, op. 132; 1st movement, bars 48–53.

There is also frequent use of a technique of abrupt shifts instead of fully executed harmonic transitions, as in the fifth movement of the C♯ minor Quartet, in bar 10. Harmonically, too, the means of tonality are used to alienate tonality, by concealing the scale steps, as at the start of the Cavatina from the Quartet op. 130, where the tonic occurs too early, not at the entry of the main theme but already in the introduction, so that the perception of where the passage actually starts is blurred.

String Quartet in B♭ major, op. 130; 5th movement, bars 1–9.

In general, in late Beethoven, the harmonic accents are frequently separated from the rhythmical accents. Something like a dissociation between the different strata of the material occurs.

But there is yet another phenomenon in late Beethoven that I would bring to your attention, which is, perhaps, the most enigmatic of all. It involves seemingly conventional passages which are shrunken and overloaded with meaning, and which have something of the quality of magic spells. For example, the start of the *Presto* of op. 130, the first eight bars:

String Quartet in B♭ major, op. 130; 2nd movement, bars 1–8.

The trio theme from the *Scherzo* of the Ninth Symphony and even the 'Joy' theme, 'Freude, schöner Götterfunken', also have, when compared to these themes, this somewhat uncanny quality of a magic incantation. The trans-subjective element, which seems to have come down from tradition, is juxtaposed harshly, without coalescence, to the musical composition. Such quasi-allegorical, formula-like elements seem to me to play a certain role in very many late styles in music, even in that of Schoenberg, in a way which is comparable to what Lewy, in the book I mentioned about the language of the old Goethe, referred to as the emphasis on the abstract. If, according to a statement by Haydn which was modified by the musical historian Alfred Einstein, the popular and the erudite were intimately associated and merged in Viennese classicism, in late Beethoven these aspects diverge again. He does not seek to cleanse music of ready-made formulae, but to make these formulae transparent, to make them speak.

The principle of compression is also inherent in this style. The forms seldom run their whole course as in the middle period. The classical principle no longer prevails whereby each theme must be carried as far as its own intrinsic tendency demands, must be expanded, developed; often, it is enough to state a theme to exhaust it. For example, the first movement of the Sonata op. 101, a relatively short piece of two pages, nevertheless, through its compressed content, carries the weight of a large first movement of a sonata.

Finally, I would like to point out, without being able to deal with the matter at length, that the treatment of large forms in late Beethoven deviates widely from the norm, in that the importance of the development is reduced – as in the Quartet in A minor; the development section – and this is bound up with what I said about the anti-dynamic quality of this music – is no longer really decisive, ending in a kind of 'draw', and its contribution is only completed in the coda. Beethoven did much the same with form as with tonal harmony. Although he did not eliminate or violate the recapitulation in the last works, through the treatment of form he allowed its negative aspect to emerge; this manifested itself in the fact that the section after the recapitulation, the so-called coda, which was otherwise a mere appendage, took on decisive importance. Perhaps I could draw your attention to the first musicological study which has done justice to these matters, the work by the Göttingen lecturer Rudolf Stephan on the Finale of the B♭ major Quartet composed after the event,[319] the movement which will not be played today.[320]

Now, I will content myself with what I have already said, without daring to say anything about content, although this ought to be done. Or I shall say only this: in this process of musical demythologization, in the abandonment of the illusion of harmony, there is an expression of hope. In Beethoven's late style this hope flourished very close to the margin of renunciation, and yet is not renunciation. And I would think that this difference between resignation and renunciation is the whole secret of these pieces. I should like to illuminate this with a few bars. The dying hand – for all this really is bound up with death – releases what it had previously clutched fast, shaped, controlled, so that what is released becomes its higher truth. To gain a certain impression of this, listen to a short passage from the cavatina from the Quartet in B♭ major op. 130.

String Quartet in B♭ major, op. 130; 5th movement, bars 23–30.

Impromptu radio talk with musical examples; Norddeutscher Rundfunk, Hamburg – date of recording: 1966

ABBREVIATIONS

Unless they exist in an English translation, Adorno's writings are quoted from the German edition, *Gesammelte Schriften* (edited by Rolf Tiedemann in collaboration with Gretel Adorno, Susan Buck-Morss and Klaus Schultz), listed below. The English translations from which quotations are taken are also listed. The following abbreviations are used:

GS 1   *Philosophische Frühschriften*, 2nd edition, 1990
GS 2   *Kierkegaard. Konstruktion des Ästhetischen*, 2nd edition, 1990
GS 3   Theodor W. Adorno and Max Horkheimer, *Dialektik der Aufklärung. Philosophische Fragmente*, 2nd edition, 1984
        Translation: *Dialectic of Enlightenment*, transl. by John Cumming, London, Verso, 1979
GS 4   *Minima Moralia. Reflexionen aus dem beschädigten Leben*, 1980
        Translation: *Minima Moralia. Reflections from Damaged Life*, transl. by Edmund Jephcott, London, Verso, 1974
GS 5   *Zur Metakritik der Erkenntnistheorie/Drei Studien zu Hegel*, 3rd edition, 1990
GS 6   *Negative Dialektik/Jargon der Eigentlichkeit*, 4th edition, 1990
        Translation: *Negative Dialectics*, transl. by E.B. Ashton, London, Routledge & Kegan Paul, 1973
GS 7   *Ästhetische Theorie*, 5th edition, 1990
        Translations: *Aesthetic Theory*, transl. by C. Lenhardt, London, Routledge & Kegan Paul, 1984; *Aesthetic Theory*, transl. by Robert Hullot-Kentor, London, Athlone Press, 1997
GS 8   *Soziologische Schriften I*, 3rd edition, 1990
GS 10.1 *Kulturkritik und Gesellschaft I: Prismen/Ohne Leitbild*, 1977
        Translation: *Prisms*, transl. by Samuel and Shierry Weber, London, Spearman, 1967
GS 10.2 *Kulturkritik und Gesellschaft II: Eingriffe/Stichworte/Anhang*, 1977
GS 11 *Noten zur Literatur*, 3rd edition, 1990

GS 12   *Philosophie der neuen Musik*, 2nd edition, 1990
Translation: *Philosophy of Modern Music*, transl. by Anne G. Mitchell
and Wesley V. Blomster, New York, Seabury Press, 1973

GS 13   *Die musikalischen Monographien*, 3rd edition, 1985
Translation of monograph on Mahler: *Mahler. A Musical
Physiognomy*, transl. by Edmund Jephcott, Chicago and London,
University of Chicago Press, 1992

GS 14   *Dissonanzen/Einleitung in die Musiksoziologie*, 3rd edition, 1990
Translation: *Introduction to the Sociology of Music*, transl. by E.B.
Ashton, New York, Continuum, 1976

GS 15   Theodor W. Adorno and Hanns Eisler, *Komposition für den Film/
Theodor W. Adorno, Der getreue Korrepititor*, 1976

GS 16   *Musikalische Schriften I–III: Klangfiguren/Quasi una
fantasia/Musikalische Schriften III*, 2nd edition, 1990
Translation: *Quasi una fantasia: Essays on Music and Culture*, transl.
by Rodney Livingstone, London, Verso, 1992

GS 17   *Musikalische Schriften IV: Moments musicaux/Impromptus*, 1982

GS 18   *Musikalische Schriften V*, 1984

GS 19   *Musikalische Schriften VI*, 1984

Bibliographical data on two works on Beethoven frequently quoted by Adorno
should also be given here; from the second quotation onwards they are referred
to only by the author's name, followed by the title:

Paul Bekker, *Beethoven*. 2nd edition, Berlin undated [1912].

Wolfgang A. Thomas-San-Galli, *Ludwig van Beethoven. Mit vielen Porträts,
Notenbeispielen und Handschriftenfaksimiles*, Munich 1913.

Numbers preceded by 'fr.' refer to the sequential numbering of the individual
fragments; in the text section of this edition, these numbers are to be found in
square brackets at the end of each fragment.

EDITOR'S NOTES

1 Colourful travel tickets and place names are among the mundane things into which, for Adorno as for Walter Benjamin before him, something of the promise of metaphysics had been decanted. In 1934 he wrote to Benjamin that he was writing 'on the countless different types of multicoloured London bus tickets, a piece which has remarkable affinites with what you write on colours in *Berliner Kindheit*' (Adorno, *Über Walter Benjamin. Aufsätze, Artikel, Briefe*, 2nd edition, Frankfut/Main 1990, pp. 113f; for the text of the piece, cf. *Frankfurter Adorno Blätter II*, Munich 1993, p. 7). On place names the author of *Negative Dialectics* wrote:

> What is a metaphysical experience? If we disdain projecting it upon allegedly primal religious experiences, we are most likely to visualize it as Proust did, in the happiness, for instance, that is promised by village names like Applebachsville, Wind Gap, or Lords Valley. One thinks that going there would bring the fulfilment, as if there were such a thing. (*Negative Dialectics*, transl. by E.B. Ashton, London, Routledge & Kegan Paul, 1973, p. 373)

2 A similar argument is to be found in Thomas Mann's *Doctor Faustus*, where it is said of certain compositions that they are intended 'more for the reading eye than the ear' (Thomas Mann, *Doctor Faustus*, transl. by H.T. Lowe-Porter, Harmondsworth, Penguin, 1968, p. 61). Whether this motif was the outcome of discussions between the novelist and Adorno cannot be known. At any rate, Adorno wrote some of his notes on Beethoven in the years 1944–8, when he was advising Mann on musical questions during the writing of the novel. Mann himself reported that Adorno had read to him from his notes on Beethoven (cf. n. 275). This personal closeness must be the explanation for the parallels which occur not infrequently between Adorno's notes and the text of *Doctor Faustus*. – On Adorno's cooperation with Thomas Mann cf. Rolf Tiedemann, '"Mitdichtende Einfühlung". Adornos Beiträge zum "Doktor Faustus" – noch einmal', in *Frankfurter Adorno Blätter I*, Munich 1992, pp. 9ff; on the opposite viewpoint concerning the 'danger' of reading music, cf. fr. 239 and n. 214.

3 The Austrian violinist Arnold Josef Rosé (1863–1946), a brother-in-law of Gustav Mahler, was the leader of the string quartet named after him; in his *Introduction to the Sociology of Music* Adorno wrote that through this group he had got to know 'the entire traditional quartet literature, above all Beethoven' (GS 14, p. 278).

4 In 1925 Adorno went to Vienna to study composition under Alban Berg; he spent time in the city fairly frequently up to 1933.

5 The composer and pianist Eugen d'Albert (1864–1932), like the pianist Conrad Ansorge (1862–1930), was among the most famous interpreters of Beethoven in the first third of the century.

6 Adorno also discussed the 'child's image' of music, meaning the image of music one has as a child – which can be 'closer to the truth' than all the theory and practice of adults – in his monograph on Mahler, whose compositions contained, in a sense, such children's images. It is no accident that names of villages in the Odenwald and colourful train tickets reappear in that study too. When, in the first movement of the Fourth Symphony,

> suddenly the main theme continues from the middle of its restatement, this moment is like the child's joy at being abruptly transported from the forest to the old-fashioned market place of Miltenberg. [...] The sound of a band is to the musical sensorium of the child much like brightly coloured railway tickets to its optical sense [...]. Not lacking among the children's images in Mahler's music are the vanishing snatches from musical processions, flashing far off and promising more than they ever fulfil in deafening closeness [...]. (Adorno, *Mahler: A Musical Physiognomy*, transl. by Edmund Jephcott, Chicago and London, University of Chicago Press, 1992, p. 55)

Cf. also fr. 204, in which Adorno uses the concept of the child's image in a slightly different sense.

7 Cf. Rudolf Kolisch, 'Tempo and Character in Beethoven's Music', in *The Musical Quarterly*, vol. XXIX, no. 2 (April 1943), pp. 169ff, and no. 3 (July 1943), pp. 291ff. Adorno had been a close friend of the Austrian violinist and string quartet leader Rudolf Kolisch since the mid-1920s (cf. the article 'Kolisch und die neue Interpretation' in GS 19, pp. 460ff). Adorno's views on Kolisch's attempt to reconstruct the authentic Beethovenian tempi are to be found in his letter to Kolisch of 16 November 1943, reproduced on pp. 179–81 of this edition, and in fr. 367.

8 Among the many musical analyses published by Adorno's friend, the composer, conductor and musicologist René Leibowitz (1913–72) up to 1953 – the present note was written in that year – Adorno was probably thinking primarily of the book *Introduction à la musique de douze sous. Les Variations pour orchestre op. 31 d'Arnold Schoenberg* (Paris 1949). Adorno's library also contains other works by Leibowitz: *L'artiste et sa conscience. Esquisse d'une dialectique de la conscience artistique. Préface de Jean-Paul Sartre* (Paris 1950) and *Histoire de l'opéra* (Paris 1957). In 1964 Adorno wrote an enthusiastic review of a gramophone recording of Beethoven's symphonies conducted by Leibowitz (cf. 'Beethoven im Geist der Moderne', GS 19, pp. 535ff).

9 At about the same time as he wrote this note, Adorno was writing 'Der Artist als Statthalter', an essay occasioned by the publication of the German translation of Paul Valéry's 'Degas Danse Dessin' (cf. GS 11, pp. 114ff; also cf. n. 75).

10 At the beginning of this paragraph the manuscript contains a '1)'; as this number has no counterpart it is omitted in the printed version.

11 On the comparison with Eurydice, see n. 59, and the passage from the *Philosophy of Modern Music* quoted in that note.

12 The insignificance of the starting point – of the individual detail, the theme, and finally the musical material itself – is one of the central ideas of Adorno's theory on Beethoven (cf. frs 29, 50, 53, and so on); the idea is probably derived from the opening of Hegel's *Logic*, which posits 'pure Being' and 'pure Nothingness' as 'the same', and defines truth as 'this movement of the direct disappearance of one into the other' as 'becoming' (cf. Hegel, *Werke in 20 Bänden*, ed. by Eva Moldenhauer and Karl Markus Michel, Frankfurt/Main 1969, vol. 5, p. 83). Like a number of other motifs which Adorno's thought derived from the experience of Beethoven, it was taken over and varied in other works. In the *Philosophy of Modern Music* he writes in very Hegelian terms that 'Beethoven developed a musical essence out of nothingness in order to be able to redefine it as a process of becoming' (*Philosophy of Modern Music*, transl. by Anne G. Mitchell and Wesley V. Blomster, New York, Seabury Press, 1973, p. 77); earlier, in the 'Versuch über Wagner', he had written:

> In Beethoven the individual detail, the 'idea', is artfully insignificant, wherever the idea of totality has precedence; the motif is introduced as something quite abstract in itself, merely the principle of pure becoming; and as the whole is derived from it, the individual detail, which is engulfed in it, is at the same time concretized and confirmed by the whole. (GS 13, p. 49)

In the late, posthumously published *Aesthetic Theory*, this motif appears under the heading of the crisis of illusion:

> To appreciate the depth of the crisis of illusion, one must take into account that it has repercussions even for music, which on the face of it seems to have no use for illusion to begin with. In music fictitious elements die off even in their sublimated form; i.e. not only elements like expressions of non-existent feelings, but also structural aspects like the fiction of a totality, which has been exposed as unrealisable. In great music such as Beethoven's, but probably also in art far beyond the confines of the temporal arts, the so-called primal elements unearthed by analysis are often eminently trifling. In fact, it is only when these elements approximate nothing that they, as pure becoming, congeal into a whole. As distinct segments, they always strive to be something, such as a motif or a theme. Integral art is lured down into amorphousness by the inherent nullity of its elementary particles. And the force of this attraction increases with the degree of organization of art. It is this amorphous quality that alone enables the work of art to fulfil its integrative function. (Adorno, *Aesthetic Theory*, transl. by C. Lenhardt, London, Routledge & Kegan Paul, 1984, pp. 147–8)

On the parallel between Beethoven and Hegel with regard to the individual and the whole, cf. frs 49–57 and n. 72.

13 The notion of the aura was introduced into aesthetics and the sociology of art by Walter Benjamin. Aura, he argued, was the 'unique manifestation of something distant, however near it may be' (Benjamin, *Gesammelte Schriften*, in collaboration with Theodor W. Adorno and Gershom Scholem; ed. by Rolf Tiedemann and Hermann Schweppenhäuser, Frankfurt/Main 1972–89, vol. 1, p. 479; cf. ibid., p. 647, and vol. 2, p. 378); aura in this sense is possessed by both natural and historical objects, and especially traditional works of art. Auratic appearance is the basis of the 'beautiful illusion' attributed to art by the idealist aesthetic. Adorno took over Benjamin's theory of aura, discussing it and developing

it in many of his own writings: '[. . .] what is called aura is known to artistic experience as the atmosphere of the artwork, that whereby the nexus of the artwork's elements points beyond this nexus and allows each individual element to point beyond itself' (*Aesthetic Theory*, transl. by R. Hullot-Kentor, London, Athlone Press, 1997, p. 274). On Adorno's concept of aura see, above all, the quotation from the *Philosophy of Modern Music* in n. 170. – Taking up Adorno's idea, Jürgen Uhde and Renate Wieland discuss aura in music in *Denken und Spielen. Studien zu einer Theorie der musikalischen Darstellung*, Kassel 1988, pp. 24ff.

14 Cf. fr. 61

15 For example, the well-known definition by Hanslick: 'The content and subject matter of music consist solely of patterns of sound in motion' (Eduard Hanslick, *Vom Musikalisch-Schönen. Ein Beitrag zur Revision der Ästhetik der Tonkunst*, Darmstadt 1976 [reprint of 1st edition, Leipzig 1854], p. 32); Adorno criticized the thesis of sound patterns in motion in 'Music and Language: A Fragment' (cf. *Quasi una fantasia: Essays on Music and Culture*, transl. by Rodney Livingstone, London, Verso, 1992, pp. 1–6).

16 The Austrian music critic Ernst Decsey (1870–1941) described

> how I came to be on a friendly footing with Mahler [. . .]. In an essay on his Third Symphony I had remarked that, in order to understand the trumpet passage in the C minor movement, you need to think of Lenau's poem: 'Lieblich war die Maiennacht, Silberwölkchen flogen'; just as a solitary sound came through the forest in the poem, so it does in the music. Mahler was quite surprised by this. He invited me to call on him: 'That's what I thought of too, the same poem, the same mood. How did you know?' From that hour I was admitted to his circle, and also became a *socius malorum*. (Ernst Decsey, 'Stunden mit Mahler', in *Die Musik*, vol. 10 [1910/11], p. 356 [no. 18; 2 June 1911])

17 Like that of the aura, Adorno took over the idea of the dialectical image from Benjamin; however, in his theory he adapted it in a characteristic way. At an early stage, in his inaugural lecture of 1931 (cf. GS 1, pp. 325ff), he developed a programme of philosophy as *interpretation*: he argued that in history it was necessary to decipher enigmatic figures; the images into which Being condensed, when viewed in terms of physiognomy, were to reveal themselves as script through their dialectic. Beethoven's dialectical image, which was to be sketched in the book planned by Adorno, is discussed in fr. 250. – On Benjamin's use of the term cf. Rolf Tiedemann, *Dialektik im Stillstand. Versuche zum Spätwerk Walter Benjamins*, Frankfurt/Main 1983, pp. 32ff; on Adorno's use of the term, Rolf Tiedemann, 'Begriff Bild Name. Über Adornos Utopie der Erkenntniss', in *Frankfurter Adorno Blätter II*, Munich 1993, pp. 92ff.

18 For a time Adorno kept two notebooks simultaneously: one in which, in the manner of a diary, he continuously noted diverse ideas, and less frequently events, and a second one reserved for notes on special, usually large-scale works he was planning. The following notes, written in 1951 and 1952, were recorded first in the so-called Notebook II, an exercise book bound in brown cardboard in octavo format, which was used for ongoing notes from 1949 to 1953. In early 1953 Adorno copied them into the brown leather-bound book (=Notebook 14) which he used for notes on Beethoven and a number of projects from 1953 to 1966. – The printed edition follows the texts of Notebook 14 as the later version. Their

arrangement here is a makeshift solution: on one hand, the individual notes refer to the most divergent subjects, but, on the other, they should not be torn apart. In the present context, the reader may take them – with the notes in the following fragment 19 – as anticipatory sketches of themes and tasks which the author would have filled out in the text yet to be written.

19 The formulation stems from a letter of August 1812, allegedly by Beethoven, to Bettina von Arnim: 'Your applause is dearest to me in the whole world. I told Goethe what I thought about the affect applause has on people like us, and that we want to be heard with understanding by our own kind. Emotion is a matter for females (pardon me), but music has to strike fire from a man's soul' (Beethoven, *Sämtliche Briefe*, ed. by Erich Kastner, reprinted from the new edition by Julius Kapp, Tutzing 1975, p. 228). The letter as a whole is undoubtedly a forgery, as has long been recognized by the Goethe and Beethoven literature. However, some of its formulations – including the one quoted, which Adorno probably adduced from Kolisch ('Tempo and Character in Beethoven's Music' [n. 7], p. 293) – may be authentic.

20 On the distinction, fundamental to Adorno's philosophy of music, between tonality as the most universal structural element in traditional music and something located below it, which Schoenberg called subcutaneous, cf.: 'What he [that is, Schoenberg] designated as the "subcutaneous" – the fabric of individual musical events, grasped as the ineluctable moments of an internally coherent totality – breaks through the surface, becomes visible and manifests itself independently of all stereotyped forms' (Adorno, *Prisms*, transl. by Samuel and Shierry Weber, London 1967, p. 153; cf. also GS 18, p. 436).

21 A source for Jemnitz's remark has not been discovered. – Sándor (Alexander) Jemnitz (1890–1963), Hungarian composer, conductor and musicologist; Adorno may possibly be recalling a remark by Jemnitz, whom he knew well, in a letter or a conversation.

22 Cf. Heinrich Schenker, *Beethoven: Fünfte Symphonie. Darstellung des musikalischen Inhaltes nach der Handschrift unter fortlaufender Berücksichtigung des Vortrages und der Literatur*, Vienna 1925 (reprinted 1970).

23 Cf. Paul Bekker, *Beethoven*, 2nd edition, Berlin 1912, p. 298: Beethoven was interested in

> a text by Rudolph vom Berge. The work, which a friend from the composer's youth, Amenda, sent him with extravagant praise from Kurland in March 1815, is entitled 'Bacchus. Grand lyrical opera in three acts'. Beethoven seriously considered [. . .] this plan. Among his sketches he even made a number of strange notes. 'It must be derived from the Bacchus motif', we read in one place. And in another: 'Dissonances perhaps not resolved in the whole opera, or quite differently; since our refined music is quite inconceivable in these times, the subject must be treated in a thoroughly pastoral way.' However, he seems to have gradually formed misgivings about the play. It was displaced by other plans and forgotten.

24 Benjamin uses this expression in his 'Deutsche Menschen' of the old Goethe, when analysing a subjunctive in one of Goethe's last letters (cf. Walter Benjamin, *Gesammelte Schriften* [n. 13], vol. 4, p. 211).

25 Beethoven's irritation is reported by Gerhard von Breuning, who wanted to have a lithograph of Haydn's birthplace framed for Beethoven.

[He] took the picture to his piano teacher, who made a frame for it and added in the bottom border: 'Jos. Hayden's birthplace in Rohrau'. Beethoven was furious when he saw that the name Haydn had been misspelled. His face grew red with anger, and he asked me fiercely: 'Who wrote that? . . . What is the ass's name? Such an ignoramus wants to be a piano teacher, a musician, and doesn't even know how to spell the name of a master like Haydn.' (Maynard Solomon, *Beethoven. Biographie*, transl. by Ulrike von Puttkamer, Frankfurt/Main 1990, pp. 329f)

26 Date at foot of note: 'Los Angeles, 25 June 1944 at Franz Röhn's'. – Röhn was a friend of both Adorno and his wife, probably from their youth; he lived in Los Angeles and visited Adorno in Frankfurt in the 1960s when he was almost seventy. His few letters surviving among Adorno's posthumous papers reveal scientific and artistic interests. No further information on him has been obtained.

27 Fr. 21 was written in June or July 1948. – In January 1969, at a meeting with the publisher Siegfried Unseld, Adorno developed a plan for eight books that he still intended to write; the last was the book on Beethoven, which was to be given the title *Beethoven. The Philosophy of Music*; the Editor has chosen this for his own edition.

28 Adorno's source has not been identified. His posthumous papers include the edition of Clemens Brentano, *Gesammelte Werke*, ed. by Heinz Amelung and Karl Vietör, Frankfurt/Main 1923; the lines quoted are in vol. 1, p. 141.

29 At the beginning of the note: '(for Chapter 1)'.

30 At the beginning of the note: '(?)'.

31 Syntactical error in manuscript.

32 Syntactical error in manuscript.

33 Adorno gave more thought to the definition of music as the 'logic of the judgement-less synthesis'; for example, in 'Music and Language: A Fragment', he writes:

> In contrast to philosophy and the sciences, which impart knowledge, the elements of art which come together for the purpose of knowledge never culminate in a decision. But is music really a non-decisive language? Of its various intentions one of the most urgent seems to be the assertion. 'This is how it is', the decisive, even the magisterial confirmation of something that has not been explicitly stated. In the supreme moments of great music, and they are often the most violent moments – one instance is the beginning of the recapitulation in the first movement of the Ninth Symphony – this intention becomes eloquently unambiguous by virtue of the sheer power of its context. Its echo can be heard, in a parodied form, in trivial pieces of music. Musical form, the totality in which a musical context acquires authenticity, cannot really be separated from the attempt to graft the gesture of decision on to the non-decisive medium. On occasion this succeeds so well that the art stands on the brink of yielding to assault from the dominating impulse of logic. (*Quasi una fantasia*, p. 4; cf. GS 16, pp. 651f)

And in his *Aesthetic Theory* he writes, referring to the work of art in general:

> The notion of judgment then becomes modified when we move from communicative utterances to poetic ones. To be sure, works of art are like judgments in that they, too, effect a synthesis. But art's synthesis is non-judgmental. It is impossible to tell what any single work of art states or what might be its so-called message. (1984 edition, p. 180)

34 Date at foot of note: 'Christmas 1944'.

35 For example, in the *Phenomenology of Mind*: 'What matters [...] in the study of science is to engage in conceptual exertion.' Hegel, *Werke* [n. 12], vol. 3, p. 56). And: 'True thoughts and scholarly insight are gained only through conceptual work' (ibid., p. 65).

36 'Heterogenous continuum' is a term Adorno found in Rickert:

> What comes into our consciousness when we think of the representational cognition of a reality existing in space and time consists in the fact that this reality is at each point *different* to what it is at every other point, so that we never know how much more new and unknown material it still has to show us. We can therefore only call the real, in contradistinction to the unreal homogeneous continuum of mathematics, a *heterogeneous continuum* [...]. (Heinrich Rickert, *Die Grenzen der naturwissenschaftlichen Begriffsbildung. Eine logische Einleitung in die historischen Wissenschaften*, 3rd and 4th editions, Tübingen 1921, p. 28)

37 In his essay on Hegel, 'Skoteinos oder Wie zu lesen sei', Adorno conceived the relationship between Hegel and Beethoven more in terms of an analogy:

> Music of the Beethovenian type in which, ideally, the recapitulation, that is, the recollection of complexes set out earlier, is intended as the outcome of the development and therefore of the dialectic – such music has a character analogous [to the dynamic of Hegel's thought], but one which transcends mere analogy. Even highly organized music must be listened to multidimensionally, both forwards and backwards at the same time. This is demanded by the principle of its organization in time: time can be articulated only through differences between the known and the not yet known, the existent and the new; a regressive consciousness is a condition of progression itself. One must know a whole movement, be retrospectively aware at each moment of what has gone before. The individual passages are to be understood as its consequences; the meaning of divergent repetition must be realized, the recurrent perceived not merely as an architectonic correspondence but as something that has come about through a compelling necessity. It may be helpful to an understanding of this analogy, which seems to relate to Hegel's innermost thought, to appreciate that the conception of totality as an identity mediated within itself by non-identity translates a formal law of art to the sphere of philosophy. This translation is itself philosophically motivated.' (GS 5, pp. 366f)

38 The idea of the *tour de force* is formulated most trenchantly in *Aesthetic Theory*:

> That authentic works, too, are a *tour de force* realizing the unrealizable can also be demonstrated. Bach [...] was a virtuoso in his ability to reconcile the irreconcilable. [...] An equally compelling case could be made for the paradox of a *tour de force* in Beethoven; more precisely, in his case the paradox would be that something emerges out of nothing, which would be an aesthetical-bodily verification of the first few conceptualizations of Hegel's *Logic*. (1984 edition, p. 156)

39 This note is related to another written shortly before: 'What I called in Beethoven the *tour de force*, the paradox of something arising from nothing, is precisely the floating quality of Hegel's philosophy – its way of keeping itself in the air – the "absolute"' (Notebook B, p. 51). – In Adorno's work on Hegel, 'Aspekte der Hegelschen Philosophie', the idea of 'floating' is developed further:

> Hegel's subject–object is a subject. This explains the contradiction, unresolved according to Hegel's own demand for consistency on all sides, that while the subject–object dialectic, devoid of any superordinate abstract con-

cept, constitutes the whole, it is yet fulfilled as the life of the absolute spirit. According to this view, the quintessence of the conditional is the unconditional. The floating aspect of Hegel's philosophy, the keeping-itself-aloft, its permanent *skandolon*: the name of the highest speculative concept, that of the absolute, of that which is utterly detached, is, literally, the name of that floating quality. (GS 5, p. 261)

40 On the meaning of 'maxims' in Beethoven's late work, that is, on *Beethoven's relationship to proverbial wisdom*, cf., for example, frs 322 and 340, but above all Text 9 above, pp. 192f. – On Hegel's elimination of the 'axiom' without contradiction, cf. *Negative Dialectics*: 'It is not up to philosophy to exhaust things according to scientific usage, to reduce the phenomena to a minimum of propositions; there are hints of that in Hegel's polemic against Fichte, whom he accused of starting out with a "dictum"' (p. 13). In another place Adorno wrote that it was a 'fundamental motif of Hegel's philosophy that it could not be distilled down to any "axiom" or general principle' (GS 5, p. 252). No equivalent formulation could be found in Hegel. Adorno was probably thinking of statements like the following:

> This delusion that something posited merely for the sake of reflection must stand at the head of a system as its highest absolute principle, or that the essence of every system can be expressed in a sentence that would be absolute for thought, does scant justice to a system to which its judgement is applied. (Hegel, *Werke* [n. 12], vol. 2, p. 36)

41 Date at end of note: 'Frankfurt, Oct. 56'.
42 Hegel formulates it as: 'The true is the whole' (Hegel, *Werke* [n. 12], vol. 3, p. 24); Adorno's *Minima Moralia* rebuts this with: 'The whole is the false' (*Minima Moralia Reflections from Damaged Life*, transl. by Edmund Jephcott, London, Verso, 1974, p. 50). And as late as the essay 'Erfahrungsgehalt' of 1958 he argues as if Hegel had declared the whole to be the true: 'The claim that the particular is burst asunder by the whole becomes illegitimate, since that whole itself is not, as the famous statement in the *Phenomenology* asserts, the true, and because the affirmative and self-assured reference to the whole, as if it were something securely possessed, is fictitious' (GS 5, p. 324). – Regarding the dating, it should be noted that the text of fr. 29 was written in 1939, and Adorno's statement that the whole is the untrue only in 1942 (cf. Adorno, 'Aus einem "Scribble-In Book"', in *Perspektiven Kritischer Theorie. Eine Sammlung zu Hermann Schweppenhäusers 60. Geburtstag*, ed. by Christoph Türcke, Lüneburg 1988, p. 9).
43 Schoenberg's formulation regarding the *history* of a theme, which is also quoted in fr. 32 as the *fate* of a theme, has not been traced.
44 Adorno gave a different interpretation of the same passage from op. 59,1 in *Aesthetic Theory*; cf. Text 6 above, pp. 171f.
45 This follows the manuscript. What Bekker wrote is: '[...] – everything together gives the impression of a conjuration of spirits, a scene in which a gigantic shadow suddenly bursts out like a demon which has been called up, shows itself in its terrifying majesty and then, after painfully screeching dissonances, slides back soundlessly into the abyss.' (Bekker, *Beethoven*, p. 271).
46 Bekker's 'good formulation' referred to in the footnote reads:

> The main theme [of the first movement of the Ninth Symphony] itself, on its first appearance, defines the content of the whole piece in lineaments of

bronze. What follows is mere demonstration. Just as the basic idea reappears almost unchanged at the end, we, too, stand at the same point from which we started out. We have not moved forwards as in the other symphonies. But we have sounded the regions above and below this point up to the furthest heights, down to the most mysterious depths. It is in this principle of a structure constituted not by expansion of the thematic content but by its analysis and dissection that the novelty of this contemplative rather than experiential symphonic work lies, its inspirational power for later generations.' (Ibid., p. 273; underlined in Adorno's copy and marked 'Good' in the margin)

– In his copy of Hegel's *Aesthetics*, the page also referred to in the footnote has a marginal note by Adorno: 'Raising of negativity to consciousness as something positive. "Standing firm".' The passage which follows has triple underlining and is marked 'Very fine':

> Even if art confines itself to offering paintings of the passions for contemplation, indeed, even if it were to flatter these passions, it would still have, at least, the mitigating effect of making the human being conscious of what, otherwise, he merely, directly, *is*. For now the human being *contemplates* his impulses and inclinations; and whereas, otherwise, they carry him along without reflection, he now sees them outside himself and begins, since they confront him as something objective, to exercise his freedom with regard to them. (Hegel, *Vorlesungen über die Ästhetik*, in *Werke* [n. 12], vol. 13, p. 74)

47 The 'Note on Rembrandt', probably written in late 1939, reads:

> 'Herewith ends all human desire'. On Rembrandt's self-portrait in the Frick Gallery: this painting seems to me to record a primal bourgeois experience. It could almost be called that of the law of value. Here the exchange of equivalents means: there is no happiness which is not paid for by an equal measure of sorrow. In this work, life's wisdom means the knowledge that, for every desire for happiness, a bill will be presented. But the painter is one who shows himself equal to this knowledge. His happiness is to witness the balance sheet of happiness, on which no residue remains. The stoical gaze of the physician is that of the painter as it rests on its object. All happiness is balanced by decay. There is a peculiar power of consolation in this close-up, unemotional – one might say: practical – manner of coming to terms with decay and death. The greatness of such paintings lies in the fact that they have been *painted* in face of such experience. ('*Buntes Buch*' [= Notebook 12], p. 7)

48 Cf. fr. 29 and n. 43.

49 In *Philosophy of Modern Music* Adorno writes: 'As mere derivation, continuation disavows the inescapable claim of twelve-tone music that it is equidistant in all its moments from a central point' (p. 73). And also, earlier: 'In any music, in which every single tone is transparently determined by the construction of the whole work, the difference between the essential and the coincidental disappears. Such music maintains in all its moments the same distance from a central point' (p. 59).

50 This idea is adumbrated, for example, in ibid., p. 102, where the abolition of the theme in twelve-tone music is discussed, and this kind of music is compared to the 'form of variation prior to Beethoven, which engaged in circumscription without any particular goal'.

51 Cf. the lecture 'Das Altern der Neuen Musik':

> Beethoven's most powerful formal effects are produced when a recurrent element, which once existed merely as a theme, now emerges as a result, thus taking on an entirely different meaning. Frequently, the meaning of what has

gone before is created only retrospectively by the return of such an element. The opening of a recapitulation can engender the feeling of something enormous that has gone before, even though this enormous thing was never present at its supposed place of origin. (GS 14, p. 152)

52 Date at end of note: '1 June 1950'.

53 Further discussions of the problem of the recapitulation in Beethoven are to be found in later works by Adorno, for example, the monograph on Mahler of 1960:

> The classicism of Beethoven's first movements – in the Eroica, the Fifth, and the Seventh – was no longer a model for Mahler because Beethoven's solution of recreating the subjectively weakened objective forms from further subjectivity could no longer be repeated with truthfulness. [. . .] Even in Beethoven the static symmetry of the recapitulations threatened to disown the dynamic intent. The danger of academic form that increased after him is founded on the content. Beethovenian solemnity, the accentuation of meaning in the moment of symphonic release, reveals a decorative, illusory aspect. Beethoven's mightiest symphonic movements pronounce a celebratory 'That is it' in repeating what has already existed in any case, present what is merely a regained identity as the Other, assert it as significant. The classical Beethoven glorifies what is because it cannot be other than it is by demonstrating its irresistibility. (*Mahler*, p. 63)

And later, also in the Mahler monograph:

> The recapitulation was the crux of the sonata form. It revokes what since Beethoven had been the decisive element, the dynamic of the development, in a way comparable to the effect of a film on a spectator who stays in his seat at the end and watches the beginning again. Beethoven mastered this by a *tour de force* that became a rule with him: at the fertile moment at the beginning of the recapitulation he presents the result of the dynamic, the evolution as the affirmation and justification of what has been, what was there in any case. That is his complicity with the guilt of the great idealistic systems, with the dialectician Hegel, for whom in the end the essential character of negations, and so of becoming, amounted to a theodicy of being. In the recapitulation, music, as a ritual of bourgeois freedom, remained, like the society in which it is and which is in it, enslaved to mythical unfreedom. It manipulates the natural relationship circling within it as if what recurs, by virtue of its mere recurrence, were more than it is, were metaphysical meaning itself, the 'idea'. (Ibid., p. 94)

Finally, in the essay 'Form in der neuen Musik', written in 1966, we read:

> The recapitulation is already latently problematic in the work of Beethoven. That he, the subjectively dynamic critic of all musical ontology, did not sacrifice the recapitulation is not to be explained by his respect for custom. He registered the functional connection between the recapitulation and tonality, which still held primacy for him, and the possibilities of which he worked out fully. Admittedly, there is also the report of Beethoven's curious dictum that one should give no more thought to the basso continuo than to the catechism – almost as if he were trying by an act of will to suppress his doubts about the precondition of everything he produced. That he drew back at that point is not evidence of an unshakable tradition. It may have dawned on him that once the language of music and the musical form had diverged, they could not easily be forced together into a unity again. For the sake of realizing individual impulses he preserved the idiom as a restriction on freedom, in a way deeply akin to Hegel's idealism. As in Hegel, the problem left its marks on his procedure. Only within a time dimension which has been

liberated and made in the strictest sense thematic does Beethoven's recapitulation find its legitimation. The recurrence of the same element after a dynamic development which strives to transcend repetition must, in its turn, be motivated by its antithesis, the dynamic. For this reason the large-scale developments in Beethoven's movements, which in spirit are really symphonic, revolve almost always around the turning points, the critical moments at the start of the recapitulation. Because the recapitulation is no longer possible, it becomes a *tour de force*, the focal point. Beethoven's classicism, despite its seemingly strict adherence to musical logic, harbours a paradox. Its greatest achievements are wrested from its own impossibility, while at the same time, through the sense of contrived effects regularly conveyed by those moments, it prophesies the impossibility which by now has been heightened to a total crisis of musical form. (GS 16, p. 612)

– On the recapitulation in Beethoven, see also Text 1 above, pp. 41f.

54 Just as the idea that Beethoven reproduced the traditional forms based on tonality out of subjective freedom is central in Adorno's thought, a comparison of this idea with his synthetic *a priori* judgements derives from Adorno's earliest conceptions, about which his 'theory' on Beethoven crystallized only later. He probably formulated the comparison for the first time in the following aphorism, published as early as 1928:

> On the relationship between what was meant by both Kant and Beethoven, neither reliably moral attitudes nor the long since defunct pomp of the creative personality can decide. Kant himself once said of the latter that there was little dignity to be had from it, and its duplicity is fully exposed by the alienated constructions of the late Beethoven. Perhaps only the emphatic personality, detached from the social base, is able to form such works. However, that person is forced out of the work by its planned design as the mighty creation cools. Something of this is present in both Beethoven and Kant, uniting them in the same historical location. Just as, in the hierarchy of Kant's system, the slender region of *a priori* synthetic judgements preserved the contour of vanishing ontology within a narrower compass, freely re-creating it in order to preserve it; and just as such production succeeds and is swallowed up in the neutral point between the subjective and the objective – so, in Beethoven's work, the images of submerged forms rise from the abyss of abandoned humanity to illuminate it. The work's pathos lies in the gesture of the hand lighting the torch, while its success resides in the depth of shadow into which the mourning figure withdraws from the ending of the light. Its sorrow is reflected in the stony gaze which receives the failing light, as if to harbour it for the rest of time. Its joy resembles the flickering glow on walls which are closing. (GS 16, pp. 206f)

55 Adorno expressly classified fr. 36 with the material on Beethoven. In Kant's *Critique of Pure Reason* we read:

> In accordance with reason's legislative prescriptions, our diverse modes of knowledge must not be permitted to be a mere rhapsody, but must form a system [...]. By a system I understand the unity of the manifold modes of knowledge under one idea. This idea is the concept provided by reason – of the form of a whole – in so far as the concept determines *a priori* not only the scope of its manifold content, but also the positions which the parts occupy relatively to one another. (*Immanuel Kant's Critique of Pure Reason*, transl. by Norman Kemp Smith, London, Macmillan, 1990, p. 653, A832, B860)

Clearly, Adorno intended tonality in Beethoven to be understood as a rational idea in the sense used by Kant.

56 Cf. Otto Fenichel, *The Psychonalytic Theory of Neurosis*, New York, W.W. Norton & Company Inc., 1945, p. 12:

The assumption has been made in various forms by many biologists that there is a basic vital tendency to abolish tensions that have been brought about by external stimulation and to return to the energy state that was effective before the stimulation. The most fruitful conception in this respect is Cannon's formulation of the principle of 'homoeostasis'. Organisms, composed of material which is characterized by the utmost inconstancy and unsteadiness, have somehow learned the methods of maintaining constancy and keeping steady in the presence of conditions which might reasonably be expected to prove profoundly disturbing. The word homoeostasis does not imply something set and immovable, a stagnation; on the contrary, the living functions are extremely flexible and mobile, their equilibrium being disturbed uninterruptedly, but being re-established by the organism equally uninterruptedly.

– Adorno's critical use of the concept of aesthetic homoeostasis can be found, above all, in his *Aesthetic Theory* (cf. the passages referred to under 'homeostasis' in the index, 1984 edition, p. 524).

57   In Schoenberg's text Adorno had read:

I myself consider the totality of a piece as the *idea*: the idea which its creator wanted to present. But because of the lack of better terms I am forced to define the term idea in the following manner: Every tone which is added to a beginning tone makes the meaning of that tone doubtful. [. . .] In this manner there is produced a state of unrest, or imbalance which grows throughout most of the piece, and is enforced further by similar functions of the rhythm. The method by which balance is restored seems to me the real *idea* of the composition. (Arnold Schoenberg, *Style and Idea*, New York, Philosophical Library, 1950, p. 49)

– In the (earlier) German version of the text we always find the word *Gedanke* in place of 'idea' (cf. Schoenberg, *Stil und Gedanke. Aufsätze zur Musik*, ed. by Ivan Vojtěch, Frankfurt/Main, 1976, p. 33).

58   No such passage occurs in the Preface to the *Phenomenology*. Adorno was undoubtedly thinking of the conclusion of the following passage:

It is [. . .] not difficult to see that our time is one of birth and of transition to a new period. [. . .] Of course, it [the mind] is never at rest, but is caught up in ever-advancing motion. But just as a child's first breath, after long, peaceful suckling, interrupts the gradual, merely cumulative process – and is thus a qualitative leap – so that the child is now born, the evolving mind slowly and quietly ripens towards the new form, discards one part of its previous *world* after another; that world's crumbling is only hinted at by particular symptoms, by frivolity and boredom. These break into the established order, the uncertain premonition and precursors of something unknown and different which is approaching. This gradual crumbling, which has not changed the physiognomy of the whole, is interrupted by the sudden flash which reveals the image of the new world. (Hegel, *Werke* [n. 12], vol. 3, pp. 18f)

Adorno's memory probably linked this passage with a preceding one in which the philosopher argues against an 'opinion' which

does not understand the difference between philosophical systems as part of the advancing development of truth, but sees in their differences only contradiction. The bud vanishes as the bloom bursts forth, and it might be said that the former is contradicted by the latter; likewise, the fruit pronounces the bloom to be a false existence of the plant, the former replacing the latter as its truth. (Ibid., p. 12)

59   *Faust* I, v. 748. – The same quotation, in more complete form, is used in the *Philosophy of Modern Music* to summarize the way in which music

transcends 'the realm of intentions, of meaning and subjectivity', and to characterize the 'behaviour' of music in general: '"Tears dim my eyes: earth's child I am again" – This line from Goethe's *Faust* defines the position of music. Thus earth claims Eurydice again. The gesture of return – not the sensation of expectancy – characterizes the expression of all music, even if it finds itself in a world worthy of death' (*Philosophy of Modern Music*, p. 129). – On the analogy with Eurydice cf. fr. 11.

60 Example 3 as written by Adorno is not found in this form in the first movement of the Fifth Piano Concerto; it represents the simplified rhythmical notation of a passage in the *tutti* of the strings which occurs in bars 90ff.

61 Cf. Plato, *Symposium*:

> Only Agathon, Aristophanes and Socrates were still awake, drinking from a large bowl which they passed round to the right. Socrates was carrying on a conversation with them. Aristodemus said he could not recall the whole conversation as he had not followed it from the beginning and, moreover, had dozed off at times. But the main point had been that Socrates forced them to concede that the same man must be able to compose both comedy and tragedy, and that a proper tragedian was also a writer of comedies. They conceded the point, but did not pursue it further, as they were getting drowsy [...]. (St. 223d; translated from the edition used by Adorno: *Platons Gastmahl*, 4th edition, Leipzig 1922, pp. 107f)

62 Cf. Schindler's account: Beethoven 'declared religion and *basso continuo* to be closed matters which should not be disputed further' (Anton Schindler, *Biographie von Ludwig van Beethoven*, ed. by Eberhardt Klemm, Leipzig 1988, p. 430). – also see the somewhat divergent quotation from Bekker in fr. 316.

63 Adorno had been acquainted with the conductor Hermann Scherchen (1891–1966; emigrated in 1933), who was strongly committed to modern music, since the early 1920s.

64 For the text and source of this comment by Beethoven see frs 197 and 267.

65 Date at foot of text: 'S[anta] M[onica], 7 July 53'.

66 In the passage referred to (*Beethoven*, p. 278), Bekker discusses the last two movements of the Ninth Symphony:

> What makes the *Adagio* complementary in meaning to the *Allegro* and the *Scherzo* is the proclamation of peace, in contrast to the knowledge of the invincible, demonic power of fate which those sections convey. It is a peace immune to all the storms of life, attained through a confident faith in the existence of a better, purer world. [...] In the last movement the device of the musical quotation is used. The mysterious, incantatory formula of the opening, the demonically hastening *Scherzo*, the uplifting, consoling message of the *Adagio* – all these are offered to an imagination striving for new goals. And they are all thrust back by defensive interjections from the basses.

Bekker makes no *direct* reference to the negation of the details by the whole on page 278.

67 Cf. ibid.: 'The sketches reveal the originally planned texts of these bass recitatives [...] "Oh no, I ask not this, but something more pleasing" – thus is the first movement rebuffed.'

68 Adorno's friend, the composer, pianist and piano teacher Eduard Steuermann (1892–1964; emigrated to USA in 1936) had been his piano teacher in Vienna in the second half of the 1920s. – Cf. Adorno's essay 'Nach Steuermanns Tod', GS 17, pp. 311ff, and the selection from the

correspondence between Steuermann and Adorno in *Adorno-Noten. Mit Beiträgen von Theodor W. Adorno, Heinz-Klaus Metzger, Mathias Spahlinger u.a.*, ed. by Rolf Tiedemann, Berlin 1984, pp. 40ff.
69 Incorrect formulation in the manuscript.
70 Date at foot of text: '14 Aug. 1949'.
71 Syntactical error in original.
72 The theory of the mediation between part and whole, individual detail and totality in Beethoven was a constant preoccupation of Adorno's; the relevant discussion in his *Aesthetic Theory* should be regarded as an authoritative statement of his view:

> Beethoven, showing an elective affinity for the spirit of the mature bourgeois spirit of the natural sciences, faced the antinomy of the universal and the particular by qualitatively neutralizing the particular. He thus did more than merely integrate music as a continuum of what is in the process of becoming, more than merely shield the form from the emerging threat of empty abstraction. In foundering, the particular elements dissolve into each other and determine the form through the process of their foundering. In Beethoven the particular is and is not an impulse toward the whole, something that only in the whole becomes what it is, yet in itself tends toward the relative indeterminateness of basic tonal relations and toward amorphousness. If one hears or reads his extremely articulated music closely enough, it resembles a continuum of nothing. The tour de force of each of his great works is literally Hegelian, in that the totality of nothing determines itself as a totality of being, though it does so only as semblance and not with the claim of absolute truth. (*Aesthetic Theory*, 1997 edition, p. 185)

Cf. also n. 12.
73 Cf. fr. 14 – In the edition preserved in Adorno's papers (*Beethoven, Sämtliche Lieder. Neue revidierte Ausgabe,* Leipzig [n.d.], p. 89), the passage of sextuplets is written in triplets.
74 Cf. Theodor Mommsen, *Römische Geschichte*, vol. 1: *Bis zur Schlacht von Pydna*, 11th edition, Berlin 1912, pp. 911f:

> The unbelief which is a despairing belief speaks from this poet [that is, Euripides] with daemonic power. Of necessity, therefore, the poet never achieves a plastic conception transcending himself, or a truly poetic effect conveyed by the whole. For this reason he showed a kind of indifference towards the composition of his tragedies, not infrequently botching his works and failing to provide them with a central action or character. It was really Euripides who instigated the slovenly device of introducing the crux of the play in a prologue and resolving it by divine intervention or some such crude artifice.

75 Cf. Adorno's essay 'Der Artist als Statthalter':

> The paradox around which Valéry's work is organized [...] is that while each artistic utterance and each piece of scientific knowledge is addressed to the whole person and to the whole of humanity, this intention can yet be realized only by an oblivious division of labour which is heightened to the point of ruthlessly sacrificing the individual. (GS 11, pp. 117f; cf. the passages quoted from Valéry's 'Degas Danse Dessin', ibid., pp. 118 and 124)

76 Adorno is thinking of a letter from Jens Peter Jacobsen to Edvard Brandes of 6 February 1878:

> The novel [that is, *Niels Lyhne*] is progressing, though not by giant steps, but I fear that I have become involved too soon with people of the present day or even of posterity. [...] The prestige conferred by distant cultural epochs is worth a great deal. On the other hand, one is given a wretchedly

accurate measure of how far one has progressed when one takes on a task like mine. The book is badly composed, at all events. That does not mean that I am discouraged or racked by doubt; on the contrary, I am in good heart with regard to Niels Lyhne. (J.P. Jacobsen, *Gesammelte Werke*, vol. 1: *Novellen Briefe Gedichte*, Jena 1911, p. 247)

That Adorno had this passage in mind can be inferred from the monograph on Mahler, in which the same passage is cited as evidence of 'what Jacobsen selected expressly as a principle of "bad composition"' (*Mahler*, p. 98), although the passage actually bears witness to the opposite intention on the novelist's part.

77 "Musical" is a term [...] proper to the Germans and not to culture in general, and its meaning is false and untranslatable. "Musical" is derived from music, just as "poetic" is from poetry and "physical" from physics. If I say: Schubert was one of the most musical of people, it is the same as saying: Helmholtz was one of the most physical. [...] People have gone so far as to refer to a piece of music as itself "musical", or even to maintain that a great composer like Berlioz was not sufficiently so. [...] Music is still so young and is eternal; its time of freedom will come. When it stops being "musical". (Ferruccio Busoni, *Entwurf einer neuen Ästhetik der Tonkunst*, Wiesbaden 1954, pp. 25f)

78 Cf. the chorus in the finale of Act 2 of *Fidelio*: 'Wer ein holdes Weib errungen,/Stimm' in unsern Jubel ein!' [Who a lovely wife has won, let him join in our rejoicing]. Similarly in the last movement of the Ninth Symphony: 'Wer ein holdes Weib errungen, mische seinen Jubel ein!'

79 Lines from the first poem ('Auf dem Hügel sitz' ich') of the song cycle *An die ferne Geliebte*.

80 In the manuscript the word *Feindschaft* [hostility] is inserted above the word *Natur*. The meaning of this later addition must lie in the equating of 'sovereignty over nature' with 'hostility towards nature'.

81 This formulation is found in the manuscript; however, cf. Florestan in the vocal trio in Act 2 of *Fidelio*: 'Euch werde Lohn in bessern Welten' [May you (plural) be rewarded in better worlds]. The meaning of the quotation for Adorno in this context cannot even be guessed at. Cf. also fr. 84, and, above all, *Philosophy of Modern Music*, in which the quotation is used to define the content of traditional as against modern music:

> No music today [...] could possibly speak in the accents of 'reward'. Not only has the mere idea of humanity, or of a better world no longer any sway over mankind – though it is precisely this which lies at the heart of Beethoven's opera. Rather the strictness of musical structure, wherein alone music can assert itself against the ubiquity of commercialism, has hardened music to the point that it is no longer affected by those external factors which caused absolute music to become what it is. (pp. 19–20)

82 Cf. fr. 20, and GS 3, p. 326 regarding the quotation from Chopin.

83 Cf. Karl Kraus, *Beim Wort genommen*, Munich 1955 (vol. 3 of *Werke*, ed. by Heinrich Fischer), p. 68. Adorno's quotation contains a minor deviation from the original.

84 This reference is given in the manuscript. The only edition available to the editor was Georg Groddeck, *Der Seelensucher. Ein psychoanalytischer Roman*, Wiesbaden 1971 (reprint of Leipzig edition of 1921); the passage quoted is on p. 150 of this edition.

85 A term used by Marx and Engels in the *Holy Family*: 'Real humanism has no more dangerous foe in Germany than [...] speculative idealism, which

substitutes "self-consciousness" or "spirit" for the real individual human being' (Marx/Engels, *Werke*, vol. 2, Berlin 1957, p. 7). The young Adorno took over the idea, whereas at a later stage he generally reacted idiosyncratically to its ideological element. Not the least interesting aspect of this fragment is that it was written in July or August 1953, indicating that Adorno was still using the affirmative sense of 'real humanism' at a relatively late stage.

86 Redundant repetition in manuscript.

87 In the text 'Fortschritt', written in 1962, Adorno formulates the matter still more trenchantly:

> The passage from Schiller's 'Ode to Joy', in which those who are not accorded all-embracing love are banished from it, involuntarily betrays the truth about the idea of humanity, which is at once totalitarian and particular. What happens to the unloved or those incapable of love in the name of the idea in these lines unmasks that idea, as does the affirmative force with which Beethoven's music hammers it home. It is hardly by chance that, by using the word *stehlen* [steal] in connection with the humiliation of the joyless, who, for that very reason, are denied joy twice over, the poem calls up associations from the spheres of property and criminality. (GS 10.2, p. 620)

88 Adorno's essay 'Musikalische Diebe, unmusikalische Richter', of 1934 (*Stuttgarter Neues Tagblatt*, 20.8.1934 [vol. 91, no. 386], p. 2; now GS 17, pp. 292ff).

89 Poem by Goethe, probably written shortly before the turn of the century; a model of Goethean classicism. – Cf. Goethe, *Werke*, Hamburg edition, ed. by Erich Trunz, vol. 1: *Gedichte und Epen I,* 2nd edition, Hamburg 1952, pp. 243f.

90 In his essay 'Zukunftsmusik', Wagner wrote:

> Mozart often, indeed, almost habitually, lapsed into the banal phrases which make his symphonic movements seem to us often like so-called *Tafelmusik* – a music, which, along with attractive melodies, provides pleasant sounds as a background to conversation. To me, at any rate, the half-cadences recurring so regularly and so noisily in Mozart's symphonies sound like a musical translation of the clatter of dishes being served and cleared away from a princely table. (*Wagner-Lexikon. Hauptbegriffe der Kunst- und Weltanschauung Richard Wagners in wörtlichen Anführungen aus seinen Schriften zusammengestellt*, compiled by Carl F. Glasenapp and Heinrich von Stein, Stuttgart 1883, p. 262)

> – Cf. Adorno: 'All music was once a service to relieve the boredom of people of rank, but the Last Quartets were no *Tafelmusik*' (GS 5, p. 47).

91 Cf. *Wagner-Lexikon* [n. 90], p. 439:

> In no symphonic movement are two themes of absolutely antithetical character opposed to each other. However different they may seem, they always complement each other like the masculine and feminine aspects of the same basic character. But how diversely these elements can refract each other, take on new forms and combine and re-combine, can be seen from a movement from a Beethoven symphony: the first movement of the *Eroica* shows this diversity even to the extent of misleading the uninitiated, whereas, to the initiated, precisely this movement reveals the unity of its basic character most convincingly.

92 Cf. n. 81.

93 In 1940, when he wrote fr. 84, the formulation was still fresh in Adorno's mind as a self-quotation from the 'Versuch über Wagner' written shortly before:

The metaphysical-psychological structure of *Tristan* must, to justify death from the standpoint of individuation, equate it with joy. Yet as positivity the image of joy lapses into the quotidian. It becomes an *élan* of the individual who wants it to be so, who precisely in this wish participates in life, and in this participation proclaims his assent to life. Thereby Wagner's metaphysics of death also paid its tribute to the unattainability of joy, which holds good for all great music since Beethoven. (GS 13, p. 101)

94 The bibliographical references are to Friedrich Rochlitz, *Für Freunde der Tonkunst*, vol. 3, Leipzig 1830, and vol. 4, Leipzig 1832. – The *passage on Fichte* reads:

> Picture a man of about fifty, of short rather than medium height but very strongly built. A stocky man with a strong bone structure, much like Fichte's, only more fleshy and with a fuller, rounder face; a ruddy, healthy complexion; eyes which were restless and bright – indeed, almost piercing when he fixed his gaze. His movements were few and hasty; in his facial expression, especially in his eyes, which were full of wit and life, there was a mixture, or sometimes a momentary alternation, of friendly candour and timidity. In his whole bearing was the tension, the anxious attentiveness of a deaf person who has very lively feelings: now he would say something frankly and cheerfully, then lapse into brooding silence. On top of all that, the awareness always in the onlooker's mind: that this was the man who brought nothing but joy to millions – pure, spiritual joy! (Ibid., vol. 4, pp. 350f)

– On 'Über Beethoven und die französische Revolution', he writes:

> With regard to music in the age preceding the most recent one, it had been more difficult to do justice to spirit – in the present epoch, to the letter. [...] The causes of this or that predisposition of one epoch or the other; the causes of the difference between the periods in this respect, and of the change between them – all these are rooted, first of all, in the course of the world and its influences on minds in general. (There would be much to say on that subject; and this could be aptly introduced and vividly presented by referring to factors which are anything but harmonious. For you cannot believe, any more than I do, that [...] as far as music is concerned, Beethoven's more recent works could have been written four decades ago; or, to state the matter bluntly – however strange this may seem in the present context – that they could have been written before the French Revolution with its mighty influence on the whole world?) (Ibid., vol. 3, pp. 314f)

– Rochlitz's 'Physiognomik Beethovens als des Idealisten':

> If you want to see him in a relaxed and cheerful mood, said Schubert, you should go straight away to buy him a meal at the inn, where he always goes with the same intention. – He took me there. Most of the seats were occupied: Beethoven was surrounded by several of his acquaintances whom I did not know. He seemed really to be happy. [...] It was not an actual conversation that he was carrying on; he was speaking alone, often at some length, wherever his thoughts took him. Those around him added little, just laughed or nodded approval. He was philosophizing – on politics as well – in his own way. He talked of England and the English, both of which he pictured as incomparably splendid – which sounded odd enough at times. Then he told a number of stories about the French at the time when Vienna was captured twice over. He had no love for them. He said all this quite heedlessly without the slightest restraint – all spiced with highly original, naive opinions and droll comments. To me he seemed like a man with a rich, penetrating mind and unlimited, never-resting imagination, who, as a highly gifted adolescent had been deposited on a desert island with everything he had learned or experienced up to then, and any other knowledge he may have picked up,

and who had pondered and brooded there on all this material until his fragments had become wholes and his fantasies convictions, which he was now
proclaiming to the world contentedly and confidently. (Ibid., vol. 4,
pp. 352ff)

95 Cf. Hegel, *Werke* [n. 12], vol. 12: *Vorlesungen über die Philosophie der
    Geschichte*, pp. 147–74. – Which *passages* Adorno was thinking of in con-
    nection with Rochlitz's 'physiognomy' of Beethoven (or with Beethoven
    himself) is not at all evident. On the contrary, Hegel describes the charac-
    ter of the Chinese as distinguished by the fact that 'everything which con-
    stitutes mind – free manners, morality, soul, inward religion, scholarship
    and real art – is foreign to them' (ibid., p. 174) – that is, it was as unlike
    Beethoven as can be imagined.

96 Seume, in his *Spaziergang nach Syrakus*, paints an attractive picture of Vienna
    as it was when Beethoven arrived there [in 1792]. The book came out in 1803
    and was banned by the censor; but we find a copy among Beethoven's post-
    humous papers, which makes us even more interested in Seume's report. The
    master also owned Seume's *Apokryphen*, a collection of aphorisms advocating
    political freedom, also banned. We can see from this how avidly the republican
    Beethoven read the writings of the zealot of freedom (Wolfgang A. Thomas-
    San-Galli, *Ludwig van Beethoven*, Munich 1913, p. 68).

97 Adorno writes in similar terms in the study 'Über epische Naivetät' of
    1943 (cf. GS 11, pp. 36f). – In fr. 89, written in 1942, he naturally means
    the Marxian theory by the 'wholly true' theory.

98 On aesthetic progress, he writes in *Aesthetic Theory*, with regard to
    Beethoven:

    Progress in art must not be denied; nor should it be proclaimed. Subsequent to
    Beethoven, there has not been a single work that matches his late quartets in
    terms of truth content. But the reasons for this are objective: the status of these
    quartets in terms of material, spirit and technique was unique and will never be
    duplicated, not even by an artistic talent greater than Beethoven's. (p. 298)

99 He is referring to the Schoenberg section of what was to become the
    Philosophy of Modern Music (the only part written by 1941) (cf. pp. 29ff;
    regarding his critique of music's domination of nature, cf. especially, ibid.,
    pp. 64ff).

100 Orthographic error in manuscript.

101 Above the text: 'Perhaps re. Beethoven'.

102 Cf. GS 17, pp. 295f, where the difference between Schubert and Wagner is
    discussed in detail.

103 The relationship between idealism and myth had been a central question in
    Adorno's philosophy since the book on *Kierkegaard* (cf. GS 2, pp. 151ff).
    Regarding Adorno's concept of the mythical – probably originally derived
    from Benjamin – the 'Versuch über Wagner' is especially relevant, together
    with *Dialectic of Enlightenment*. In the Wagner essay, that composer's
    myth-making tendency is contrasted to Beethoven:

    With astonishing insight, Vischer excluded Beethoven as 'too symphonic'
    from his programme of a mythical opera. Just as everything mythical is abol-
    ished in face of the character of: *O Hoffnung, lass den letzten Stern*; just as
    each bar of Beethoven transcends the natural context from which it springs
    and to which it is reconciled, the symphonic form, which Schoenberg called
    the principle of the 'developing variation', is fundamentally anti-mytholo-
    gical. (GS 13, p. 119)

104 Date at head of text: '1 February 1945'.
105 Cf. n. 13. – Benjamin discusses the 'decay' or 'destruction' of aura by the reproducibility of the art-work in, for example, *Gesammelte Schriften* [n. 13], vol. 1, pp. 478ff; ibid., pp. 439ff and vol. 7, pp. 354ff.
106 Between 1938 and 1941 Adorno was collaborating on the Princeton Radio Research Project, as director of the so-called Music Study, an empirical-sociological investigation (cf. GS 10.2, pp. 705f); he planned to write a book on the results, to be entitled *Current of Music. Elements of a Radio Theory*. Although extensive drafts exist, it remained a fragment (it will be published within the framework of the *Nachgelassene Schriften*). A manu-script exists of the essay 'Likes and Dislikes in Light Popular Music', which was to form chapter 5; a kind of summary of it was printed as 'On Popular Music' (cf. *Studies in Philosophy and Social Science*, vol. 9, no. 1, 1941, pp. 17ff). – On the 'concept of the New', cf. 'On Popular Music':

> The musical sense of any piece of music may indeed be defined as that dimension of the piece which cannot be grasped by recognition alone, by its identification with something one knows. It can be built up only by sponta-neously linking the known elements – a reaction as spontaneous by the lis-tener as it was by the composer – in order to experience the inherent novelty of the composition. The musical sense is the New – something which cannot be traced back to and subsumed under the configuration of the known, but which springs out of it, if the listener comes to its aid. (p. 33)

107 Cf. the reference in n. 19.
108 The juxtaposition of *Fidelio* to the Kantian 'doctrine of marriage', devel-oped in §§ 24–6 of *Metaphysik der Sitten*, parallels Benjamin's study of Goethe's *Elective Affinities*, which relates Kant to Mozart's *Magic Flute* in the same context (cf. Benjamin, *Gesammelte Schriften* [n. 13], vol. 2, pp. 128f). – On Hegel's dialectic, which, in the *Elements of the Philosophy of Right*, defines marriage as the transition from subjectivist morality to an objective, substantial ethical standpoint, cf. the wrongfully neglected dis-sertation of Roland Pelzer, written under Adorno's supervision ('Studien über Hegels ethische Theoreme', in *Archiv für Philosophie*, vol. 13, no. 1/2, December 1964, pp. 3ff).
109 Adorno found this thesis set out in Bekker's lecture *Die Sinfonie von Beethoven bis Mahler*:

> The criterion of great symphonic art [...] does not reside in 'beauty' of con-struction or invention, as identified by scholarly concepts. Nor does it lie in any property of what we are accustomed to call the 'work of art' in the nar-rower sense. It lies in the special kind and degree of the power with which this art-work is able to form communities of feeling. This power enables it to create a unified, specifically individual entity from the chaotic mass of the public – an entity which recognizes itself, at the moment of listening, of experiencing art, as a unity moved by the same feelings and striving towards the same goals. Only this *sociogenetic* capacity of the work of art determines its meaning and its value. I therefore consider its ability to form a society the highest quality of the symphonic work. (Paul Bekker, *Die Sinfonie von Beethoven bis Mahler*, Berlin 1918, p. 17; a similar view is expressed by Bekker, *Beethoven*, p. 201; also cf. Text 2b, p. 118 above)

110 A somewhat enervated report on the conversation by Thomas Mann, in his diary entry of 9.4.1949:

> In the afternoon a long session at Horckheimer's [sic] with Adorno. A curi-ous, strenuously eloquent and fatiguing discussion covering the world situa-

tion. (Thomas Mann, *Tagebücher 1949–1950*, ed. by Inge Jens, Frankfurt/ Main 1991, p. 47)

111 Probably stated most clearly in the account of Kretschmar's lecture 'Beethoven and the Fugue', cf. Thomas Mann, *Doctor Faustus* [n. 2], pp. 53ff. – In *Negative Dialectics*, Adorno took up the motif with reference to Beethoven and Bach: 'The autonomous Beethoven is more metaphysical, and therefore more true, than Bach's *ordo*. Subjectively liberated experience and metaphysical experience converge in humanity' (p. 397).

112 Syntactical error in manuscript.

113 Syntactical error in manuscript.

114 Adorno does not follow Kant's wording exactly here.

115 In *Aesthetic Theory* Adorno extended the definition of the sublime, which Kant had restricted to natural phenomena in the *Critique of Judgment*, to beauty in art, arguing that, indeed, it only became self-conscious through such beauty:

> [. . .] there is one other aspect that shows especially the historical limitations of [Kant's] aesthetics, and that is the doctrine of the sublime. According to Kant, the sublime is a feature of nature and not of art. Now it is precisely in Kant's time that we see artists consciously adopting the ideal of sublimity, presumably without knowing the Kantian position on this question. The prime example of this tendency may be Beethoven, whose name was never mentioned by Hegel. [. . .] Paradoxically, it is in his depiction of the sublime in nature that Kant has most in common with the young Goethe and the artists from the period of the bourgeois revolution. The young poets who were Kant's contemporaries experienced nature as he did. But, and this is the paradox, by giving expression to the sentiment of sublimity in their poems, they identified the sublime as belonging to art rather than to morality [. . .]. (pp. 509–10)

Also:

> Kant's theory of the sublime, sketched in reference to the beautiful in nature, anticipates that spiritualization which only art can actualize. What is sublime in nature, says Kant, is the autonomy of spirit in the presence of a prepotent empirical world, and that autonomy comes into its own only in the spiritualized work of art. (Ibid., pp. 136–7; also cf. ibid., pp. 280ff)

– Also cf. fr. 349, and the quotations from Kant in n. 284.

116 Georgiades's 'idea of the festive' may be inferred from his ceremonial address 'Das musikalische Theater':

> In the musical theatre which, taking its cue from the theatre of speech, seems to have been conceived from the standpoint of the person, the person fades into insignificance. All the more strongly is the other, festive aspect brought to the fore: the love of lustre, splendour, or of heightening through myth; the predilection for apotheosis. Turned inwards, this aspect is manifested as a tendency towards solemnity, transfiguration and redemption. Unreal, visionary or transcendental elements are incorporated. All this stems not only from opera's origins in the musical feasts of the Renaissance, but is favoured by the nature of music itself. [. . .] In Mozart's musical theatre – and therefore also in Beethoven's *Fidelio* – we encounter [. . .] all the aspects of music as harmony that we have also found in serious opera: the festive (*The Marriage of Figaro* closes with: 'Away to the feast!'); the happy outcome, and thus concord, apotheosis and transfiguration (*The Magic Flute*); and the summing up of the situation. (Thrasybulos G. Georgiades, *Kleine Schriften*, Tutzing 1977 [*Münchner Veröffentlichungen zur Musikgeschichte*, vol. 26], pp. 136 and 143)

– The first edition of this address is among Adorno's posthumous papers (cf. Georgiades, 'Das musikalische Theater', ceremonial address held at the public session of the Bavarian Academy of Sciences in Munich, 5 December 1964, Munich 1965), though it is dated nine years later than the writing of fr. 107. In this fragment, Adorno refers to a lecture by Georgiades on Mozart's 'Jupiter' Symphony, which he had heard the same year and about which he wrote to the author on 4 April 1956: 'how much I was impressed [. . .] by your lecture and also – without immodesty – how much the ideas you developed touched on those of my book on Beethoven, which has been in progress literally for decades.' (Cf. also the essay 'The Alienated *Magnum Opus*' [Text 5 above, p. 151] and Text 2b above, p. 122.)

117 See reference in n. 19.

118 This is put still more incisively in *Aesthetic Theory*: 'For the subjective art of Beethoven, what is constitutive is the highly dynamic form of the sonata, and along with that the late-absolutist style of Viennese classicism, which reached its peak in Beethoven. Nothing of the sort is conceivable again because style has been annulled' (1984 edition, p. 295).

119 Adorno is thinking primarily of Halm's book *Von zwei Kulturen der Musik*, the first edition of which (Munich 1913) is preserved in his library.

120 Cf. *Philosophy of Modern Music*, p. 69.

121 The complete bibliographical data are as follows: Robert Schumann, *Gesammelte Schriften über Musik und Musiker*, ed. by Heinrich Simon, vol. I, Leipzig, undated [*c*.1888].

122 The numbers 1–3 were accidentally omitted from the manuscript and have been reinstated by the Editor.

123 Cf. the text of the baritone solo written by Beethoven himself, which precedes Schiller's 'Ode to Joy' in the Ninth Symphony: 'O friends, no more these sounds. Let us give more pleasing, happier voice' (bars 216–36) – cf. frs 183 and 339: the 'sounds' rejected by Beethoven are, in Adorno's interpretation, those of mythical *fate*.

124 In the passage mentioned, Thomas-San-Galli quotes Anton Schindler on the Piano Sonatas, op. 14:

> The content of both sonatas [. . .] is a dialogue between a man and a woman or a lover and his beloved. In the sonata in G major this dialogue, and its meaning, are more incisively expressed, and the opposition between the two main voices (or principles) is introduced more perceptibly. Beethoven called these two principles the *beseeching* and the *resisting*. The counter-movement in the first bars (G major sonata) already shows the opposition between the two. In bar eight, with a quiet, soothing transition from seriousness to a more tender feeling, the *beseeching* principle appears, entreating and flattering until the middle movement in D major, where the two principles are again opposed, but no longer with the seriousness of the beginning. The *resisting* element becomes more pliant, allowing the first voice to end the phrase it has begun without interruption.

Adorno's handwritten note on the quotation reads: 'That would indicate that the wide intervals derived from the triad are the resisting ones, while the seconds, the beseeching ones, come from song and belong (initially) to subjectivity.'

125 Cf. Schindler on the Piano Sonata in G major op. 14, 2: 'The agreement is only satisfactorily expressed by a clearly enunciated Yes! of the resisting principle at the end of the work (the last five bars of the last movement)' (Thomas-San-Galli, *Ludwig van Beethoven*, p. 115). In his copy of

Thomas-San-Galli's book Adorno underlined this sentence several times, adding 'the affirmative moment' in the margin.

126 Cf. Paul Hindemith, *Unterweisung im Tonsatz. Theoretischer Teil*, Mainz 1937, passim. In the section on seconds, he writes: 'The performer's power is aroused by the rising interval; the spatial and material resistance to be overcome releases energy, and has an invigorating, refreshing effect on the listener. This is reinforced by the size of the intervals [...]' (p. 213). Adorno criticized Hindemith as a

> furious rationalist, as soon as he had to do with chords, or even just intervals, in which historical experience had been precipitated, which bore the traces of historical pain. He has to demonstrate them at all costs from pure principles, even if they have long since been so far consolidated socially that they have become second nature and need no demonstration through principles. (GS 17, p. 230)

127 Cf. n. 7; Beethoven's comments on the metronome are quoted at the beginning of Kolisch's essay. – Adorno, who wrote fr. 122 in February 1943, probably had access to the manuscript of Kolisch's essay, which was not published until April and July 1943.
128 Cf. fr. 353 and the quotation from Däubler's poem in n. 286.
129 Cf. fr. 66.
130 Cf. Hegel, *Werke* [n. 12], vol. 6: *Wissenschaft der Logik II*, p. 250:

> Furthermore, the refutation must not come from outside, that is, it must not be based on assumptions lying outside the system which are alien to it. [...] The true refutation must draw on the strength of the antagonist and fall within the sphere of his power; to attack him from outside oneself, and to be proved right where he is absent does not advance the cause.

(In GS 5, p. 14, Adorno quotes this passage to characterize the procedure proper to immanent criticism.)
131 Date at foot of text: '4.IV.1949'.
132 The pianist Artur Schnabel (1882–1951; emigrated 1933) was a leading interpreter of Beethoven, whose piano sonatas he edited and recorded for gramophone in the 1930s. – Schnabel's personal relationship to Adorno does not seem to have been of the best, as emerges from the diary of Ernst Krenek, who notes on 26.2.1938 regarding Schnabel: 'Curiously, he has a real hate-complex towards Wiesengrund[-Adorno]. Difficult.' (Ernst Krenek, *Die amerikanischen Tagebücher 1937–1942. Dokumente aus dem Exil*, ed. by Claudia Maurer Zenck, Vienna, etc., 1992, p. 50). Adorno, for his part, in his notes for the 'Theorie der musikalischen Reproducktion', treats Schnabel as a rather intimidating example of a pianist.
133 Actually, it is put even less felicitously by Bekker (*Beethoven*, p. 163): 'Here we have Beethoven's testament in F minor.'
134 Cf. Adorno's text with this title (GS 18, pp. 47f), in which he writes, on the one hand: 'that characterization of the keys leads nowhere is beyond doubt', but, on the other: 'one will concede even to Paul Bekker that Beethoven was frequently mistaken in his choice of D minor, F minor and $E^\flat$ major' (ibid., p. 47).
135 See the reference in n. 7.
136 Adorno paraphrased this term, which is not to be found, at least in dictionaries in common use, in his monograph on Mahler: 'Mahler's major–minor manner has its function. It sabotages the established language of music with dialect. Mahler's tone has the flavour evoked by the

Austrian dialect term *schmeckert* as applied to the Riesling grape. Its aroma, at once mordant and fugitive, assists spiritualization by its evanescence.' (*Mahler*, p. 23).

137 Adorno himself wrote in his essay on Schubert of 1928: 'Schubert's language here is dialect: but it is a dialect without a soil. It has the concreteness of a homeland; but this homeland is not present but remembered. Nowhere is Schubert further from native soil than when he quotes it.' (GS 17, p. 33).

138 'La Prière d'une Vierge', salon piece for piano by the Polish composer Tekla Badarzewska-Baranowska (1834–61), written at eighteen.

139 Music as the antagonist of repetition, which is seen as a behaviour profoundly enmeshed in myth, is one of the most fertile motifs in Adorno's thought. Karl Heinz Haag, to whom Adorno dedicated his 'Drei Studien zu Hegel', formulated, perhaps more incisively than the teacher himself, what are the concerns of a philosophy of negative dialectics, and how that philosophy is connected to Beethoven:

> The unrepeatable presents itself as something particular which is not subsumable to any generality, or rather as that which vanishes when encompassed by the general. Still less is the uniqueness of things independent of their conceptual fixation. This uniqueness is not a quality existing in itself, but appears only as the antithesis of the general, which tolerates it only as something non-conceptual. Music, which knows neither concepts nor names, is expected – especially in its highest productions – to be able to realize the unrepeatable. But just as philosophical reflection can present immediacy only as refracted through its mediation, the same is true of music, which knows it only as its own variation. The musical idea is no less dialectical than the philosophical. In Beethoven's music, as the most intensive attempt to repeat the unrepeatable, it is able to invoke only that which the Self and Nature have lost in alienation. A union of both, which Hegel believed to be attained in the absolute Idea, would be the unrepeatable as the apotheosis of the subject against time, the *chorismos* of possibility and reality. In truly overcoming the repeatable, people would become for the first time that which a world predicated on repetition already proclaims them to be: that which each individual is. (Karl Heinz Haag, 'Das Unwiederholbare', in *Zeugnisse. Theodor W. Adorno zum sechzigsten Geburtstag*, ed. by Max Horkheimer, Frankfurt/Main 1963, pp. 160f)

140 Date at foot of text: '(September 1944)'.

141 In his *Aesthetic Theory* Adorno defines the difference between Mozart and Beethoven from the standpoint of the philosophy of history in terms of their different attitudes to the principle of unity as a constituent of form:

> For Mozart, who in turn inherited an older tradition, the unity of form is still unshakable and able to endure extreme strain. For Beethoven, who saw the substantiality of oneness erode before the nominalistic onslaught, there is a need to tense unity much more tautly, so that it preforms the moments *a priori* in order then to be able to tame them all the more triumphantly. (1984 edition, p. 204)

142 Cf. the more detailed definition of this idea in *Aesthetic Theory*:

> The incomparable achievement of Beethoven, whose music is as deeply affected by the nominalistic motif as is Hegel's philosophy, was to have injected into intervention (which is demanded by the problem of form) the autonomy and freedom of an increasingly self-conscious subject. What, in the eyes of a self-subsistent work of art, looked like repression, Beethoven legitimated in terms of its substance.' (Ibid., p. 315)

143 The Editor relates the word 'this' to precisely this reconstruction by Beethoven of traditional forms out of subjective freedom.

144 Only a similar-sounding passage in 'Über die Anwendung der Musik auf das Drama' could be traced:

> Beethoven changed nothing in the structure of the symphonic movement, as he found it already formed by Haydn. He could not change it for the same reason that an architect cannot move around the pillars of a building at will, or use the horizontal as a vertical. [...] It has been noted very rightly that Beethoven's innovations are to be found far more in the field of rhythmic arrangement than in harmonic modulation. (Richard Wagner, *Gesammelte Schriften und Dichtungen*, 2nd edition, vol. 10, Leipzig 1888, pp. 177f)

145 This view is perhaps most clearly expressed in *Philosophy of Modern Music*, pp. 54f.

146 Syntactical error in manuscript.

147 See the passage from 'Zukunftsmusik' quoted from the *Wagner-Lexikon* in n. 90.

148 A comparison – often quoted by Adorno – which Kant used to characterize his 'revolution in thought'; this involved the founding of objective cognition in subjectivity:

> We must therefore make trial whether we may not have more success in the tasks of metaphysics, if we suppose that objects must conform to our knowledge [...]. We should then be proceeding precisely on the lines of Copernicus' primary hypothesis. Failing of satisfactory progress in explaining the movements of the heavenly bodies on the supposition that they all revolved round the spectator, he tried whether he might not have better success if he made the spectator to revolve and the stars to remain at rest. (*Critique of Pure Reason*, p. 22, B XVI)

149 In the Preface to the *Phenomenology of Mind*, cf. the passage arguing that science, that is, philosophy as understood by Hegel, is 'the ruse which, seeming to abstain from action, observes how determined being and its concrete life believes itself to be serving its own self-preservation and its special interests, while, quite to the contrary, it dissolves itself and becomes a part of the activity forming the whole.' (Hegel, *Werke* [n. 12], vol. 3, pp. 53f).

150 Cf. Hölderlin, *Sämtliche Werke* (Kleine Stuttgarter Ausgabe), vol. 5: *Übersetzungen*, ed. by Friedrich Beissner, Stuttgart 1954, pp. 213ff. ('Anmerkungen zum Oedipus').

151 Cf. Ibid.

152 Cf. the discussion of the same passage in fr. 42.

153 Later, in connection with Mahler's 'tendency to introduce new themes into his symphonic movements', Adorno set out this theory as follows:

> Proust is said to have pointed out that in music new themes sometimes take over the centre in the same way as previously unnoticed minor characters in novels. The formal category of the new theme derives paradoxically from the most dramatic of all symphonies. But precisely the singular case of the *Eroica* throws Mahler's formal intention into relief. In Beethoven the new theme comes to the aid of a deliberately overextended development, as if the latter could no longer clearly recall the distant exposition. Nevertheless, the new theme does not really cause surprise, but enters as something prepared, something familiar; not by chance have analysts repeatedly attempted to derive it from the material of the exposition. The classicist idea of the symphony takes for granted a definite, closed multiplicity just as Aristotelian poetics assumes the three unities. A theme appearing as absolutely new

offends its economic principle, that of reducing all events to a minimum of postulates, an axiom of completeness that integral music has made as much its own as have systems of knowledge since Descartes's *Discours de la méthode*. Unforeseen thematic components destroy the fiction that music is a pure tissue of deductions, in which everything that happens follows with unambiguous necessity. (*Mahler*, pp. 71–2)

154 Redundant pronoun in manuscript.

155 'The Poetic Idea' in Bekker's book is the title of the first chapter of part II, itself entitled: 'Beethoven the Tone Poet'. While Bekker is able to support this terminology with a number of Beethoven's own formulations, in general he brings the latter's music itself fatally close to programme music. Adorno criticized the 'hazy' term 'poetic ideas' on the first page of his monograph on Mahler (*Mahler*, p. 3), in doing which he was in surprising agreement with Hans Pfitzner's *Neue Ästhetik der musikalischen Impotenz* (cf. n. 217).

156 On this question cf. 'Das Altern der Neuen Musik':

Beethoven's most powerful formal effects are produced when a recurring element, which was once just a theme, now reveals itself as a result, thus taking on an entirely different meaning. Often, the meaning of what has gone before is only established by these recurrent elements. The opening of a recapitulation can give the feeling of something immense that has gone before, even though that immense event was not detectable at the point where it supposedly occurred. (GS. 14, p. 152)

157 A letter from Adorno to Sándor Jemnitz of 10 February 1926 gives an idea of how long he was preoccupied with this question:

As far as the confusion between the rondo and the variation form is concerned, I'm sure I do not need to remind you that the two forms are far more closely related than a schematic classification would allow. The elaboration of a partial and *self-contained* thematic element is common to both. And while the rondo since Beethoven has varied the recapitulation more and more radically, under the influence of the idea of the development, which resists any static thematic existence [...], variations, no longer securely founded on the theme, show an ever-increasing tendency towards 'functionalization', towards a sonata-like openness, thus transcending themselves in the direction of the rondo, which, as it were, mediates between variation and sonata. (Quoted from Vera Lampert, 'Schoenbergs, Bergs und Adornos Briefe an Sándor [Alexander] Jemnitz', in *Studia musicologica*, vol. XV, fasc. 1.4, Budapest 1973, p. 366)

158 The Fantasia op. 77 is dedicated to Count Franz von Brunswik, a friend of Beethoven.

159 Date at foot of text: '18 June 1948'.

160 'Pocket score' refers here and in what follows to the *Taschenpartituren* published by Eulenburg.

161 'Eh ihr den leib ergreift auf diesem sterne / Erfind ich euch den traum bei ewigen sternen' [Before your bodies take upon this star, I shall invent you dreams in stars eternal] – wrote Stefan George in *Der Siebente Ring*, in the poem 'Haus in Bonn' on Beethoven's birthplace (cf. *Gesamt-Ausgabe der Werke. Endgültige Fassung*, vol. 6/7, Berlin, undated [1931], p. 202).

162 That is, Adorno's edition of *Eulenburg's kleine Orchester-Partitur-Ausgabe* (Leipzig, undated).

163 Cf. n. 123.

164 'Cf. 79' was clearly added later. It concerns a page number, referring to Notebook 12, in which fr. 183 is on p. 28; fr. 339 is on p. 79.

165 The 'scene in Karlsbad', which is said to have taken place in August 1812 and not in Karlsbad but in Teplitz, was recorded in an (unauthentic) letter from Beethoven to Bettina von Arnim:

> [...] when two such as I and Goethe come together, the great lords have to take note of what greatness can mean among our kind. On the way home yesterday we met the whole imperial family. We saw them coming a good way off, and Goethe let go of my arm so that he could stand aside, and, say what I might, I could not persuade him to take a single step further. So I pressed my hat down on my head, buttoned my overcoat and walked with folded arms right through the thickest crowd of them. Princes and toadies made way for me, Archduke Rudolph raised his hat, and the Empress greeted me first. The lords and ladies know me. To my great amusement I saw the procession file past Goethe, who stood to one side with his hat off, bowing deeply. Then I gave him a piece of my mind, showed no mercy and berated him for all his sins [...]. (Beethoven, *Sämtliche Briefe* [n. 19], pp. 227f)

Regarding the authenticity of the letter quoted, see n. 19. – The 'lawsuit over "van"' was no such thing, but a case brought by the mother of Beethoven's nephew Karl regarding a right of custody under a provincial law which applied only to nobles. Under this law Beethoven was referred in 1818 to

> the civil court responsible for ordinary citizens. If we are to believe Schindler – and the notebooks recording conversations seem to support him on this point – this had a devastating effect on the composer. [...] He was so deeply offended that he would have liked to leave the country. (Solomon, *Beethoven* [n. 25], pp. 110, 279f)

– The 'brain-owner' anecdote is told by Bekker as follows:

> When he [Beethoven's younger brother Nikolaus Johann] had in later years become the owner of the Gneixendorf estate and sent Ludwig a card with the words: 'Johann van Beethoven, Landowner', he received the reply: 'Ludwig van Beethoven, Brain-owner'. A self-characterization by both brothers which aptly reflects the difference between them. (Bekker, *Beethoven*, pp. 37f)

166 Beethoven 'gradually [...] broke off even his personal ties, visiting the gravely ill Haydn "less and less often". The old Haydn missed Beethoven. [Ignaz von] Seyfried writes that Haydn often enquired about him: "What is our Grand Mogul up to now?", he would ask, knowing that Seyfried would tell his friend that Haydn had asked after him' (Solomon, *Beethoven* [n. 25], p. 98) – Cf. *Aesthetic Theory*, 1997 edition, p. 198, and *Introduction to the Sociology of Music*, transl. by E.B. Ashton, New York, Continuum, 1976, pp. 94–5 (that is, Text 2a above, p. 117).

167 To the extent that the bombastic element comes together with the titanic, a comment from *Aesthetic Theory* might also be quoted for comparison: 'Beethoven could probably be heard as a composer only after the gesture of the titanic – his primary effect – was outstripped by the crasser effects of younger composers like Berlioz.' (*Aesthetic Theory*, 1997 edition, p. 195).

168 A pronouncement by Beethoven three days before his death; according to Thomas-San-Galli, incorrectly linked to his acceptance of last rites (cf. *Ludwig van Beethoven*, p. 434).

169 Regarding the substance of this pun, cf. *Aesthetic Theory*: 'Works like the Ninth Symphony exert a mesmerizing influence; the power they have by virtue of their structure is translated into power over people. After

Beethoven, art's power of suggestion, originally borrowed from society, has rebounded on to society and become propagandistic and ideological.' (1984 edition, p. 347).

170 Such are the references in the manuscript. – The allusion to the 'book with Max' is undoubtedly to the *Dialectic of Enlightenment*; the notation *I A 3*, however, cannot be deciphered with sufficient certainty. In April 1942 Horkheimer began work on the first chapter, 'The Concept of Enlightenment'; in June or July, or possibly August, Adorno then turned to the chapter on 'The Culture Industry', whereas he does not seem to have started the excursus 'Odysseus or Myth and Enlightenment' until early 1943. As fr. 196 was written on 10 July 1942 the reference can only be to 'The Concept of Enlightenment'. It cannot therefore be ruled out that Adorno was referring by the doubtful abbreviation to a passage like the following:

> Enlightenment has always taken the basic principle of myth to be anthropo-morphism, the projection onto nature of the subjective. In this view, the supernatural, spirits and demons, are mirror images of men who allow them-selves to be frightened by natural phenomena. Consequently the many mythic figures can all be brought to a common denominator, and reduced to the human subject. (T.W. Adorno and Max Horkheimer, *Dialectic of Enlightenment*, transl. by John Cumming, London, Verso, 1989, pp. 6–7)

– The second reference is to a typescript (preserved in Adorno's posthum-ous papers) of the Schoenberg section of his later *Philosophy of Modern Music*. The footnote cited states:

> Benjamin's concept of the 'aural' work of art corresponds by and large with that of the hermetic work. The aura present therein is the uninterrupted sym-pathy of the parts with the whole, which constitutes the hermetic work of art. Benjamin's theory emphasizes the manner in which circumstances are mani-fested as phenomena from the perspective of the philosophy of history; the 'aural' content of the hermetic work of art underscores the aesthetic perspect-ive. This concept, however, permits deductions which the history of philo-sophy does not necessarily draw. The result of the decline of the aural or hermetic work of art depends upon the relationship of its own decline to epi-stemology. If the decline takes place blindly and unconsciously, it degenerates into the mass art of technical reproduction. It is not a mere external act of fate that the remnants of the aura remain throughout mass art. It is rather an expression of the blind obduracy of the structures, which, to be sure, results from their suppression by the present circumstances of domination. The work of art as a means of perception, however, becomes critical and fragmentary. Agreement on this fact prevails today in all works of art which have a chance of survival: the works of Schoenberg and Picasso, Joyce and Kafka, and even Proust offer unified support of this contention. This, in turn, perhaps allows further speculation in the field of the philosophy of history. The hermetic work of art belongs to the bourgeoisie, the mechanical work belongs to fas-cism, and the fragmentary work, in its state of complete negativity, belongs to utopia. (*Philosophy of Modern Music*, pp. 125–6, n. 55)

171 Date at foot of text: '10 July 1942'.

172 In the notebook which Adorno called the 'Grünes Buch' we find the fol-lowing two notes on the philosophy of music under the dates indicated:

> In one of its dimensions, music is to be assigned to the realm of natural beauty rather than of art. The ineffable quality of a gentle dusk, the depth of night, dawn – these and the speechlessness of music are deeply related. Manifestations of a beauty which has not been absorbed into the sphere of meaning.

And:

> The barbaric element in music: in traditional music I often find myself wondering how much of an effect is due to a particular chord or connection itself – as something intrinsically given, as second nature – and how much to the composition as such. In Reger, for example, one has the constant feeling that the former is a surrogate for the latter. The actual chord resounds deeply, carries the aura of meaning with it, whereas this ought really to be done by the composition. When a child strikes a bass chord in B minor, it thinks the chord is already music, and all music, especially Romantic, has something of this. Perhaps the deepest impulse of modern music springs from its inability to endure the lie that the natural material could speak by itself. Only now has that material become really no more than an element. (Green-brown leather-bound book [=Notebook 1], pp. 50f)

173 Although the Stravinsky section of the *Philosophy of Modern Music* had already been written in mid-1949, when fr. 199 was noted down, Adorno might well have been thinking of the close of the (earlier) Schoenberg section in this passage. He wrote there of traditional music:

> Music is an ideology insofar as it asserts itself as an ontological being-in-itself beyond social tensions. Even Beethoven's music – bourgeois music at its very height – echoed the turmoil and the ideal of the heroic years of the middle class in merely the same way that a morning dream echoes the noise of beginning day. It is not actual sensory listening but only the conceptually mediated perception of the elements and their configuration which assures the social substance of great music. [...] Music down to this very day has existed only as a product of the bourgeois class, a product which, both in the success and failure of its attempts at formulation, embodies this society and gives aesthetic documentation of it. (*Philosophy of Modern Music*, pp. 129–30)

174 Date at end of text: '30 June 1949'.
175 On Beethoven's classicism, cf. the comment in *Aesthetic Theory*: 'Beethoven's late works mark a revolt against the false principle of classicism by one of the most powerful classical artists.' (1984 edition, p. 414).
176 Regarding Beethoven and Kant from the viewpoint of moral philosophy, cf. Adorno's aphorism written as early as 1930:

> Beethoven and Kant really do meet up in Schiller. But in a more specific way than simply under the umbrella of a formal ethical idealism. In the 'Ode to Joy' Beethoven composed, programmatically, the Kantian postulate of the Categorical Imperative. In the line *'muß ein lieber Vater wohnen'* [must a dear Father dwell], he emphasized the *'muß'*. Thus God becomes in his eyes a mere postulate of the autonomous ego, which makes an appeal beyond the starry heaven above us to something which did not seem to be fully contained in the moral law. But joy fails to respond to such an appeal, joy, which the ego impotently chooses, instead of its rising above him like a star. (*Quasi una fantasia*, pp. 22–3)

177 Cf. frs 148–50.
178 Cf. the last of the 'Scenes from Childhood', op. 15
179 Adorno probably means the *Arioso dolente* in the third movement of the Piano Sonata in A♭ major, op. 110; cf. bars 9ff in that work. Although no literal quotation is to be found in the 'Harp' Quartet, Adorno might have been thinking of a passage which appears at the top of p. 14 of the Eulenburg pocket score.
180 Adorno discussed the relationship between classicism and Romanticism at length in the essay 'Klassik, Romantik, Neue Musik' of 1958:

In the strict sense, the Romantic moment is an *a priori* postulate of classicity. Just as the evolution of Wilhelm Meister would lack force without the contrasting figure of Mignon; just as Hegelian phenomenology bears Romantic consciousness within itself and at the same time criticizes it in Schelling, great music, especially Beethoven's, behaves in the same way. The most tangible example, if not the most significant, is the first movement of the Piano Sonata in C♯ minor, famous as the 'Moonlight' Sonata. It defines the character of the late Nocturnes of Chopin once and for all and lets the matter rest. But in a subtler and more sublimated form this moment imbues Beethoven's entire *oeuvre*. It survives even in the harsh, unconciliatory late work. Wagnerian biographers of Beethoven such as Ludwig Nohl have not been slow to criticize short forms, such as the Cavatina from the great String Quartet in B♭ major, for resembling the Romantic genre piece in the style of the song without words. No doubt this was a misunderstanding on the part of an over-zealous partisan. Unmistakably, however, the *Andante con moto quasi Allegretto* of the String Quartet in C major, op. 59 no. 3, presents in its most characteristic passage a thematic figure which sounds like an idea of Schubert's. In general, the intimate middle movements of the Quartets – and the *Adagio* of op. 74 – are especially rich in such phrases. In addition, the lyricism of piano works, as in the first movement of the Sonata in A major op. 101, or even the Rondo of the small E major sonata op. 90, would be specifically Romantic, were it content to remain mere lyricism; were it not taken up into the subjectively engendered objectivity of the total form. The cycle *An die ferne Geliebte* measures out the whole path from the Romantic *Lied* to the symphonic element of the postlude. (GS 16, pp. 130f)

181   Carus discusses the Fifth Symphony; for the Goethe quotation, cf. Goethe, *Werke*. Hamburg edition [n. 89], vol. 10: *Autobiographische Schriften II*, p. 413 ('Sankt-Rochus-Fest zu Bingen').

182   Of Beethoven's Fifth Symphony, Carus writes: 'heard on Palm Sunday 1835':

> Did not the first part of this symphony already float like a great thunder cloud, lit up in beautiful colours and casting a broad shadow? The clouds were strangely interlaced, split here and there by lightning, and now and then a distant roll of thunder was heard; but soon the *Adagio* burst forth, as a clear beam of moonlight breaks through the parting clouds at nightfall. To feel and reflect on all this causes us to revere such a creation as more than a work of nature; although it arouses many thoughts in us as we listen, we cannot truly exhaust it by any thought, nor would we wish to do so.

– For the ideas noted down by Adorno 'very early' – in late 1941 or early 1942 – cf. n. 172.

183   This refers to the *Neun Briefe über Landschaftsmalerei* by Carl Gustav Carus, Leipzig 1831. Adorno seems to have known Carus only from the selection edited by Paul Stöcklein (cf. the reference in fr. 209); this contains 'Zukünftige Idee romantischer Landschaftsmalerei' taken from the *Briefe*, and an aphorism from *Friedrich der Landschaftsmaler. Zu seinem Gedächtniss nebst Fragmenten aus seinen nachgelassenen Papieren*, Dresden 1841.

184   In the still unpublished 'Aufzeichnungen zu einer Theorie der musikalischen Reproduktion' Adorno writes on the opening bars of the 'Appassionata': 'From a certain stage of reflection onwards the notation, going beyond the mensural and neumic moment, wishes to say something on its own account, as a subjective intention, and it is the performer's task to read what this is. In the "Appassionata" the difference between:

and

decides the character of the composition' (Black notebook with cloth spine [=Notebook 6], p. 109).

185 On this point cf. *Aesthetic Theory*:

> The harmonic variant of the main theme in the coda of the first movement of Beethoven's 'Appassionata', op. 57, with the gloomy effect of its diminished seventh chord, is as much a product of fantasy as the brooding triadic theme that opens this movement. Regarding their genesis, it makes sense to think that what occurred to Beethoven first was not the main theme as it appears in the exposition but that all-important variant of it in the coda, and that he, as it were, retrospectively derived the primary theme from its variation. (1984 edition, pp. 248–9)

186 Cf. Alfred Kerr, *Liebes Deutschland. Gedichte*, ed. by Thomas Koebner, Berlin 1991, p. 353: 'Beethoven. Der Wirbel schweigt. Die Totenuhr / tickt stumm den Takt der Kreatur; / ein Tupfen nach dem Tosen. / Das Sterbe-Scherzo der A-Dur: / Choral der Glaubenlosen.' [Beethoven. The vortex stilled. The death-clock mutely ticks the beat of creaturely life. A tapping after the raging. The Death Scherzo of the A major: chorale of the faithless.] The use of this phrase is *surprising*, above all, because it is taken from Kerr, a writer condemned by Karl Kraus and not rated very highly by Adorno.

187 Bekker, *Beethoven*, pp. 441f., writes of the 'Kreutzer' sonata:

> Though inferior in poetic value to the C minor Sonata [op. 30,2], the Ninth Sonata for Piano and Violin in A major which followed it has, through its virtuoso brilliance, outstripped its predecessor in public acclaim and is generally regarded as the crowning achievement among Beethoven's Duo Sonatas. This evaluation may be justified in that the A major Sonata represents the purest type of concert duo and, in providing effects which are equally congenial to both instruments, has become a favourite piece among duo virtuosi. [...] If, in this [first] part the poetic element holds its own with the *concertante* aspect, the two parts which follow are devoted entirely to virtuoso effects. The simple, singing *andante* theme of the variations movement is embellished with the most daring trappings of virtuoso art, without, however, taking on more than a figuratively paraphrasing meaning. The tarantella-like Finale, too, [...] though outwardly one of the most brilliant concert pieces ever written by Beethoven, aims first of all to produce rousing, impetuous effects.

188 Cf. the following passage, translated from the Insel-Verlag edition (in Adorno's library):

> After this *Presto* [the first movement] they played the beautiful, but ordinary, in no way new *Andante* with its banal variations and the quite feeble Finale. [...] All this was very fine, but did not make on me a hundredth part of the impression I had had from the first piece [the first movement of the 'Kreutzer' Sonata]. I heard everthing against the background of my impression from the first piece. (Leo N. Tolstoy, *Sämtliche Erzählungen*, vol. 2, Frankfurt/Main 1961, p. 777)

189 Incorrect formulation in manuscript.

190 In collecting his poems for the last two editions of the complete works of 1815 and 1827, Goethe entitled the second section 'Gesellige Lieder' [Convivial Songs].

191 'The *Shekinah*, that is, [...] the personification and hypostatization of the "immanence" or "presence" of God in the world, is a conception' which has accompanied the spiritual life of the Jewish people for 2000 years in all its 'manifold ramifications' and 'equally manifold transformations'

(Gershom Scholem, *Von der mystischen Gestalt der Gottheit. Studien zu Grundbegriffen der Kabbala*, Zurich 1962, p. 136). 'God's "dwelling", his *Shekinah* as literally understood, means [...] his visible or hidden existence in a place, his presence' (ibid., p. 143). Though originally by no means identical to the *female element*, the concept of the *Shekinah* was given an 'entirely new twist' by the Cabbala: 'However the Talmud and the Midrashim may talk of the *Shekinah* [...], it never appears as a feminine element in God. No single parable speaks of it in female images'; such images

> are, to be sure, frequently used in connection with the community of Israel in its relationship to God, but for these authors the Community of Israel is not yet a mystical hypostasis of a force within God Himself, but only a personification of the historical Israel. Nowhere is the *Shekinah* contrasted as a female element to the 'Holy One, let Him be praised', as a masculine element in God. The introduction of this idea is one of the most influential and important innovations of the Cabbala. (Scholem, *Die jüdische Mystik in ihren Hauptströmungen*, Zurich 1957, pp. 249f)

– In 1942, when he wrote fr. 216, Adorno knew of the idea of the *Shekinah* both from the English first edition of Scholem's history of Jewish mysticism (*Major Trends in Jewish Mysticism*, Jerusalem 1941), which the author had sent him with a dedication dated 1 April 1942, and from his translation of the Sitre Torah from the Zohar (cf. *Die Geheimnisse der Tora. Ein Kapitel aus dem Sohar von G. Scholem*, Berlin 1936 [3rd Schocken private imprint], esp. the Afterword, pp. 123ff), for the translation of which he expressly thanked Scholem in April 1939; cf. fr. 370 and n. 305.

192 Bekker (*Beethoven*, p. 254) writes of the Seventh and Eighth Symphonies: 'What is characteristic of these new symphonies is the absence of a slow movement.'

193 On the repetitions in Stravinsky, cf. the section on 'Catatonia' in *The Philosophy of Modern Music*, p. 178.

194 On the category of Beethoven's 'maxims', cf. n. 40 and the references given there.

195 Cf. the last aphorism in 'Zweite Nachtmusik' of 1937:

> What distinguishes Haydn and Beethoven from all music in the style of the *Divertimento* is the fact that their technique, in commanding long time intervals through the temporal differential represented by the motif, does not so much fill time as draw it together; time is not passed, but subjugated. For they, too, are concerned with linear time, instead of the arrested time created by the motif-technique of the fugue, in which the temporal locations of entries are largely interchangeable, or are governed not by progression but by relationships of equilibrium. The symphony, however, goes further; it has its own temporal progression yet lasts, through its concept, for only a moment. [...] Paradoxically, passing time, which passes also for musical form, is syncopated by the moment of the identical motif, which in itself is timeless; through its heightened tension time is abbreviated to the point of standing still. At the same time, the displacement within the antiphonal interplay of motifs prevents their repetition from lapsing into monotony. Certainly, through its heightened or diminished repetition as an exorcizing or exorcized moment, the motif brings about a temporal extension. Yet through antiphony it appears as something ever new, and in its metamorphoses obeys the demands of historically passing time, the passage of which its identity virtually suspends. This paradox predominates in the first movements of the Fifth and Seventh Symphonies, and in the 'Appassionata': the latter's many

hundred bars seem like one, as seven years in the mountain of the fairy tale seem like one day; and even in Wagner Alfred Lorenz detected traces of the same tendency, when he experienced the whole 'Ring' cycle as present in a single moment. But in the strict sense, symphonic time belongs to Beethoven alone, and is the reason for the exemplary purity, the superior formal power of his work. (GS 18, pp. 51f)

196 An attempt to lighten this darkness can be found in the following passage from the last part of the *Philosophy of Modern Music*, in which Adorno postulates two types of hearing, one expressive and dynamic and the other rhythmical and spatial:

> The idea of great music lay in a mutual penetration of both modes of listening and in the categories of composition suited to each. The unity of discipline and freedom was conceived in the sonata. From the dance it received its integral regularity, and the intention regarding the entirety; from the Lied it received that opposing and negative impulse which, out of its own consequences, again produces the entirety. In so doing, the sonata fulfils the form which preserves this identity as a matter of principle – even if not in the sense of a literal beat, or tempo. It does this with such a multiplicity of rhythmic-melodic figures and profiles that the 'mathematical' pseudo-spatial time, which is recognized as tendential in its objectivity, coincides with the psychological time of experience in the happy balance of the moment. This conception of a musical subject–object was forcibly extracted from the realistic dissociation of subject and object. Consequently, a paradoxical element was present in the conception from the beginning. Beethoven – closer, from the perspective of such a conception, to Hegel than to Kant – had need of the most extraordinary configurations of the formal spirit to attain so complete a musical synthesis as he did in the Seventh Symphony. In his late phase he added a paradoxical unity, permitting the unreconciled characters of these two categories to merge openly and eloquently as the highest truth of his music. It might be felt that the history of music after Beethoven – Romantic music as well as that which is actually modern – indicates a decline parallel to that of the bourgeois class; it does this in a more meaningful sense than in mere idealistic phrases regarding beauty. If this is in any way true, then this decline is conditioned by the impossibility of resolving the conflict between the defined categories. (*Philosophy of Modern Music*, pp. 198–9)

197 Cf. the references in n. 7. – Although this fragment was written before the publication of Kolisch's book, the theory contained in the latter was undoubtedly familiar to Adorno through conversation; he also appears to have had access to a manuscript before publication (cf. n. 127).

198 Adorno reverts to the typologies of the intensive and extensive styles in the monograph on Mahler, in connection with the epic character of the latter's symphonies:

> His musical outlook was by no means lacking in tradition, a quasi-narrative, expansive undercurrent that in him strove toward the surface. Again and again in Beethoven the symphonic concentrates, which virtually supplant time, are matched by works whose duration is that of a joyous life both animated and reposing in itself. Among the symphonies the *Pastoral* represents this interest most ingenuously; the most important movements of this type include the first of the F major quartet, op. 59, no. 1. Toward the end of his so-called middle period it becomes more and more central to Beethoven's work, as in the first movements of the great B-flat major trio, op. 97, and the last violin sonata, pieces of supreme dignity. In Beethoven himself, confidence in extensive amplitude and in the possibility of passively discovering unity in multiplicity stylistically held in balance the tragic-classical idea of a music of the active subject. Schubert, for whom this idea had already paled,

is all the more attracted to Beethoven's epic style. (*Mahler*, Chicago and London 1992, p. 65)

199 Adorno used the first volume of the edition (preserved in his posthumous papers) of Beethoven's *Trios für Pianoforte, Violine und Violoncell*, ed. by Ferdinand David, C.F. Peters Verlag, Leipzig.

200 'See above' seems to refer to the composition, not to Adorno's notes.

201 Adorno's essay 'Spätstil Beethovens', written in 1934, was first published in 1937; cf. Text 3 above, pp. 123ff. – The essay was originally entitled: 'Über Spätstil. Zum letzten Beethoven'.

202 Adorno's study 'Zweite Nachtmusik', written in 1937; cf. reference and quotation in n. 195.

203 Unpublished second chapter of the book *Current of Music*, which remained a fragment (cf. n. 106). A shortened version appeared as 'The Radio Symphony. An Experiment in Theory' (in *Radio Research* 1941, ed. by Paul F. Lazarsfeld and Frank N. Stanton, New York 1941, pp. 110ff. A German version formed the last chapter of *Der getreue Korrepetitor* (GS 15, pp. 369ff; see Text 2b above, pp. 118ff).

204 Adorno is probably referring to a remark of Bekker's which he quoted approvingly; cf. fr. 271.

205 Hugo Leichentritt (1874–1951; emigrated 1933), German musicologist and composer who also published orchestral works by Beethoven (New York 1938). Adorno's source has not been identified.

206 On the relationship of the development to the exposition in first movement of the *Eroica*, cf. *Aesthetic Theory*:

> It is, for example, impossible to interpret in terms of a so-called succession of shapes the recondite links between the developmental section of the first movement of Beethoven's *Eroica* symphony to the exposition, or the extreme contrast posed by the introduction of the new theme. This work is intellective *per se* and does not need to be ashamed or afraid of interference by integration. (Adorno, *Aesthetic Theory*, 1984 edition, p. 144)

On the development in general:

> A no less impressive achievement of fantasy [than the harmonic variant of the main theme of the coda of the first movement of the 'Appassionata'] is the transition to terse harmonic periods towards the end of the long development section of the first movement of the *Eroica* Symphony. [. . .] it looks as though Beethoven, having run out of steam at this point, simply did not care to do any additional sustained work. (Ibid., p. 249)

207 Cf. Schoenberg, *Style and Idea* [n. 57], p. 67:

> Mozart has to be considered above all as a dramatic composer. Accommodation of the music to every change of mood and action, materially or psychologically, is the most essential problem an opera composer had to master. Inability in this respect might produce incoherence – or worse, boredom. The technique of the recitative escapes this danger by avoiding motival and harmonic obligations and their consequences.

Adorno comments on this passage in his 'Versuch über Wagner': 'Schoenberg writes very logically, and with splendid insight into the seriousness of the process of composition, [. . .] about the motival and harmonic obligations which the fully developed work has to meet.' (GS 13, p. 113).

208 Bekker (*Beethoven*, p. 223) writes of the fourth movement of the *Eroica* as 'a much-disputed and often underrated movement'.

209 This probably refers to the essay 'Arnold Schoenberg. 1874–1951', written a year earlier than the present text, which Adorno included in the collection *Prisms*. He was probably thinking of discussions of polyphony in Schoenberg, who

> thinks Classicism's unfulfilled promise through to its conclusion [...]. He reasserted Bach's challenge, which Classicism, including Bach, had evaded. Classicism had neglected Bach out of historical necessity. The autonomy of the musical subject took priority over all other considerations and critically excludes the traditional form of objectivization. [...] Only today, when subjectivity in its immediacy can no longer be regarded as the supreme category since its realization depends on society as a whole, does the inadequacy of even Bach's solution, which extended the subject so as to cover the whole, become evident. The development-section, which even at its heights in Beethoven, in the *Eroica*, remains 'dramatic', not totally composed, is transformed through Schoenberg's polyphony; the subjective melodic impulse is dialectically dissolved into its objective multivocal components. (Adorno, *Prisms*, pp. 156–7)

210 Date at head of text: 1953.
211 *Empririscher Stil* in manuscript – no doubt meaning '*Empire* style'.
212 In *Aesthetic Theory* he writes more generally:

> Beethoven's symphonies in their most arcane chemistry are part of the bourgeois process of production and express the perennial disaster brought on by capitalism. But they also take a stance of tragic affirmation towards reality as a social fact; they seem to say that the status quo is the best of all possible worlds. Beethoven's music is as much a part of the revolutionary emancipation of the bourgeoisie as it anticipates the latter's apologia. (1984 edition, p. 342)

213 Cf. Georg Lukács, *Goethe and his Age*, transl. by Robert Anchor, London 1968. – Lukács discusses 'idealism and realism in classicism' in, for example, his essay 'Schiller's Theory of Modern Literature' (ibid., pp. 101ff).
214 The 'danger of reading' (itself mainly empirical) is matched by a danger of performance, against which Adorno argues in fr. 2. Cf. also the following passage, which takes up ideas from the late Schoenberg:

> Mature music becomes suspicious of real sound as such. Similarly, with the realization of the 'subcutaneous', the end of musical interpretation becomes conceivable. The silent, imaginative reading of music could render actual playing as superfluous as, for instance, speaking is made by the reading of written material; such a practice could at the same time save music from the abuse inflicted upon the compositional content by virtually every performance today. The inclination to silence, which shapes the aura of every tone in Webern's lyrics, is related to the tendency stemming from Schoenberg. Its ultimate result, however, can only be that artistic maturity and intellectualization abolish not only sensuous appearance, but with it, art itself. (*Prisms*, pp. 169–70)

215 Obviously, Adorno did not intend to attribute the following example to the Fifth Symphony. It comes from the Fifth Piano Concerto, E♭ major, op. 73; cf. 1st movement, bars 97ff, and so on.
216 Adorno discusses the third movement, the *Scherzo*, of the Fifth Symphony in the essay 'On Popular Music':

> According to current formalistic views the scherzo of Beethoven's Fifth Symphony can be regarded as a highly stylized minuetto. What Beethoven takes from the traditional minuetto scheme in this scherzo is the idea of out-

spoken contrast between a minor minuetto, a major trio, and repetition of the minor minuetto; and also certain other characteristics such as the emphatic three-fourth rhythm often accentuated on the first fourth and, by and large, dance-like symmetry in the sequence of bars and periods. But the specific form-idea of this movement as a concrete totality transvaluates the devices borrowed from the minuetto scheme. The whole movement is conceived as an introduction to the finale in order to create tremendous tension, no only by its threatening, foreboding expression but even more by the very way in which its formal development is handled.

The classical minuetto scheme required first the appearance of the main theme, then the introduction of a second part which may lead to more distant tonal regions – formalistically similar, to be sure, to the 'bridge' of today's popular music – and finally the recurrence of the original part. All this occurs in Beethoven. He takes up the idea of thematic dualism within the scherzo part. But he forces what was, in the conventional minuetto, a mute and meaningless game-rule, to speak with meaning. He achieves complete consistency between the formal structure and its specific content, that is to say, the elaboration of its themes. The whole scherzo part of this scherzo (that is to say, what occurs before the entrance of the deep strings in C-major that marks the beginning of the trio), consists of the dualism of two themes, the creeping figure in the strings and the 'objective', stone-like answer of the wind instruments. This dualism is not developed in a schematic way so that first the phrase of the strings is elaborated, then the answer of the winds, and then the string theme is mechanically repeated. After the first occurrence of the second theme in the horns, the two essential elements are alternately interconnected in the manner of a dialogue, and the end of the scherzo part is actually marked, not by the first, but by the second theme which has overwhelmed the first musical phrase.

Furthermore, the repetition of the scherzo after the trio is scored so differently that it sounds like a mere shadow of the scherzo and assumes that haunting character which vanishes only with the affirmative entry of the Finale theme. The whole device has been made dynamic. Not only the themes, but the musical form itself have been subjected to tension: the same tension which is already manifest within the two-fold structure of the first theme that consists, as it were, of question and reply, and then even more manifest within the context between the two main themes. The whole scheme has become subject to the inherent demands of this particular movement. (*Studies in Philosophy and Social Science*, vol. 9, no. 1, 1941, pp. 20f)

217 In *Die neue Ästhetik der musikalischen Impotenz. Ein Verwesungssymptom?* (Munich 1920, pp. 64f) Hans Pfitzner wrote:

> When we stand before something incomprehensible that wholly defeats our explanations, we readily loosen the strict sequence of thought, surrender the weapons of reason and abandon ourselves quite defencelessly to *feeling*. Hearing a genuinely inspired musical idea we can only cry out: 'How beautiful that is!' [. . .] Listening to such a melody, one is suspended in mid-air. Its quality can only be recognized, not demonstrated. On it no agreement can be reached by intellectual means. Either one shares the delight it produces, or one does not. To anyone who does not join in no arguments are availing, and to his attacks there is no response except to play the melody and say: 'How beautiful!' What it expresses is as deep and as clear, as mystical and as obvious as truth.

Although Pfitzner's polemic is directed largely against Bekker's book on Beethoven, in the passages quoted he is not referring to Beethoven. – Alban Berg mordantly criticized such 'effusions' in his essay 'Die musikalische Impotenz der "Neuen Ästhetik" Hans Pfitzners' (cf. *Musikblätter des Anbruch*, vol. 2, nos 11–12, June 1920).

218 Incorrect formulation in manuscript.
219 Date before text: 'Los Angeles, 11 January 1953'.
220 The *Freischütz* was performed in a new production at the Frankfurt Opera in 1952, the première being on 18 July. The conductor was Bruno Vendenhoff, stage direction was by Wolfgang Nufer, stage set was by Frank Schultes; the main parts were sung by Lore Wissmann (Agathe), Ailla Oppel (Ännchen), Otto von Rohr (Caspar) and Heinrich Bensing (Max).
221 Thus in manuscript.
222 However, cf. in *Aesthetic Theory*:

> Many a situation in Beethoven is a *scène à faire* and therefore flawed. The onset of the reprise in the Ninth Symphony is a celebration of the unity of the original thesis and the symphonic process of development. It resounds like an overwhelming 'This is how it is'. Now, subjective tremor is a response to the fear of being overwhelmed. While the music is mainly affirmative, it also exposes untruth. (1984 edition, p. 347)

Cf. also the passage from the '*Fragment über Musik und Sprache*' quoted in n. 33.
223 'With the Ninth Beethoven had supplanted the symphonic drama by the psychological symphonic epic' (Bekker, *Beethoven*, p. 280; sentence underlined in Adorno's copy).
224 Similar comment in a note from 1939: 'Impurities of composition in Beethoven, as in the second theme group of the finale of op. 59,1 (octaves) and main theme op. 130 (fifths in 4th bar after definitive entry of the *allegro* [1st movement, bar 28]).' (Notebook 12, p. 13).
225 Adorno is thinking of 'Pacific 23', Arthur Honegger's 'Mouvement symphonique' of 1923, which Adorno criticized in a concert note of 1926: 'What happens in musical terms is meagre enough, and the imitation of the natural object entirely lacks the dreamlike over-distinctness which might be able to invoke the lost thing surrealistically. [. . .] Locomotives are better.' (GS 19, p. 65).
226 Adorno is referring to the Preface in which Strauss speaks of 'the beautiful line of the four equal melody carriers of the classical string quartet, which in the ten last quartets of Beethoven developed a freedom equal to that in Bach's choral polyphony – a freedom which none of his nine symphonies can muster.' (Hector Berlioz, *Instrumentenlehre*, enlarged and revised by Richard Strauss, part I, Leipzig, undated [c. 1904], p. II).
227 Schelling's theory of rhythm is in §§ 79ff of his *Philosophie der Kunst*; in the edition in Adorno's posthumous papers (*Schellings Werke. Nach der Originalausgabe in neuer Anordnung hrsg. von Manfred Schröter*, 3rd supplementary vol., Munich 1959) on pp. 142ff.
228 On Beethoven's *idea of the symphonic* cf. the essay on Stravinsky of 1962 from *Quasi una fantasia*:

> Beethoven's symphonies, unlike his chamber music, achieve their specificity through the unity of two elements which can only be reconciled with difficulty. His success was due not least to his ability to use each to counterbalance the other. On the one hand he remains true to the general idea of Viennese Classicism with its belief in thematic development and hence the need for a process unfolding in time. On the other hand, his symphonies exhibit a characteristic accentual dialectic [*Schlagstruktur*]. By both compressing the unfolding of time and mimicking it, time is abolished and, as it were, suspended and concentrated in space. The idea of the symphonic, which has since established itself as if in a platonic realm, can be found in

the tension between these two elements. In the nineteenth century they broke apart, like the systems of German Idealism. (*Quasi una fantasia*, pp. 165–6)

229 In 1968, in the essay 'Wissenschaftliche Erfahrungen in Amerika', Adorno wrote of the original version of the treatise, written in 1941 (the German version, written twenty years later, is translated here):

> The thesis was that serious symphonic music as broadcast on the radio is not what it is when performed, so that the radio industry's claim to bring serious music to the people proves dubious. [...] I included the core of this work in the last chapter of *Der getreue Korrepetitor*, on the musical use of the radio. Admittedly, one of its central ideas proved obsolete: my thesis that the radio symphony was not a symphony, an idea based technically on changes to the sound caused by limitations of radio reproduction at that time which have now been largely eliminated by high fidelity and stereophonic sound. Nevertheless, I believe that the theory of atomistic listening is unaffected by this, nor is that of the peculiarly 'image-like' character of music on the radio, which has survived the earlier technical limitations. (GS 10.2, p. 717)

230 Recognition of the inadequacy of the concept of harmony in relation to Beethoven's later works was at the origin of Adorno's study of the composer; it remained important up to the *Aesthetic Theory*:

> Without this reminder, without contradiction and non-identity, harmony would be irrelevant aesthetically, just as in Hegel's early work on the difference between Schelling's and Fichte's system identity can be conceived only in conjunction with non-identity. The more deeply works of art become engrossed by the idea of harmony, of appearing essence, the less they can feel content with it. It is hardly an over-generalization or a misuse of philosophy of history to say that such divergent phenomena as the antiharmonistic postures of Michelangelo, of the mature Rembrandt and Beethoven are all attributable to the inner development of the concept of harmony and in the last analysis to its insufficiency. They have nothing to do with the subjective pain and suffering experienced by these artists. Dissonance is the truth about harmony. (1984 edition, pp. 160–1)

231 Thomas Mann had access to Adorno's essay 'Spätstil Beethovens', written in 1934, when he wrote Chapter VIII of *Doctor Faustus* in 1945; the passages used by the novelist for Wendell Kretschmar's lecture on the Piano Sonata op. 111 have been repeatedly demonstrated in detail in the secondary literature (cf. Hansjörg Dörr, 'Thomas Mann und Adorno. Ein Beitrag zur Entstehung des "Doktor Faustus"', in *Literaturwissenschaftliches Jahrbuch der Görres-Gesellschaft*, new series, vol. II, 1970, pp. 285ff, esp. pp. 312f).

232 'Ach neige' (in the lines: 'Ach neige,/Du Schmerzenreiche, / Dein Antlitz gnädig meiner Not!' [Incline / thou rich in grief, oh shine / Thy grace upon my wretchedness] in the dungeon scene, the seventh before the last of part I (cf. *Faust I*, lines 3587ff); however, Adorno's comparison is with the *closing* scene of part II. In it 'a penitent, otherwise called Gretchen', speaks lines which take up the monologue in Part I: 'Neige, neige, / Du Ohnegleiche, / Du Strahlenreiche, / Dein Antlitz gnädig meinem Glück!' [Incline / Thou past comparing / Thou radiance bearing / Thy grace upon my happiness] (*Faust II*, lines 12069ff, transl. by Walter Arndt, New York and London 1977)

233 Date at end of note: '14 June 1948'.
234 Possible orthographic error in original.
235 Allusion to the poem 'Melancholey redet selber' by the Baroque poet Andreas Tscherming, which Adorno knew from Benjamin's *Ursprung des*

deutschen Trauerspiels (English: *The Origin of German Tragic Drama*, transl. by John Osborne, London 1977, p. 147).

236 Adorno developed the concept of 'complementary harmonics' to characterize the vertical dimension of twelve-tone music (cf. *Philosophy of Modern Music*, pp. 81ff).

237 Adorno wrote his text for the *Vossische Zeitung*, which published a series of articles 'Hausmusik, die wir empfehlen' in 1934; the newspaper was forced to cease publication before Adorno's text appeared.

238 Cf. Alfred Lorenz, *Das Geheimnis der Form bei Richard Wagner*, vol. 2: *Der musikalische Aufbau von Richard Wagners 'Tristan und Isolde'*, Berlin 1926, pp. 179f:

> If we concentrate the drama in us so intensely that, without jumping over what lies between, we can hold together beginning and end in a single moment, we realize that the whole of 'Tristan' is nothing other than a Phrygian cadence: °S–D worked out in gigantic dimensions

> The longing, the subdominant primal ground of Being, instead of being resolved and purified in the E major tonic, leaps straight to the heightened ecstasy of the dominant. [. . .] In the gigantic dimensions of this 4–hour work the E major tonic will come to consciousness as the unstated but complete release [. . .] though, admittedly, only to someone who has the ability to think together such a large work in one moment.

239 Date at end of note: '9.XI.48'.

240 Also see fr. 260, and the comment by Bekker quoted in n. 223.

241 Incorrect formulation in manuscript.

242 However, the theme in the first violin is noted by Beethoven as follows:

(String Quartet in C♯ minor, op. 131, 5th movement, *Presto*; Eulenburg score, p. 20)

243 Cf. Text 3, pp. 123ff above; first published in *Der Auftakt* (Prague), vol. 5/6, no. 17, 1937, pp. 65ff.

244 Cf. in *Philosophy of Modern Music*:

> That which Goethe commended in his old age – the step-by-step withdrawal from the phenomenon – can be understood in artistic concepts as the process by which material becomes no more than a matter of indifference. In Beethoven's last works barren conventions – through which the compositional stream flows only hesitantly – play approximately the same role as the one performed by the twelve-tone system in Schoenberg's most recent works. (p. 120)

– The Goethe quotation is taken from *Maximen und Reflexionen*: 'Alter: stufenweises Zurücktreten aus der Erscheinung' (*Gedenkausgabe der Werke, Briefe und Gespräche*, ed. by Ernst Beutler, vol. 9, 2nd edition, Zurich 1962, p. 669).

245 Cf. the letter of 1.6.1801 to Carl Amenda: 'Don't pass on your quartet [op. 18,1, which was dedicated to Amenda in the manuscript], as I have

changed it a lot, since I have only just found out how to write quartets, as you will see when you receive it' (Beethoven, *Sämtliche Briefe* [n. 19], p. 44).

246 Cf. the letter of 10.3.1824 to Verlag Schott: 'Difficult as I find it to talk about myself, I consider it [that is, the Mass] my greatest work' (Beethoven, *Sämtliche Briefe* [n. 19], p. 706).

247 Date at head of text: '19.X.57'.

248 Frs 289 and 305 represent direct preliminary studies for the essay 'The Alienated Magnum Opus'; the chronology of its composition has been retained in the version printed. – In Notebook C, in which the notes are contained, the last note (that is, fr. 305) is followed by the entry, very unusual for Adorno: 'Dictated first draft of essay on *Missa* on 19 and 20 October 1957. Thank heaven I have done it at last' (Notebook C, p. 83).

249 'The Alienated Magnus Opus' was broadcast on 16.12.1957 by Norddeutscher Rundfunk, Hamburg; it was first printed in January 1959 in *Neue Deutsche Hefte*. When Adorno included the text in *Moments musicaux* in 1964, he wrote in the Preface:

> 'The Alienated Magnum Opus' [...] forms part of the complex of the philosophical work on Beethoven projected since 1937. It has yet to be written, mainly because the author's efforts have continually foundered on the *Missa Solemnis*. He has therefore tried at least to set out the reasons for these difficulties, and to state the question more precisely, without presuming to have answered it. (GS 17, p. 12)

250 Grillparzer, who wrote a 'Melusina' for Beethoven as an opera libretto, had originally thought of a different subject, which seemed 'to permit treatment for the opera if need be', although it moved 'in the sphere of the most exalted passion'. This subject, fragments of which are to be found in Grillparzer's works under the title 'Drahomira', is discussed in the passage quoted from Thomas-San-Galli. (Cf. Franz Grillparzer, *Sämtliche Werke, ausgewählte Briefe, Gespräche, Berichte*, ed. by Peter Frank and Karl Pörnbacher, Munich 1965, vol. 4, pp. 198f and vol. 2, pp. 1107ff.)

251 Orthographic error in original.

252 From the second song 'Er, der Herrlichste von Allen' in the cycle *Frauen-Liebe und Leben* after Adalbert von Chamisso.

253 Last lines of Isolde.

254 Thus in manuscript ['That I cannot reward you' – in singular]; but cf. Florestan in the terzetto of the second act of *Fidelio*: 'O dass ich Euch nicht lohnen kann!' [plural].

255 He is referring to the essay 'Arnold Schoenberg. 1874–1951' (cf. GS 10.1, pp. 152ff); cf. the passage quoted in n. 209.

256 Not traced.

257 Cf. the reference in n. 7 and Adorno's letter to Kolisch, pp. 179ff above.

258 Adorno also discusses the relation between late style in art and discursive thought in *Philosophy of Modern Music*, in connection with late Schoenberg and not without bringing in Beethoven and axiomatic wisdom:

> The liquidation of art – of the hermetic work of art – becomes an aesthetic question, and the growing indifference of material itself brings about the renunciation of the identity of substance and phenomenon in which the traditional idea of art terminated. The role of the chorus in Schoenberg's recent works is the visible sign of such concession to knowledge. The subject sacrifices the clarity of the work, forces it to become doctrine and epigram, con-

ceiving of itself as the representative of a non-existent fellowship. The canons of late Beethoven are an analogy, and this fact in turn sheds light upon the canonic practices of Schoenberg's choral works. (pp. 126–7)

259 See reference in n. 19.

260 The edition of *Faust* by Georg Witkowski quoted by Adorno was published in nine editions between 1907 and 1936. – In the *Gedenkausgabe der Werke, Briefe und Gespräche*, ed. by Ernst Beutler, the lines quoted are in vol. 5 (2nd edition, Zurich and Stuttgart 1962), p. 618; they are under 'Paralipomena zum zweiten Teil' with the heading 'Zweifelhaftes'.

261 From the 'Kinderlieder' forming the appendix to *Des Knaben Wunderhorn*, here under the title 'Gelegenheitsverse', with the introductory remark: 'When the boys, at play, stake the last thing they have, they sing: etc.' (cf. *Des Knaben Wunderhorn. Alte deutsche Lieder, gesammelt von L. Achim von Arnim und Clemens Brentano. Mit einem Nachwort von Willi A. Koch*, Darmstadt 1991, p. 856).

262 Cf. 'On Language as Such and on the Language of Man' – still unpublished in 1948, when Adorno wrote this note:

> There is a language of sculpture, of painting, of poetry. Just as the language of poetry is partly, if not solely, founded on the name language of man, it is very conceivable that the language of sculpture or painting is founded on certain kinds of thing languages, that in them we find a translation of the language of things into an infinitely higher language, which may still be of the same sphere. We are concerned here with nameless, nonacoustic languages, languages issuing from matter; here we should recall the material community of things in their communication. (Walter Benjamin, *Reflections. Essays, Aphorisms, Autobiographical Writings*, transl. by Edmund Jephcott, New York and London, Harcourt Brace Jovanovich, 1978, p. 330)

– On fr. 327 cf. the formulation, only slightly modified, in *Minima Moralia*:

> Just as, according to Benjamin, painting and sculpture translate the mute language of things into a higher but similar one, so it might be supposed that music rescues name as pure sound – but at the cost of severing it from things. (*Minima Moralia*, pp. 222–3)

263 On the question of the superiority of Bach or Beethoven, Adorno writes in *Aesthetic Theory*:

> To ask which of the two ranks more highly is therefore a moot question. It is only when we use the criterion of truth content – the emancipation of the subject from myth and the reconciliation of both – that Beethoven emerges as the more advanced composer. This criterion outweighs all others in importance. (1984 edition, p. 303)

264 Adorno is probably referring to the Sonata op. 42, D 845. – In his essay on Schubert of 1928 'Schubert's form' is described as a 'circling journey'; Adorno goes on:

> Both the Impromptus and the 'Moments musicaux', and especially the works in sonata form, are constructed in this way. Not only the underlying negation of all thematic-dialectical development, but equally the repeatability of unchanged characters, make them quite different to the Beethovenian sonata. For example, in the first Sonata in A minor, the fact that the movement is based on two ideas which are not opposed as first and second theme but are each contained in both the first and second theme groups [applies to op. 42] is not to be ascribed to a motival economy which manipulates the material

for the sake of unity, but to the recurrence of the same in the enlarged diversity. One can find here the origin of the idea of mood which was valid for the art of the nineteenth century and particularly for landscape painting [...]. (GS 17, p. 26)

265 'The March of the Priests and Sarastro's invocation (no. 10, *O Isis und Osiris*) introduced a new sound to opera, far removed from churchliness: it might be called a kind of secular awe.' (Alfred Einstein, *Mozart. His Character, His Work*, transl. by Arthur Mendel and Nathan Broder, London, New York and Toronto 1945, p. 466). – 'Secular awe' is the translation for Einstein's German coinage *Weltfeierlichkeit*, which itself seems to be based on Goethe's *Weltfrömmigkeit* [secular piety].

266 In Benjamin's commentary, which was central to Adorno's concept of humanity, he writes on the letter of Johann Heinrich Kant:

> There is no doubt that it breathes true humanity. But like everything perfect it also says something about the conditions and limits of that to which it gives such perfect expression. Conditions and limits of humanity? Certainly, and it seems that these are perceived just as clearly by us as, on the other side, they stand out against medieval conditions of life. [...] Now let us look back to the Enlightenment, for which natural laws were nowhere in contradiction to a palpable order of nature, which understood this order as a set or rules which assigned the lower orders to boxes, the sciences to pigeonholes, goods and chattels to other little boxes, but included *Homo sapiens* among the creatures, from which he was distinguished only by the gift of reason. Such was the narrow-mindedness against which humanity unfurled its sublime function and without which it was condemned to shrivel. If this interdependence of meagre, confined existence and true humanity emerges nowhere more clearly than in Kant (who marks the strict mid-point between the schoolmaster and the popular orator), this letter of his brother's shows how deeply rooted in the people was the feeling of life which attained consciousness in the writings of the philosopher. In short, whenever there is talk of humanity, we should not forget the cramped bourgeois room into which the Enlightenment shed its glow. (Walter Benjamin, *Gesammelte Schriften* [n. 13], vol. 4, pp. 156f)

267 Of a performance directed by Webern himself, in December 1932 in Frankfurt/Main, Adorno wrote: '[...] then the German Dances of 1824, masterfully arranged by Webern in a procedure which makes transparent not only the architecture of the work, which is fully instrumented, but also the classical method of instrumentation, which is here, as it were, brought to consciousness of itself.' (GS 19, p. 237).

268 The idea of the chthonic took on a certain importance in the mid-nineteenth century through Johann Jakob Bachofen: in his *Mutterrecht* (Stuttgart 1861) a prehistoric gynaecocracy is described, which was distinguished by an archaic, 'chthonic' religiosity. Adorno – whose posthumous papers include the volume *Bachofen, Mutterrecht und Urreligion. Eine Auswahl*, ed. by Rudolf Marx, Leipzig, undated [1926], with numerous underlinings and marginal notes – uses 'chthonic' (subterranean, grounded in the earth) in a sense largely synonymous with 'mythical' and 'bound to nature'.

269 The giant Suckelborst in Mörike's poem 'Märchen vom sichern Mann' – 'Mere nothings are his deeds and full of foolish whims' – who reads to the dead from his 'World-Book', his 'mighty manuscript', and who pulls out the devil's tail (cf. Eduard Mörike, *Sämtliche Werke*, ed. by Johst Perfahl, vol. 1, Munich 1968, pp. 715ff), seems, for Adorno, to converge in places

with the motifs of the ogre and Rübezahl [Sprite of the Mountains], whom he mentions a number of times in connection with Beethoven (cf. frs 278f, 340 and 342).

270 The 'mythology study' refers to the first part of *Dialectic of Enlightenment*, which was given this title only later. The passage Adorno is referring to is as follows:

> Just as the name of Zeus, in non-exclusive cults, was given to a god of the underworld as well as to a god of light; just as the Olympian gods had every kind of commerce with the chthonic deities: so the good and evil powers, salvation and disaster, were not unequivocally distinct. They were linked together like coming up and passing away, life and death, summer and winter. The gloomy and indistinct religious principle that was honoured as *mana* in the earliest known stages of humanity lives on in the radiant world of Greek religion. Everything unknown and alien is primary and undifferentiated: that which transcends the confines of experience; whatever in things is more than their previously known reality. What the primitive experiences in this regard is not a spiritual as opposed to a material substance, but the intricacy of the Natural in contrast to the individual. The gasp of surprise which accompanies the experience of the unusual becomes its name. It fixes the transcendence of the unknown in relation to the known, and therefore terror as sacredness. The dualization of nature as appearance and sequence, effort and power, which first makes possible both myth and science, originates in human fear, the expression of which becomes explanation. It is not the soul which is transposed to nature, as psychologism would have it; *mana*, the moving spirit, is no projection, but the echo of the real supremacy of nature in the weak soul of primitive men. The separation of the animate and the inanimate, the occupation of certain places by demons and deities, first arises from this pre-animism, which contains the first lines of the separation of subject and object. When the tree is no longer approached merely as tree, but as evidence for an Other, as the location of *mana*, language expresses the contradiction that something is itself and at one and the same time something other than itself, identical and not identical. Through the deity, language is transformed from tautology to language. [...] It is in the nature of the work of art, or aesthetic semblance, to be what the new, terrifying occurrence became in the primitive's magic: the appearance of the whole in the particular. In the work of art that duplication still occurs by which the thing appeared as spiritual, as the expression of *mana*. This constitutes its aura. As an expression of totality art lays claim to the dignity of the absolute. This sometimes causes philosophy to allow it precedence to conceptual knowledge. (*Dialectic of Enlightenment*, pp. 14–15, 19)

271 According to Schindler, Beethoven said this of the opening bars of the Fifth Symphony (cf. Anton Schindler, *Biographie von Ludwig van Beethoven* [n. 62], p. 188).

272 With the question of an 'intertwinement of the chthonic with humanity', Adorno's notes on Beethoven impinge on a debate which was occupying German intellectuals in the pre-Fascist period; it arose from a number of selections from Bachofen's main works which were published at that time. In 1929 Thomas Mann, in his lecture 'Die Stellung Freuds in der modernen Geistesgeschichte', recognized a reactionary element in a sympathy 'directed towards the chthonic, night, death, the demonic, in short, towards a pre-Olympic, primal, earth religion' (Thomas Mann, *Leiden und Grösse der Meister*, Frankfurt/Main 1982, p. 884). – Adorno, who could conceive of the overcoming of myth only as a reconciliation with it, took up this motif in an unexpected context, in his essay 'Balzac-Lektüre':

Balzac had a special liking for the Germans, for Jean Paul, Beethoven [...]. From his description of the musician Schmucke we can see where his germanophilia had its source. It is of the same kind as the influence of German Romanticism, from the *Freischütz* and Schumann to the anti-rationalism of the twentieth century. However, in contrast to the terror exerted by Latin *clarté*, German obscurity, in Balzac's labyrinthine sentences, harboured utopia, just as the Enlightenment was repressed in German writings. In addition, Balzac may have responded to the constellation of the chthonic and humanity. For humanity is the remembrance of nature by man. [...] The universal human being, the transcendental subject behind Balzac's prose, who becomes the creator of a society for which bewitchment is second nature, is akin to the mythical self of great German philosophy and of the music corresponding to it, which posits everything that exists from itself. While the human grows eloquent in such subjectivity through the force of its original identification with the Other, which it knows itself to be, it is, at the same time, always inhuman in the violence which makes that Other subject to its will. Balzac draws closer to the world the further he removes himself from it by creating it. The anecdote according to which he turned his back on political events during the March Revolution, going to his writing desk with the words: 'Let's get back to reality', describes him faithfully even if it is invented. His gesture is that of the late Beethoven, in shirtsleeves, furiously humming to himself, writing notes from the C♯ minor string quartet enormously enlarged on the wall of his room. As in paranoia, rage and love are intertwined. In the same way elemental spirits play their pranks on human beings and help the poor. (GS 11, pp. 142ff)

273 Cf. Johann Karl August Musäus, *Volksmärchen der Deutschen*, ed. by Norbert Miller, Munich 1976, p. 174.

274 'Waldmisanthrop' is the name given by Musäus, in the first of the Rübezahl legends, to Prince Ratibor, whose beloved was taken away by the mountain gnome and who then 'wandered in lonely woods, shunning his fellow men' (cf. ibid., pp. 189 and 172).

275 In Thomas Mann's *Genesis of a Novel [Entstehung des Doktor Faustus]* we read:

> Early in October [1943] [...] we spent an evening at the Adornos'. [...] I read three pages concerning the piano that I had recently interpolated in my alarmingly hypertrophic chapter [that is, ch. VIII of *Doctor Faustus*], and our host read to us from his studies and aphorisms on Beethoven – in which a certain quotation from Musaeus' *Rübezahl* played a part. The ensuing conversation passed from humanity as the purified chthonian element to parallels between Beethoven and Goethe, to humaneness as romantic resistance to society and convention (Rousseau) and as rebellion (the prose scene in Goethe's *Faust*). Then Adorno sat down at the piano and, while I stood by and watched, played for me the entire Sonata Opus 111 in a highly instructive fashion. I had never been more attentive [...]. (Thomas Mann, *The Genesis of a Novel*, transl. by Richard and Clara Winston, London, Secker & Warburg, 1961, pp. 41–2)

– Adorno wrote fr. 342 in 1941.

276 Cf. the text of the closing chorus of the Ninth Symphony from Schiller's 'Ode to Joy', and Adorno's aphorism quoted in n. 176.

277 The 'l.c.' refers to a quotation from *Deutsche Mythologie* contained in the same notebook as fr. 345, but in a note which does not form part of the Beethoven fragments.

278 In the essay 'Zum Gedächtnis Eichendorffs', written more than a decade later, Adorno writes:

'Language as the expressive means of poetry', as something autonomous, is his divining rod. It is served by the self-extinction of the subject. He who does not want to preserve himself makes his own the lines: 'Und so muss ich, wie im Strome dort die Welle, / Ungehört verrauschen an des Frühlings Schwelle.' [And so must I, like yonder river's wave, expire upon the shore of spring]. The subject makes himself the rushing of the water; makes himself language, surviving only in its dying away, like this language. The act of man's becoming language, of the flesh becoming word, informs language with the expression of nature and transfigures its movement into life once again. *Rauschen* [rushing, murmur] was his favourite word, almost a formula; Borchardt's 'Ich habe nichts als Rauschen' [I have only a rushing in my ears] might stand as a motto above the poetry and prose of Eichendorff. However, this sense of rushing is effaced by an over-hasty association with music. *Rauschen* is not a sound but a noise, more related to language than to musical sound, and Eichendorff himself presents it as resembling language. (GS 11, p. 83)

– On Borchardt's idea of *Rauschen* cf. ibid., p. 536 and GS 5, p. 326.

279 The 'reason study' is Adorno's name for Max Horkheimer's treatise *Vernunft und Selbsterhaltung*, on which he collaborated in 1941/2; Horkheimer discusses the 'survival of the matriarchal' in connection with the fate of sexuality under fascism:

The social authority forbids the girl to deny herself to the wearer of a uniform just as strictly as the taboos in their old form prohibited compliance. The image of the Virgin Mary was never able entirely to absorb the archaic cult of woman. In the collective collusion against the old maid as in the sympathy of literature for the abandoned girl, the repressed popular consciousness had constantly reasserted itself, long before the National Socialists made an issue of the coy outcasts and the unmarried mothers. But even the excesses fed on memories of a buried prehistory and authorized by the regime do not equal the blessedness of the Christian Virgin who is betrothed to the heavenly bridegroom. For the regime is taking prehistory into its power. For by being brought by the regime into daylight, by being named and mobilized for large-scale industrial exploitation, what was buried is destroyed. Even while it shrank from violating its Christian form and declaring itself Germanic, it set the tone of German philosophy and music. Only the unleashing of the soul, summoned up as a genotype, has completely mechanized it. However futile it is to dismiss the mythical content of National Socialism as merely fraudulent, no less untrue is the National Socialist claim to preserve that content. The searchlights they direct at the surviving myth finish off at one stroke the work of destruction that was elsewhere performed by culture over centuries. For this reason the intoxication dispensed by order of the Party does not lead back to promiscuity from fear of the exogamous order, but is only a mockery of love. For love is the unreconciled foe of the prevailing reason. (Max Horkheimer, *Gesammelte Schriften*, ed. by Alfred Schmidt and Gunzelin Schmid Noerr, vol. 5: *Dialektik der Aufklärung und Schriften 1940 bis 1950*, Frankfurt/Main 1987, pp. 343f)

280 Adorno may possibly be thinking of fr. 31 or fr. 251.

281 Cf. n. 155.

282 The pages referred to are in the introduction, where the purpose of art is discussed: 'As the first such purpose, the idea comes to mind that art has the ability and the calling to soften the wildness of the desires'; cf. the reference in n. 46 and the quotation included there.

283 'Sophocles. – Many have tried, but in vain, with joy to express the most

joyful; / Here at last, in grave sadness, wholly I find it expressed'
(Hölderlin, *Poems and Fragments*, transl. by Michael Hamburger,
Cambridge, Cambridge University Press, 1980, p. 71).

284 The passage, frequently quoted by Adorno (cf., for example, *Aesthetic
Theory*, 1997 edition, p. 334), is from § 28 of the *Critique of Judgment*:

> Nature considered in an aesthetical judgment as might that has no dominion
> over us, is *dynamically sublime*. If nature is to be judged by us as dynam-
> ically sublime, it must be represented as exciting fear. [...] But we can regard
> an object as *fearful*, without being afraid *of* it; viz. if we judge of it in such a
> way that we merely *think* a case in which we would wish to resist it, and yet
> in which all resistance would be altogether vain.

(In connection with the last sentence Adorno noted on his copy of the
Critique of Judgment: 'Rather: the image mediates the fear concealed
within reality'.)

> Bold, overhanging, and as it were threatening, rocks; clouds piled up in the
> sky, moving with lightning flashes and thunder peals; volcanoes in all their
> violence of destruction; the boundless ocean in a state of tumult; the lofty
> waterfall of a mighty river, and such like; these exhibit our faculty of resist-
> ance as insignificantly small in comparison with their might. But the sight of
> them is the more attractive, the more fearful it is, provided only that we are
> in security [...]. (*Kant's Critique of Judgment*, transl. by J.H. Bernard,
> London and New York, Macmillan, 1892, pp. 123–5)

On the last paragraph, Adorno's marginal note: 'Like the lyric poetry of
the young Goethe'. – Cf. n. 115.

285 At greater length in *Aesthetic Theory*:

> For art, the sensuous exists only in a spiritualized, discontinuous form. We
> can illustrate this in terms of the notion of 'serious significance' (*Ernstfall*) in
> important works of the past. Let us take Beethoven's 'Kreutzer' Sonata,
> which Tolstoy branded as sensuous. Just before the reprise of the first move-
> ment there is an enormously effective chord in the key of the second sub-
> dominant. Occurring anywhere outside the context of the 'Kreutzer' Sonata,
> the same chord would be more or less trivial. The passage gains its signific-
> ance only in the framework of the movement, or its place and its function
> therein. It takes on serious significance by both accentuating and pointing
> beyond the *hic et nunc*; it moreover spreads the sense of serious significance
> over the preceding and subsequent portions of the composition. (1984 edi-
> tion, p. 130)

286 'Der stumme Freund. – Vermenschter Stern, mit allen deinen Fluten /
Verlangst und bangst du blass hinan zum Mond. / [...] / Vermenschter
Stern, zu deinem freundlichen Genossen / Will unvermutet auch das
frohste Sonnenkind' [The Mute Friend. – Humanized star, with all your
rising flow / fearful and pale you yearn towards the moon / [...] /
Towards your fond companion, human star / Even sun's blithest child
yearns unawares] (Theodor Däubler, *Der sternhelle Weg*, 2nd edition,
Leipzig 1919, p. 34).

287 Cf. the first note quoted in n. 172.

288 In *Aesthetic Theory* the idea is developed:

> There are measures in Beethoven's music that sound like that sentence from
> Goethe's *Elective Affinities*: 'Hope soared away over their heads like a star
> falling from the sky'. One place is a passage in the slow movement of the
> Piano Sonata in D minor, op. 31, no. 2. Listen to it first in isolation, then in
> context. You will notice that the context is directly responsible for producing

that intangible radiance the passage has. What makes this passage uncanny, however, is the way in which its expression soars above that context by concentrating itself on a songlike, humanized melody. Thus it is individuated in its relation to the product of totality, more precisely through the medium of totality. It is a product of totality as well as of the suspension of totality. (p. 268)

– The quotation is from: Goethe, *The Elective Affinities*, transl. by R.J. Hollingdale, Harmondsworth, Penguin, 1978, p. 261.

289 Cf. Ludwig Nohl, *Beethovens Leben*, 2nd completely revised edition by Paul Sakolowski, vol. 1, Berlin 1909.

290 A quotation from *Aesthetic Theory* may be compared to the same passage:

The D flat major passage in the slow movement of Beethoven's op. 59, no. 1, for example, would not radiate spiritual solace were it not for the balanced euphonia of the string quartet sound. Here as elsewhere the promise of the reality of content – which makes that content true – is tied up with the sensuous. This is what is materialistic about art, and this moment is as valid in art as the materialistic moment is in metaphysics. (p. 389)

– Cf. the first paralipomenon of Text 6 and the quotation from a letter of Adorno's included in n. 291.

291 The prehistory of this paralipomenon, which deals with a subject which occupied Adorno continually, includes a letter he wrote to Rudolf Kolisch on 10.7.1942:

When you write that the beauty of the D♭ major passage in the *Adagio* of op. 59, no. 1 is due to its position and not to itself as such, this touches on a universal state of affairs which plays a decisive role in my notes on Beethoven, which can be explicated, for example, from the entry of the recapitulation of the 'Appassionata' or the funeral march of the *Eroica*. The latter is so magnificent only because the formal impetus of the development extends beyond the limits of the schema, carrying the recapitulation with it; however, the recapitulation is discernible as such, but no longer as a section of a 'march' but as a moment of an integral symphonic form. I believe that this twofold character of the formal elements plays a decisive role in Beethoven and that, in particular, his superiority probably stems from the fact that all the individual musical parts stand in a dialectical relationship to the whole. The particular releases the whole from itself and is itself defined only by the whole. I also believe that for just this reason the concept of the banal cannot be applied even to the simplest details in Beethoven, such as that D♭ major melody. For only the insignificant which puffs itself up as Being, as an 'idea' or 'melody', is banal; but this never happens in Beethoven, where the particular is insignificant – one might almost say in Hegelian fashion, is abolished – for the sake of the whole. The concept of the banal is a complementary part of Romanticism: countless themes in Wagner and Strauss, many in Mendelssohn and some in Chopin are banal. But banality is bound up with the illusion of importance, and never to have allowed this to occur constitutes the magnificence (in banal terms: the classical element) of Beethoven. (From a carbon copy in the Theodor W. Adorno Archiv, Frankfurt/Main)

292 On Adorno's theory of name cf. fr. 327, and especially 'Music and Language: A Fragment':

The language of music is quite different from the language of intentionality. It contains a theological dimension. What it has to say is simultaneously revealed and concealed. Its Idea is the divine Name which has been given shape. It is demythologized prayer, rid of efficacious magic. It is the human attempt, doomed as ever, to name the Name, not to communicate meanings. (*Quasi una fantasia*, p. 2)

– For interpretation cf. the essay by the Editor, 'Begriff Bild Name' referred to in n. 17.

293 Benjamin discusses the connections between song and the language of birds, and between the languages of art and things, in 'On Language as Such and on the Language of Man'; cf. the quotation in n. 262 and its continuation: 'For an understanding of forms it is of value to attempt to grasp them all as languages and to seek their connection with natural languages. An example that is appropriate because it is derived from the acoustic sphere is the kinship between song and the language of birds.' (Benjamin, *Reflections*, pp. 330–1)

294 It can be concluded from fr. 370 that Adorno was thinking of Beethoven's formulation according to which 'one wants to be heard with the intellect; emotion befits only women'; however, this statement is taken from a letter which is a hoax (cf. n. 19).

295 In the Draft Introduction to *Aesthetic Theory*, Adorno used the clatter of hooves in the Piano Sonata op. 81a [cf. 1st movement, bars 223ff], identified in fr. 363 as evoking the 'moving away of the coach', to illustrate the difference in principle between philosophy and music:

> Art is mediated conceptually but in a qualitatively different way than thought. What is already mediated in art – i.e. the fact that art works are more than mere thisness – has to be mediated by reflection a second time, namely through the medium of concepts. This is accomplished not by turning away from artistic details, but by addressing them conceptually. If we take, for example, the evanescent association of clacking horse hoofs that may arise from hearing a particular three-measure phrase towards the end of the first movement of Beethoven's 'Les Adieux' sonata, we notice how this fleeting passage – which has no particular function in the movement as a whole but is simply the sound of disappearance – says more about the hope of return than could be gained by any number of general reflections on the essence of such evanescent sounds. Not until philosophical aesthetics learns to grasp such micrological figures in the structure of an artistic whole will it be able to live up to its promise. (1984 edition, p. 490)

He had written in similar terms in the essay 'Über das gegenwärtige Verhältnis von Philosophie und Musik' of 1953 (cf. GS 18, p. 156).

296 Part Three of Hegel's *Science of Logic* has the title 'Subjective Logic or the Doctrine of the Notion'.

297 Cf. n. 81.

298 Adorno refers to the second edition of the version edited by Georg Lasson (Leipzig 1921); in the section on unhappy consciousness he underlined the following sentence in his copy on the page indicated: 'That the unchangeable consciousness renounces and sacrifices its form while the individual consciousness *gives thanks*, i.e. denies itself the satisfaction of awareness of its independence and transfers the nature of activity from itself to the Beyond; admittedly, from these two moments of the reciprocal renunciation of both parts the unity of consciousness with the Unchangeable arises.' (cf. Hegel, *Werke* [n. 12] vol. 3, p. 172)

299 Cf. the reference to this line from Stefan George in n. 161.

300 Cf. the essay referred to in n. 7 and Adorno's letter to Kolisch, pp. 179ff above.

301 Cf. frs 50 and 20.

302 The manuscript contains the words 'counter Rudi's theory B'; perhaps this might mean: 'counter Rudi's theory on Beethoven'.

303 Some light is thrown on this truly enigmatic note by the inclusion of the

motif in the monograph on Mahler. Of Mahler's wild outbursts, especially in the Third, Fifth and Sixth Symphonies, his 'climate of absolute dissonance, his blackness', Adorno writes: 'the outbreak, from the place it has escaped from, appears as savage: the anti-civilizational impulse as musical character. Such moments evoke the doctrine of Jewish mysticism that interprets evil and destructiveness as scattered manifestations of the dismembered divine power [. . .]' (Adorno, *Mahler*, p. 51). It is not inconceivable that this motif was taken from Beethoven because – despite the 'immoderately wild' second movement of the F major Quartet – there are no outbursts in Beethoven comparable to those in Mahler.

304   Cf. the passage from the (inauthentic) letter of Beethoven to Bettina von Arnim quoted in n. 19.

305   Such is the reference in the manuscript; it seems to be incorrect. Scholem's translation from the Zohar was first published in 1935, as volume 40 of Bücherei des Schocken Verlags (cf. *Die Geheimnisse der Schöpfung. Ein Kapitel aus dem Sohar von G. Scholem*. Berlin 1935), and was reprinted the following year – with a different title (*Die Geheimnisse der Tora*) and with Scholem's introduction placed at the end as an afterword, but apparently using the same typesetting – as 3rd Schocken-Privatdruck (cf. exact reference in n. 191). The passage quoted from *Feuer, das Feuer verzehrt* [Fire Which Consumes Fire] – 'Nature' is Adorno's interpretation – is to be found on p. 70 of the 1935 edition and on p. 49 in that of 1936. – In its context the passage, which represents an interpretation of Psalm 104.14, is as follows:

> The line 'He causeth the grass to grow for the *behema*' points to this mystery [*behema*, actually 'beast, cattle', is the *Shekinah* previously called 'earth']. This also refers to 'the beast which lies down on a thousand mountains' [according to a scriptural quotation]. And these 'mountains' [which are the pious] bring forth their daily grass. And this 'grass' is the angels, which exert power only for a while and are created on the second day, to be consumed by that *behema* [of the *Shekinah*] which is a fire which consumes fire.

– The translator sent Adorno the version of 1936 and was thanked for it in a letter of 19.4.1939 which is worth quoting at length because it is illuminating with regard to the affinity between Adorno's thought and some motifs of Jewish mysticism (an affinity not documented in the Beethoven notes):

> Dear Herr Scholem, It is not just an empty phrase if I tell you that the translation of the extract from the Zohar which you sent me gave me the greatest pleasure I have had from any gift in a very long time. Please do not think me presumptuous in saying this: I am very far from pretending that I am qualified as a serious reader of that text. But it is of such a kind that its undecipherable aspects form part of the pleasure it gave me. And I think I can say that with the help of your Afterword I have gained at least a clearer topological idea. [. . .]
>
> All the same, I should like to note two points, even though they may be quite foolish ones. The first concerns my astonishment at the connection of the text with the neo-Platonic/gnostic tradition. [. . .] It has often seemed to me that this text owes its power to the decline itself, and perhaps such a dialectic might contribute something to understanding the aspect to which you give such emphasis: the sudden transformation of spiritualism – and, I would almost say, in line with your interpretation, of acosmism – into mythology. This would take us very close to the point around which our talks in the summer revolved, the question of mythical nihilism. The spirit

which expels the world from the act of creation calls up the demons to whom the world was set as a limit.

The other question is of a somewhat epistemological nature although, of course, it is factually connected to the mythical form of absolute spiritualism. The extract you have translated is an interpretation of the history of creation as a 'symbol'. However, the language into which the symbol is translated is itself a mere symbolic language, which calls to mind Kafka's statement that all his works were symbolic, but only in the sense that they were to be interpreted by new symbols in an endless series of steps. The question I would like to ask you is as follows: Has this series of steps got a bottom, or does it fall into a bottomless void? Bottomless because, in a world which knows nothing except spirit and in which even differentness is defined as a mere self-divestment of spirit, the hierarchy of intentions has no end. One might also say that there is nothing but intentions. If I may go back to Benjamin's old theorem of the intentionless character of truth, which does not represent a last intention but calls a stop to the flight of intentions, then, in face of the Zohar text, one cannot escape the question as to the role of myth as blinding. Is not the totality of the symbolic, however much it may appear as the expression of the expressionless, subject to the natural order because it does not know the expressionless – I would almost like to say, because it does not know nature in the true sense? [. . .]

I should like to add that the notion of the instantly transient angels touched me in the deepest and most curious way. And one last thing: the connection between your concerns and Benjamin's has never been so clear to me as during this reading. (From a carbon copy in the Theodor W. Adorno Archiv, Frankfurt/Main)

306 Cf. Rudolf Kolisch's essay 'Tempo and Character in Beethoven's Music' referred to in in n. 7.

307 Refers to Adorno's collaboration with Max Horkheimer in California, which involved *Dialectic of Enlightenment* and, above all, *The Authoritarian Personality*.

308 Cf. wording and reference of this statement in frs 197 and 267.

309 Adorno has the following passage from Kolisch's essay in mind: 'But this setting up of types does not at all undermine the individuality of particular works. Nor am I attempting a simplification of the infinite complexity of musical phenomena. I am simply isolating a single element in that complexity – tempo – and emphasizing its relationship to "character"' (Kolisch, 'Tempo and Character in Beethoven's Music' [n. 7], p. 183).

310 In his 'Versuch über Wagner' Adorno discussed *Das Geheimnis der Form bei Richard Wagner* by Alfred Lorenz (4 vols, Berlin 1924–33); cf. GS 13, pp. 30f. and passim.

311 No reply from Kolisch is among Adorno's posthumous papers. – In his 'Aufzeichnungen zu einer Theorie der musikalischen Reproduktion' Adorno also dealt with Kolisch's theory:

We discussed Rudi's theory about Beethoven's tempi. According to it, there is a countable diversity of basic types, basic characters, to each of which an identical tempo is assigned. I do not want to dispute this; it is one of the 'mechanical', contrived elements in Beethoven, supported by the abbreviations in his handwriting and the statement about natural genius and the diminished seventh chord. But leaving aside the question – to be discussed in the book [that is, in *Theorie der musikalischen Reproduktion*, which remained a fragment] – whether and how far the true interpretation should come to the aid of the work in its neediness (every true performer attempts this, and finding the right solution is inseparable from the search for the lesser evil, that which, relatively, agrees best with the composition), many distinctions should be made within the framework of the identity discovered by Rudi. I mentioned the slow movement of op. 59,2 and the Lydian one from op. 132; Rudi added that of the Ninth Symphony. Unquestionably, all three belong to the *Alla breve* type, with very slow *minims* as units; Rudi would certainly make the crotchets = 60. But the minims in the E major *Adagio* and in that of the Ninth are melodic minims, while those in op. 132 are choral minims, which are much more difficult to grasp as melody. To make the theme recognizable at all, therefore, I would play this movement most *quickly* of the three and thus in sharpest contrast to tradition. This is the only way to prevent the movement from conveying nothing more than a solemn mood based, through its unintelligibility, on something false. There are also considerations of form and proportion. If the minims in op. 132 are not played in a flowing manner, the tempo of the 3/8 part is too far away so that unity can no longer be perceived at all. And the movement of the Ninth has the great *Abgesang*, the semiquaver-sextuplets of which set an upper limit to the minims of the theme. For the sake of proportion the fact that the middle theme is 3/4, so that its unity is probably *slower* than in the Lydian movement, the middle theme of which I think of in whole bars, for harmonic reasons. But, above all, the *spiritual* characters of the three movements, the subjectively lyrical one from op. 59, the choral variations and the symphonic *adagio* type, are so fundamentally different that it seems positivistic to me to measure the tempo of them all by the same yardstick, for the sake of the relatively abstract category of the '*adagio* minim'. (Notebook 6, pp. 77f)

312 Cf. wording and reference of quotation in n. 288.
313 Cf. reference to this quotation from *Faust* in n. 59.
314 Adorno's impromptu talk preceded a discussion with Hans Mayer which was recorded by the Hessischer Rundfunk in Frankfurt on 7.1.1966 and broadcast on 27.1.1966 by the Norddeutscher Rundfunk, Hamburg, with the title 'Avantgardismus der Greise'.
315 Cf. Ernst Lewy, *Zur Sprache des alten Goethe. Ein Versuch über die Sprache des Einzelnen*, Berlin 1913. – Lewy's four-volume edition of the *Gesammelte Schriften* of J.M.R. Lenz was published by Kurt Wolff Verlag in Leipzig in 1917; the last two volumes of this edition are still to be found in Adorno's library.
316 Cf. fr. 283 and n. 244.
317 In the essay 'Parataxis' Adorno compared the constellation of tonality, subjectivity and language with Hölderlin's critical relationship to language:

Hölderlin's dialectical experience not only knows language as something external and repressive, but also knows its truth. Without alienating itself into language, the subjective intention would not exist at all. The subject becomes subject only through language. Hölderlin's critique of language therefore moves in its basic direction towards the process of subjectivization, much as one might say that Beethoven's music, in which the composing subject emancipates itself, at the same time makes its pre-established medium, tonality, speak, instead of only negating it from the standpoint of expression. (GS 11, pp. 477f)

318 Cf. the reference in fr. 199 or Karl Marx, *The Eighteenth Brumaire of Louis Bonaparte*, transl. by Eden and Cedar Paul, London 1926, pp. 24–5.
319 Such a study by Stephan has not been traced. Adorno may possibly have been thinking of Stephan's work 'Zu Beethovens letzten Quartetten', which also contains a discussion of the Finale, composed later, of the B♭ major Quartet (cf. Rudolf Stephan, *Vom musikalischen Denken. Gesammelte*

Vorträge, ed. by Rainer Damm and Andreas Traub, Mainz 1985, pp. 45f); although this work was not printed until 1970, Adorno may have read it earlier in manuscript or heard it as a lecture.

320 Refers to the *Grosse Fuge*, 'which was originally the Finale of the String Quartet op. 130' (cf. p. 187 above) and which was played at the end of the broadcast which included Adorno's talk.

EDITORIAL
AFTERWORD

Adorno wrote the notes on Beethoven, like most of his first drafts of planned works, in notebooks he kept from his youth until the day before he died; forty-five of these notebooks, of different formats and sizes, are among his posthumous papers. By far the major part of the notes on Beethoven is in the following four notebooks:

Notebook 11: School exercise book without cover; 159 pages, format 19.9 × 16 cm, partly in Gretel Adorno's handwriting. To be dated from about early 1938 to 10.8.1939.
Notebook 12: So-called 'Buntes Buch', cardboard cover; 118 pages, format 20 × 16.4 cm. A few entries in Gretel Adorno's handwriting. – Dated: 1.10.1939 to 10.8.1942.
Notebook 13: So-called 'Scribble-In Book' II, plastic cover; 218 pages, format 17.2 × 11.7 cm. – Dated 14.8.1942 to 11.1.1953.
Notebook 14: Brown leather cover with gilt edges; 72 pages with writing (of 182), format 17.3 × 12.2 cm. – Dated 11.1.1953 to 1966.

Isolated notes for the projected book on Beethoven are to be found in eight further notebooks of Adorno's, which have been used for the present edition:

Notebook 1: So-called 'Grünes Buch', green-brown leather cover with gilt edges; 108 pages, format 13.6 × 10.8 cm. – Dated: approx. 1932 to 6.12.1948.
Notebook 6: Black school exercise book with cloth spine; format 20.6 × 17.1 cm. – 1st part, pages not numbered: references for book on Kierkegaard ('finished 29.10.1932'); 2nd part: 135 pages, 'Aufzeichnungen zu einer Theorie der musikalischen Reproduktion' (to be dated from approx. early 1946 to 6.12.1959).
Notebook II: Brown octavo notebook marked 'II'; 142 pages, format 15.1 × 9 cm. – Dated: 16.12.1949 to 13.3.1956.

Notebook C: Black octavo notebook, marked 'C'; 128 pages, format 14.9 × 8.9 cm. – Dated: 26.4.1957 to 26.3.1958.
Notebook I: Black octavo notebook, marked 'I'; 144 pages, same format as 'C'. – Dated: 25.12.1960 to 2.9.1961.
Notebook L: Black octavo notebook, marked 'L'; 146 pages, same format as 'C'. – Dated: 18.11.1961 to 30.3.1962.
Notebook Q: Black octavo notebook, marked 'Q'; 145 pages, same format as 'C'. – Dated: 7.9.1963 to 27.12.1963.
Notebook R: Black octavo notebook, marked 'R'; 149 pages, same format as 'C'. – Dated: 15.10.1963 to 4.3.1964.

Adorno usually wrote the entries in his notebooks in ink, less often with ballpoint pen and only exceptionally in pencil. Sometimes the notebooks contain entries in Gretel Adorno's handwriting together with his own: Adorno dictated such notes to his wife in shorthand; she then wrote them out in the notebook in use at the time.

The text of the present edition is based on exact and repeated perusal of all the manuscripts in the Theodor W. Adorno Archiv; the relevant notes have been included and printed in full. The attribution of the notes to the material of the Beethoven book was as a rule unproblematical. Adorno worked through his notebooks afterwards and marked the fragments belonging to the Beethoven complex with a *B* at the beginning, or, less often, by writing out the name of the composer. Where such a mark by Adorno's hand is missing, it was put in by Gretel Adorno, undoubtedly on behalf of her husband, if not on his instructions. In the printed version such markings are referred to in the footnotes only if they make attribution of a note to the Beethoven book seem provisional or not yet entirely certain.

On the arrangement of the fragments by the Editor, this has already been explained in the Preface (see above, pp. ixf). To justify the procedure selected, Karl Löwith – in a similar case relating to the late work of Nietzsche – has produced convincing arguments which will be quoted here:

> Anyone who wants not only to *read* successively notes made at different times, but to *understand* the ideas in their context, and in their variations and discontinuities, must himself seek out and 'compile' those which belong together in terms of their content, and keep apart those which are together only by chronological accident. But for the proper guessing and combining, collating and distinguishing, penetrating and clarifying of a scattered train of thought, mere philological and historical pointers are wholly inadequate supports. (Karl Löwith, *Sämtliche Schriften*, vol. 6: *Nietzsche*, Stuttgart 1987, p. 517)

– However, a chronological list of Adorno's notes is also important, and indispensable for the clarification of certain questions, and the reader will find this in a comparative table (see below, pp. 253ff); at least the relative dating of the individual fragments is guaranteed by their sequence in Adorno's notebooks, which were always filled chronologically. Where Adorno has dated fragments individually – which, clearly, he usually did if a note was especially important to him – this is stated in the Notes section.

The orthography of the fragments has been unified and coordinated with current usage. Adorno kept his notebooks solely for himself; they were never intended to be read by others. In addition, the Beethoven notes were written over a period of more than thirty years: both these circumstances explain the not infrequent irregularities and inconsistencies in their handwritten form. The Editor has decided not to preserve these in the printed version, as this would unnecessarily have made the book considerably less legible. The equation of scholarly editions with transcripts of handwritten diplomatic notes, which has been widely adopted recently, was refuted a good while ago by Rudolf Pannwitz – in the same context which provoked the comments by Löwith just quoted. Pannwitz calls such a practice a 'photocopy not of the sequence within consciousness, but of the sequence of its conversion into pencil and ink' (Rudolf Pannwitz, 'Nietzsche-Philologie?', in *Merkur* 117, vol. 11, 1957, p. 1078). The Editor could not be content with such a photocopy, with regard either to the orthography or to the arrangement of Adorno's fragments on Beethoven. An edition, and particularly the *editio princeps*, of a work uncompleted by the author has to support and assist the text, not to make its reception as difficult as possible and finally to stand in its way.

In contrast to this, but with the same intention, Adorno's punctuation has been taken over almost unchanged from his manuscripts. For Adorno each punctuation mark had 'its own physiognomic value, its own expression, which cannot be separated from its syntactical function but is not exhausted by it either' (GS 11, p. 106). This applies all the more to first drafts, in which Adorno was not yet thinking about punctuation in detail, but letting himself be carried along by the flow of ideas and language, trusting that these would find their own expression. [Naturally, this physiognomic character of punctuation, and some of the punctuation errors which might have thrown light on the author's thought processes in the original, could not be carried over into the English translation – tr.]

All additions by the Editor are enclosed in square brackets. Where corrections have been made by the Editor, this is stated in the endnotes. – In his notes Adorno often used the letter *B* instead of writing the name *Beethoven*; this has been tacitly written out in the printed version. – Factual explanations have, as far as possible, been included in the text, again in square brackets; only where the need for more lengthy formulations prohibited this are the explanations included in the endnotes. – The unambiguous identification of Beethoven's works, often referred to by abbreviations in the text, posed a certain problem. When Adorno uses the opus number or familiar names ('Appassionata', 'Kreutzer' Sonata, *Eroica*, and so on) the identification is regarded as given. In all other cases the Editor has added the corresponding opus numbers in square brackets. – Examples of notation, which Adorno seems always to have written from memory, are printed from the facsimile of his handwriting.

The Editor thanks Elfriede Olbrich and Renate Wieland: the former produced the roughly deciphered copy of large sections of the manuscript; the latter gave help and information on technical musical questions. But, above all, thanks are due, from the reader as well as the Editor, to Maria Luisa Lopez-Vito, without whose committed collaboration this edition could not have been produced.

March 1993

COMPARATIVE TABLE
OF FRAGMENTS

Column C: Chronological numbering. The serial number corresponds to the temporal sequence in which the individual notes were written by the author.

Column S: The source of the note. The number or symbol before the oblique stroke gives the page number in the notebook. Fragments recorded in Gretel Adorno's handwriting are marked with an asterisk *.

Column N: Numbering of the fragments in the present edition. This number, allocated by the Editor, is added in square brackets at the end of each fragment.

C	S	N	C	S	N
	1938		38	12/25	335
			39	12/25	11
1	11/25*	81	40	12/26	1
2	11/28*	228	41	12/26	365
3	11/31*	221	42	12/26	102
4	11/41	278	43	12/26	128
5	11/53	330	44	12/28	260
6	11/54	331	45	12/28	183
7	11/55	185	46	12/28	8
8	11/72	142	47	12/28	117
9	11/73	172	48	12/28	112
10	11/74	366	49	12/29	72
11	11/75	274	50	12/30	313
12	11/76	275	51	12/30	192
13	11/76	53	52	12/30	344
14	11/78	164	53	12/30	195
15	11/78	335	54	12/30	35
16	11/78	334	55	12/31	133
17	11/78	332	56	12/31	121
			57	12/32	131
	1939		58	12/33	114
			59	12/33	88
18	11/154	350	60	12/34	99
19	11/158	141	61	12/34	52
20	11/159	184	62	12/34	31
21	12/8	74	63	12/35	201
22	12/18	181	64	12/35	115
23	12/8*	29	65	12/35	86
24	12/12	97	66	12/35	45
25	12/13	276	67	12/35	3
26	12/13	116	68	12/35	73
27	12/13	277	69	12/35	44
28	12/14	279	70	12/36	75
29	12/14	108	71	12/36	130
30	1/43	191	72	12/36	119
	1940		73	12/36	120
			74	12/38	281
31	12/15	223	75	12/38	49
32	12/16	224	76	12/38	361
33	12/23	101	77	12/38	5
34	12/23	87	78	12/38	311
35	12/24	57	79	12/39	315
36	12/25	60			
37	12/25	61			

C	S	N		C	S	N
80	12/40	316			*1942*	
81	12/40	266		120	12/90	193
82	12/41	258		121	12/90	240
83	12/41	267		122	12/91	347
84	12/42	307		123	12/91	251
85	12/42	138		124	12/92	136
86	12/43	271		125	12/93	65
87	12/43	30		126	12/97	173
88	12/43	202		127	12/101	346
89	12/44	85		128	12/103	110
90	12/44	154		129	12/103	310
91	12/44	155		130	12/105	100
92	12/45	84		131	12/105	264
93	12/46	314		132	12/105	89
94	12/46	309		133	12/109	370
95	12/46	353		134	12/110	91
96	12/47	171		135	12/110	159
97	12/47	145		136	12/111	230
98	12/47	118		137	12/112	234
99	12/47	219		138	12/113	196
100	12/48	156		139	12/113	197
101	12/49	222		140	12/114	160
102	12/56	220		141	12/114	356
103	12/56	326		142	12/114	357
104	12/56	62		143	12/114	68
105	12/56	134		144	12/115	207
				145	12/115	261
	1941			146	12/115	351
106	12/72	76		147	12/115	341
107	12/72	6		148	12/115	144
108	12/72	280		149	12/115	182
109	12/72	342		150	12/115	352
110	12/73	82		151	12/116	216
111	12/74	58		152	12/117	54
112	12/77	64		153	12/117	208
113	12/79	339		154	12/117	318
114	12/84	139		155	13/3	338
115	12/84	46			*1943*	
116	12/84	337		156	13/8	122
117	12/85*	152		157	13/9	360
118	12/87*	153		158	13/13	187
119	12/87	263				

C	S	N		C	S	N
159	13/15	188		197	13/69	80
				198	13/70	17
	1944			199	13/70	354
				200	13/70	284
160	13/20	286		201	13/71	285
161	13/22	336		202	13/71	203
162	13/26	325		203	13/71	24
163	13/26	170		204	13/72	94
164	13/33	27		205	13/72	150
165	13/33	20		206	13/73	143
166	13/35	22		207	13/73	329
167	13/37	42				
168	13/37	4				
169	13/38	345			*1948*	
170	13/39	55				
171	13/39	140		208	13/75	15
172	13/42	348		209	13/81	47
173	13/42	324		210	13/83	113
174	13/43	23		211	13/84	282
175	13/44	92		212	13/85	132
176	13/45	59		213	13/85	272
177	13/45	148		214	13/85	319
178	13/48	126		215	13/86	320
179	13/48	212		216	13/87	321
180	13/49	103		217	13/88	322
181	13/49	147		218	13/88	323
182	13/54	26		219	13/92	273
				220	13/93	104
	1945–7			221	13/93	206
				222	13/94	369
183	13/59	93		223	13/94	265
184	13/59	96		224	13/97	308
185	13/61	71		225	13/97	328
186	13/65	109		226	13/97	165
187	13/65	194		227	13/100	67
188	13/66	70		228	13/100	111
189	13/66	217		229	13/100	127
190	13/66	218		230	13/103	213
191	13/66	161		231	13/105	225
192	13/67	157		232	13/105	21
193	13/67	151		233	13/108	359
194	13/68	149		234	13/120	327
195	13/68	77		235	13/120	358
196	13/69	317		236	13/127	186

C	S	N		C	S	N
237	13/129	146		275	II/70	362
238	13/138	13		276	13/199	349
239	13/139	83				
240	13/140	268			*1952*	
241	13/141	333		277	13/201	178
242	13/144	198		278	13/202	189
243	13/145	269		279	13/203	231
244	13/147	137		280	13/205	232
245	13/148	363		281	13/209	25
246	13/149	364		282	13/209	233
247	13/150	283		283	13/210	180
248	13/160	10		284	13/211	175
				285	13/212	190
	1949			286	13/212	235
249	13/164	105		287	13/213	236
250	13/165	123		288	13/214	19
251	13/166	166				
252	13/166	166			*1953*	
253	13/168	226		289	13/214	237
254	13/169	7		290	13/216	239
255	13/169	204		291	13/217	238
256	13/170	253		292	13/218	229
257	13/170	125		293	14/1	243
258	13/171	129		294	14/4	2
259	13/171	106		295	14/6	6
260	13/174	214		296	14/7	249
261	13/177	215		297	14/9	179
262	13/181	51		298	14/9	9
263	13/182	211		299	14/9	262
264	13/182	95		300	14/11	250
265	13/182	227		301	14/14	135
266	13/183	167		302	14/15	158
267	13/184	199		303	14/17	36
268	13/185	200		304	14/17	37
269	13/187	56		305	14/18	16
270	13/190	12		306	14/18	177
271	13/191	340		307	14/18	254
				308	14/20	255
	1950/1			309	14/20	256
272	13/195	32		310	14/21	43
273	13/197	33		311	14/22	169
274	13/198	34		312	14/23	176

C	S	N	C	S	N
313	14/23	168	344	C/78	297
314	14/23	66	345	C/78	298
315	14/27	312	346	C/79	299
316	14/27	241	347	C/81	300
317	14/29	209	348	C/81	301
318	14/29	210	349	C/82	302
319	14/29	50	350	C/82	303
320	14/31	14	351	C/82	304
321	14/32	69	352	C/83	305
322	14/32	78	353	C/94	252
323	14/34	248	354	C/94	259
	1954			*1960*	
324	14/41	124	355	14/70	38
325	14/42	367	356	14/71	39
326	14/43	174		*1961*	
327	14/44	306			
328	14/44	63	357	1/112	368
329	14/44	287		*1962*	
	1955		358	L/108	48
330	14/57	343		*1963*	
331	14/58	288			
	1956		359	Q/68	79
			360	Q/68	257
332	14/61	107	361	Q/69	244
333	14/67	163	362	Q/69	245
334	14/68	28	363	Q/69	247
	1957		364	Q/70	242
			365	Q/71	90
335	C/23	246	366	R/21	40
336	C/76	289	367	Q/11	41
337	C/77	290		*1966*	
338	C/77	291			
339	C/77	292	368	14/72	162
340	C/77	293		*Undated*	
341	C/77	294			
342	C/78	295	369	Copy	270
343	C/78	296	370	Copy	98

THEMATIC SUMMARY
OF CONTENTS

leaven; spirit and the chthonic; the giant Suckelborst and Rübezahl 165 – *Rauschen*, mimesis, standing fast 168

The category of seriousness 169 – Star and hope 170 – *Text 6: The Truth Content of Beethoven's Music* 171

Music and mastery of nature; spiritualization and animation; the instrumental as recollection of nature 172 – 'Les Adieux' 174 – Leavetaking, thanking and unhappy consciousness 175 – Power of illusion; illusion and myth 176 – Beethoven and the *Shekinah* 176

INDEXES

The indexes refer to the fragments and texts by Adorno, but not to the Editor's notes. Numbers in roman type refer to the numbering in square brackets [ ] at the end of each fragment. References to the texts are by numbers in *italics*, preceded by *p.* or *pp.*; these refer to pages in the book. Indirect mentions are identified by numbers in parentheses ( ).

I Beethoven's Works

II Names